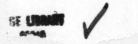

HISTORY OF RELIGION

Anglicanism in History and Today

Anglicanism in History and Today

J. W. C. WAND

Former Bishop of London

WEIDENFELD AND NICOLSON

20 NEW BOND STREET LONDON WI

Uxori Dilectissimae
Post
Quinquaginta Annos

SET IN 11-ON-13 POINT BASKERVILLE AND
PRINTED IN GREAT BRITAIN BY THE SHENVAL PRESS
LONDON, HERTFORD AND HARLOW
17/6906

CONTENTS

LIST OF ILLUSTRATIONS

PREFACE

A few months before he died Dr Garbett, then Archbishop of York, expressed the hope that I would write a book 'in praise of the Church of England'. It was the period of the 'angry young men' both inside and outside the Church, and he felt the need of a counter-balance. He had himself done much in his own judicial and objective fashion to make clear our position and claims, and his admirable books on the subject are still widely read.

Owing to other literary commitments it was impossible at the time to comply with his suggestion. Later, however, I was invited to lecture on Anglicanism in Ireland, Canada, USA and to various clerical bodies in England. The lectures were delivered *ex tempore* and in anything but literary form. When, however, the present publishers asked for a volume on the Anglican Communion for their new series, it seemed that it might be worth while to build on the basis of these lectures and so at last fulfil the request of one's old friend and colleague.

It will be noticed that the subject as now treated covers a far wider area than the Church of England. Indeed one of the points we shall have to notice is the changing position of our national Church in relation to the whole Anglican Communion. But the subject is wider in another sense. One would like to treat the Idea of Anglicanism in much the same way as Newman dealt with the Idea of a University, regarding the institution as the embodiment of an ideal, a spirit, a *weltanschauung*.

It is inevitable in view of one's own special interests that the subject should be approached from the historical angle, but preoccupation with the past should never be allowed to destroy the sense of an intensely vital organism extending over a large portion of the globe. It is immensely intriguing to the ecclesiastically minded traveller to find that the Anglican Communion, although it is everywhere recognizably one and the same, yet in no two quarters of the earth is precisely similar. It is understandable enough that countries like USA and India should have their distinctive contributions to make to the complete pattern. What is more surprising is that both in them and in countries like Canada, Australia and New Zealand, you find the same broad variations of churchmanship, yet the shades of the theological colours are all slightly different. The outward signs, for instance, that distinguish the

ix

high churchman in the Antipodes are not necessarily observable in the case of his opposite number in Ireland. It is the combination of identity with variety that makes half the fascination of Anglicanism.

The reader will not expect this book to give a detailed description of the various Anglican churches in different parts of the world. A book of that kind was published under my own editorship in 1948 by the Oxford University Press with the title *The Anglican Communion*. The essays in it covered for the most part questions of individual history, constitution, and management in the component national and missionary churches. The effort here is rather to catch the general spirit of Anglicanism and to show how it originated, how it has maintained itself in history, and how it expresses itself today.

This must be the excuse if it is complained, as it may well be, that the book is too English. The fact is that for good or ill the Anglican Communion does still reflect the prevailing influence of its British origins. That it may not always continue to do so, one may believe and even hope. The signs of change are already with us. After all, is not the Executive Officer of the whole Anglican Communion an American Bishop? The growing habit of moving from country to country for decennial Congresses must also work to the same effect. The more closely we are bound together the less strikingly shall we exhibit the idiosyncrasies of any one constituent member. But so long as we remain the Anglican Communion, we shall continue to display features that are distinctively Anglican. It is to the attempt to elucidate those distinctive traits that the present effort is devoted.

Perhaps I ought to add, in order to avoid any possible misunderstanding, that the book is intended to be entirely descriptive and not in the least apologetic. I owe so much to the Anglican Communion in every department of my own personal life that I must perforce feel that anyone who reads her story with unbiased mind will be bound to recognize that here, in what she gives and what she stands for, there is something evidently of God, something that puts us in touch with eternity in the midst of time, something that really makes life worth the living. I have, therefore, been content to sketch first the emergence of Anglicanism, then more briefly the development of its thought, and finally some of its representative activities. The sketch is far from being completely comprehensive, but I hope that, such as it is, it gives a not unfair picture of what the Anglican Communion is and does. I apologize in advance for a certain number of repetitions, but they seemed to be made inevitable by the particular method of approach.

It only remains for me to offer my thanks to those who have helped me in my formidable but happy task: Miss Ann Edmonds who has done all the typing, Dr Gordon Huelin who read both the manuscript and the proof, Canon F. Hood who also read the proof, and to the members of the Publishers' staff whose technical expertise was patiently and unstintingly placed at my disposal.

St Paul's   J. W. C. WAND

1961

Note to Second Impression

The call for a reprint gives me the opportunity of expressing my sincere thanks to kindly reviewers, particularly to those who have helped me to correct several inaccuracies in the text.

St Paul's   J. W. C. WAND

1963

INTRODUCTION

WE MUST start by defining our terms. The word Anglican comes direct from the Latin *anglicanus* which simply means English. As a term descriptive of the Christian Church in this country it is found throughout the Middle Ages: *ecclesia anglicana* was the regular title of the section of the Catholic Church to be found in the provinces of Canterbury and York. It achieved an added significance when those provinces broke off from Rome. It was then used by the apologists of the reformed church to describe a type of Catholicism distinct from the Roman. That specific meaning, however, became later attached to the hyphenated form Anglo-Catholic while Anglican was used in the wider sense of anything specifically pertaining to the churches in full organizational fellowship with the see of Canterbury.

The sum-total of those churches is generally known as the Anglican Communion. The term is not exceedingly popular, as it still carries a certain English flavour which may become irritating in countries whose patriotism or nationalism may feel itself impugned. However, no more appropriate title has yet been conceived, and there is, of course, a considerable proportion of its forty million adherents throughout the world who are happy enough on historical and sentimental grounds to see it retained. We may conclude then that the word Anglicanism

'properly applies to the system of doctrine and practice upheld by those Christians who are in religious communion with the see of Canterbury: it is especially used, in a somewhat more restricted sense, of that system in so far as it emphasizes its claim to possess a religious outlook distinguishable from that of other Christian communions both Catholic and Protestant'.[1]

It is clear that Anglicanism is an omnibus term carrying within it a variety of subjects and revealing a different aspect as each demands individual attention. It may be viewed as an organization, as a faith, as a way of life, as a movement of thought, as a system of culture. All these, and others, we shall have to deal with in turn. First we must look at it as an organization, as what, in fact, is called the Anglican Communion. How does it present itself to the world today? Fortunately we are not left in any doubt on that matter because the Anglican Bishops have themselves told us what they believe Anglicanism to be. In their Lambeth Conference of 1930 they described it as follows:

'It is a fellowship within the one Holy Catholic and Apostolic Church of those duly constituted Dioceses, Provinces or Regional Churches in communion with the See of Canterbury which have the following characteristics in common—

a They uphold and propagate the Catholic and Apostolic Faith and Order as they are generally set forth in the Book of Common Prayer as authorized in their several Churches.

b They are particular or national Churches, and as such promote within each of their territories a national expression of Christian faith, life and worship.

c They are bound together not by a central legislative and executive authority, but by mutual loyalty sustained through common council of the Bishops in conference.'

So far the Bishops. We might summarize their statement briefly by saying that Anglicanism, viewed purely as an organization, is a fellowship of free and independent churches whose Bishops meet in conference at Lambeth and recognize the Archbishop of Canterbury as their senior.

Part I

ORGANIZATION

CHAPTER ONE

HISTORICAL TURNING POINTS

It is our immediate task to trace the way in which Anglicanism as just described came into being. The story will, of course, show a considerable development. Anglicanism, as we know it today, did not come freshly minted from the hand of the Creator in the present century, nor in the sixteenth, nor even in the first. There has been continuous change, growth, adaptation to environment, in other words life. But we are not now so afraid of the idea of development in religion as we once were. Even churches that prided themselves on never changing are now prepared gladly to accept and actually to insist upon the notion of development. So Fr Cary-Elwes states the present attitude of Roman Catholic apology in his book *The Sheepfold and the Shepherd*: 'If anyone says that in the first three centuries it is impossible to find evidence of the papacy as we know it we admit their contention most readily. The doctrine of papal authority, though present in embryo both in the New Testament and in the Fathers, is far from being full grown. It is the same with all the other doctrines of the Church, from that of the Holy Trinity itself to that of Indulgences.'[1] The collocation of two such different doctrines as those of the Blessed Trinity and of Indulgences may give us pause and cause us to ask whether both can be equally legitimate results of the same process. Granted that development is inevitable so long as there is life, the important issue is to decide between true and false development. It is the Anglican contention that although its present world-wide Communion is not a precise replica of the Church of the New Testament it is, nevertheless, a true development from it, preserving intact the essential features present in the embryo. The acorn has become the oak and there has been no break in the continuity of its growth.

In tracing the development of the Anglican Communion we have to emphasize three particularly important points: its origins, its separation, its expansion. The origins account for its mixed character, the separation for its peculiarities, and the expansion for its ecumenical standing. This is not entirely true; the effects are not quite so clear-cut as is here implied. Some of its independence of spirit, for instance, which is certainly one of its peculiarities can be traced to its origins as well as to its separateness. But on the whole the analysis is accurate enough and it will help to keep the story clear.

Origins

The origins of the church in these islands are very mixed. The British have never been tempted to follow Hitler's example and claim that they are of pure blood. Ecclesiastically they are as mixed as they are racially. The first eight hundred years of Christianity in Britain show one wave of outside influence after another. It may not be easy to trace all the effects in the ultimate product, any more than it is possible to trace each particular trait of individual character to some remote ancestor. But the amalgam is there nevertheless; we cannot entirely forget the several springs from which we took our rise, even if we would.

Who first brought Christianity to these shores it is impossible to say. It is curious that in the whole course of our history we have never had a great dominating figure, no Paul or Augustine, not even a Luther or a Calvin, to lend us his name. In that at least we have remained true to our beginnings. No great apostle preached the gospel to the British on the remote outskirts of the Roman Empire. We judge from a reference in Irenaeus that Britain was still unconverted in the last quarter of the second century; we judge from the statements of Tertullian and Origen that the gospel had already arrived early in the third century and then spread widely during its first quarter.[2] It probably came with the soldiers and merchants from Gaul, or with the slaves engaged in the tin-trade with Cornwall and in the lead mines on Mendip. Considering the multi-racial extraction of Roman soldiers and slaves this in itself may already imply a cosmopolitan character for the infant church.

Christianity in these pagan islands soon acquired some of the prestige not only of the mysterious East but also of the conquering and imperial culture of Rome. After the last great persecution under Diocletian, in which probably our proto-martyr Alban suffered, Gildas tells us there was a spurt in ecclesiastical building. Archaeological evidence suggests that the Romano-British were glad to build their churches within the protective walls of Roman forts. The prestige they would thus gain was, no doubt, greatly enhanced when Constantine, who had been proclaimed Emperor at York, granted toleration and even special favour to the Church, by which he hoped to cement the unity of his empire. The position was to be still further improved when Theodosius I made Christianity the official religion of the empire in 381.

Not that Christianity enjoyed any easy victory. The thriving mission met stiff competition. We find just the same Romano-British co-operative effort in the building of heathen temples in honour of Celtic gods with Latinized names and the attributes of classical deities. Christianity made its chief conquests in the towns; there was good reason in Britain, as elsewhere, why the term pagan (i.e. countryman) should come to mean heathen. The church that resulted from this mixed origin was organized on a roughly diocesan basis, the bishop having the oversight of a town and the immediately adjacent territory. The church in Britain was important enough after a century of growth to send three episcopal representatives to the official gathering at Arles in 314, which preluded the long conciliar period in early church history. Restitutus is the only proper name that has come down to us from this deputation. He was Bishop of London; the other emissaries were the Bishops of York and possibly Lincoln. It may be significant of the lowly standing of the British Church that these signatures are found among those of the Gallic bishops and that the copyist has boggled over two of them.[3]

In 360 three British bishops were again present at a council, this time at Ariminum (Rimini). There may have been others but we know of these three because they were too poor to pay their own travelling expenses and had to depend upon aid granted by the government.[4] It does not look as if the gospel had as yet made much progress among the wealthy Romans in the lovely villas scattered up and down the country. Or they may merely have anticipated the Englishman's reluctance to contribute heavily to church funds.

It has been the common view that this young and flourishing church was destroyed at one fell swoop in the middle of the fifth century by the arrival of the Anglo-Saxon invaders. But modern research has caused considerable modification of this somewhat naïve interpretation of events. For one thing the towns show little sign of violent destruction; they seem rather to have decayed from lack of use after the Roman withdrawal. The British do not seem to have been capable of carrying on the elaborate urban organization of their Roman masters, and after the latter had withdrawn they appear to have retreated into the countryside. They took their church with them and there must be some

5

truth in the view that both it and they ultimately found their home in the remote fastnesses of Wales and the west country.

But that cannot have meant the complete and immediate elimination of Christianity in the territory formerly held by the Romans and now over-run by the Anglo-Saxons. There are far too many signs of creative activity in adjacent parts. In 397 Ninian built in Galloway his White House (Whithorn) of lime-washed stone to the astonishment of the Picts, whom he was trying to convert. Bede[5] tells us that he was 'a most reverend bishop and holy man of the British nation, who had been regularly instructed at Rome'. He was not the only Britisher to be trained on the continent for missionary work in the remote parts of his own islands. Palladius, who was consecrated by Pope Celestine I and worked first in Ireland and then in Scotland without much success in either sphere, is of doubtful nationality. But Patrick (*d.* 461), the apostle of Ireland, and Illtyd (*d.* 535), the apostle of Wales, were British (though the latter is said to have come from Brittany) and both had been pupils of Germanus of Auxerre. Gallic influence must have brought some encouragement to British Christians.

In the first half of the fifth century, curiously enough just when the Romans withdrew, there seems to have been an advance of Christianity. It was between 420 and 430 that the British Fastidius wrote in Britain for the British his Latin book *On the Christian Life*. This is a very sober and pleasant exposition of Christianity without a trace of fanaticism. For that reason it has been accused of Pelagian tendencies and even of having been written by Pelagius himself. Pelagius was another Briton, a lay monk of a cultured type, who was revolted by Augustine's determinism, and thought that Christian men ought to be able to live up to the height of their calling with no more aid than God had given them in their natural endowment. If we are looking for ancestral influence we might claim to find it here in plenty. Karl Barth, the eminent Swiss disciple of Augustine and Calvin, when asked recently why his books did not sell more readily in this country replied, 'Ah, the English, they are incurably Pelagian'. Actually there is no precise evidence that Pelagius ever taught in his native country, but there is a good deal of truth in Barth's remark. Self-reliance has always been a much lauded virtue in this country, and if pressed to a logical conclusion it is essentially Pelagian.

Certainly Pelagius was not alone in entertaining such views. In this connection it is worth noticing that even St Patrick is said to have penetrated down as far as Lerins, the island in the Mediterranean off Cannes, which became the home of semi-Pelagianism. In any case

Pelagian teaching spread so widely in Britain that appeal ror help to stem its advance was made to the Pope Celestine. In 429 he sent over Germanus of Auxerre, who dealt with it in a meeting at Verulamium (St Albans). Later the same Germanus, who in his time had had experience as a secular governor, came over again to lead the British against the Picts and Saxons, whom they defeated after rallying to the war-cry Alleluia. It is now evident that Romanized and Christianized Britain fell no easy or immediate prey to the invaders. As resistance was not led by the towns, it became very much a business for the leaders of the old tribes in the countryside, one of whom was Vortigern, and another the saintly King Arthur, whose goodness and prowess have remained a legend to glorify our literature ever since.

By the middle of the fifth century Britain seems to have been isolated from the continent. A few towns like London, Canterbury and Rochester were occupied by the Saxons, as the remaining civic rulers failed to hold them. There at least enough of the old influence remained to constrain the new masters to imbibe some of the Romano-British customs. In the countryside, church organization, deprived of the support of the towns, tended, like the civil and military organization, to fall into tribal lines. No doubt many of the British rank and file settled down under the new régime and intermarried with the Anglo-Saxons, but the leaders both in church and state retreated westwards with their immediate followers. Henceforth Celt and English developed strongly contrasted types of culture.

As far as the Church is concerned that meant the development in the West of an ecclesiastical system that was quite unique in Christendom. It had its adumbrations in Wales but its full development was seen in Ireland. The story is extremely interesting. Owing to the influence of Martin of Tours, or perhaps to contact with the Levant, where, particularly in the deserts of Egypt, monasticism had sprung up and developed enormously during the fourth century, the eremitical type of life was regarded as the ideal Christianity. Monasteries, in which the austerity of the hermit was practised as closely as possible, became the effective units of ecclesiastical organization. Bishops there were in plenty, but they were maintained in order solely to perform the spiritual duties of their grade and were not expected to exercise functions of an administrative or supervisory kind. Such privileges were in the hands of the rulers of the monasteries, the abbots and abbesses who controlled the property, exercised discipline, and practised jurisdiction. Palanque, the distinguished French historian, gets over this familiar crux by simply identifying the abbot of the tribal monastery with the bishop.

7

Since each monastery seems to have belonged to a particular tribe, the drift away from the normal diocesan system, in which the bishop was the effective superintendent of his particular area, was all the more marked. Solitude was the ideal, and even the monasteries were little more than collections of hermits' huts. The clustered foundations of the little square cells can still be seen looking over the sea from the rugged headland of Tintagel, and other sites revealing the shape of the famous beehive huts can be found in many places in Wales and Ireland. The Celtic missionaries in later days retained the same longing for solitude. The names of Iona and Lindisfarne remain as a witness to the Irish churchmen's love of nature, alone and undisturbed.

Even in these peculiarities it can be said that the Celtic Church was the heir both of Gaul and of the Romano-British Church. The cult of solitude had its parallel in the limestone caves of St Martin's monks overlooking the Loire outside Tours, in the place that still retains the name of Marmoutier (*Martini Monasterium*). At the same time we have seen how tribal organization tended to revive in the British countryside after the Roman withdrawal. Of the Romano-British Church few archæological evidences remain—the foundations of a small church at Silchester (of basilican type, forty feet by thirty feet, with an apsidal east end, transepts and aisles and detached altar); possibly another at Lullingstone; an Ogham tombstone, and the Chi Ro on a few mosaic tiles and domestic utensils. These last may be early indicators of the art that flowered later in the Celtic Church. Professor Bréhier in *L'Art Chrétien*[6] says that at the end of this period only two countries remained as centres of culture and art, Italy and Ireland. He instances the Book of Kells (eighth century) as a magnificent example of Celtic art whose many-pointed stars were to become a staple of Arab ornament. What is not generally noticed in this connection is the presence on one page of the illuminations of the Book of Kells of the *flabellum* or fly-whisk, which was, and still is, used at the altar during the celebration of the Holy Mysteries by clergy of the Orthodox Church. This takes us to the customs of the Eastern Church and is another example of that mixture of influence which marks the earliest stage of Christianity in these islands.

The blend received official recognition in the next stage of our origins when the British Church was replaced by the English. The later importance of England and the Church of England has led to an almost exclusive concentration on the mission sent to this country by Pope Gregory the Great. It must never be forgotten however that, while the territory later to be known as England lapsed into barbarism after

Rome had withdrawn its troops and civil servants, British Christianity continued in the West and developed into the very important Celtic Church of Wales and Ireland, which was largely responsible for the conversion both of England and of northern Europe.

It was from the latter country (Ireland) that about 563 the monk Columba established a monastery on Iona, where he and his companions could live in quiet and whence they could carry on their enterprising missionary journeys on the mainland of Scotland. Being of noble family himself he was well able to maintain the almost regal position of a Celtic abbot and to rule his monks as if they were a small Irish nation or tribe. Kings of the Picts and Scots were not ashamed to admit conversion by him or to receive hallowing at his hands.

During the same year in which Columba died (597) Augustine, after some hesitation, landed with his party of monks from Rome in the far south of England. The way had been prepared for him by the fact that King Ethelbert's Queen was a Christian who had brought her own chaplain from Gaul to Kent and was still practising her religion. Augustine also found at Canterbury some relics of the earlier Romano-British Christians, for Queen Bertha was worshipping in the little church of St Martin, built from a Roman ruin, which had probably once been restored as a Romano-British church. Augustine tried unsuccessfully to join up with the British Church in Wales. Even without Welsh Christians and their odd ways he found himself in some difficulty over the customs of his hosts. Bertha, in particular, had come from Gaul and was not used to Italian ways. Royal ladies, no less than others of their sex, have a strong conservative instinct in matters of religion. Augustine consulted his master Gregory, and elicited the famous reply: 'You know, my brother, the custom of the Roman Church in which you were brought up. But I advise that if you find anything in the Roman Church or in that of the Gauls or in any other church, which may be more acceptable to Almighty God, you carefully make choice of the same and teach the Church of the English, which is as yet new in the faith, whatever you thus gather from the several churches. For things are not to be loved for the sake of places, but places for the sake of good things.'[7] Following this sound advice Augustine did well in the south, himself holding Canterbury, and appointing bishops to both Rochester and London before he died in 604 or 605.

It was the failure of the Roman mission in the north that made an opening for the Celts. Edwin, King of Northumbria, had married the Christian Ethelburga from Kent; a member of the Roman mission, Paulinus, consecrated Bishop of York, had gone with her. At Goodmanham in 627 Edwin and his people accepted Christianity. Six years later, however, Edwin was defeated by the heathen Cadwalla. Paulinus had to flee, leaving only the deacon James to carry on the mission as best he could. Since this left a practically open field, the new Christian King of Northumbria, Oswald, called in the help of the Celts from Iona, where he himself had been trained. After one monk had given up the English as hopeless the saintly Aidan volunteered for the task, set up his see on the lonely island of Lindisfarne (to which pilgrims still 'plodge' across at low tide), and began the conversion of the English from the north.

There have been many friendly controversies on the respective parts played by the Roman and Celtic missions in the christianizing of England. The fact is that the honours were about as equally divided as they could be. The disadvantage of the double origin lay in the fact that the two parent churches had developed different customs. These were not matters of vital importance, but they could lead to inconvenient situations, as when, for instance, owing to differences in the method of calculating the date of Easter, the one group would be feasting while the other would be deep in the most solemn period of the Lenten fast. Under the stress of heathen pressure it was a matter of common statesmanship to bring the differences to an end. At the Synod of Whitby 663 the immense prestige of Rome carried the day and the Church of the English accepted the Roman standard of ecclesiastical propriety. The decision was important because for nine centuries it linked England with the main stream of Western Christianity.

This did not mean that the Celtic influence died out altogether. Although the Celts who remained may have abandoned their distinctive customs for the Latin, it can hardly be supposed that the whole spirit and ethos can have changed immediately. For one thing the two centuries that had intervened since the cessation of the Roman occupation had meant a definite interruption of the Latin influence. Our story is quite different from that of the continent. In France, through all the upheaval of the Dark Ages, the cities had maintained their identity and for the most part the bishops remained in them at the centre of their sees. In Britain on the contrary, as we have seen, continuity was broken. The cities for the most part lost their importance and fell into disuse. At the same time organized Christianity disappeared; all had to begin again under the Italian and Celtic missions. The Celts thus coming in at ground level had all the better opportunity to leave a permanent impress upon the style of the united Church.

On the other hand, Rome felt that she had a particular interest in the Church of the English. It was their great Pope Gregory who had sent the original mission. No part of the continent was so directly the child of Rome as England.

The result of the intermingling can be seen, appropriately enough, in ecclesiastical art, particularly in that of the Northumbrian or 'Early Saxon' (650–850) period. In it the discerning can pick out Irish, Roman and Saxon elements. In fact, it is sometimes known as the art of the Hiberno-Saxon school. There can be little doubt that in the monasteries Celtic and Saxon monks worked side by side, sometimes at parts of the same manuscript. If one were to analyse their illuminations it would be possible to show that the interlacing lines are based on classical models, the quaint fancy that turned them into writhing animals came from the Saxon inventive genius, and the heavy robes of the human figures from Celtic sources. Walter Oakeshott sums up the situation thus:

'Northumbria was the meeting place of a number of cultural influences, from Ireland, from England, and through England, from Italy. It was this meeting of different streams which gave the artistic movement its force. It is not surprising that in Bede Northumbria should have produced the greatest scholar of the early middle ages, and in the *Lindisfarne Gospels* perhaps the greatest book of the early middle ages; nor that Charlemagne at the end of the eighth century should have sent to Northumbria for his schoolmasters.'[8]

The same inter-mixture of cultures can also be seen in constitutional development. When Theodore at the age of sixty-seven came over from the continent to become Archbishop of Canterbury, he brought with him Hadrian, an African monk. Both of them had been educated in Athens but Theodore was a native of Tarsus. It is possible that the authorities at Rome thought that an eastern churchman might be too susceptible to British Pelagianism, if it still existed, and therefore sent Hadrian to care for the Archbishop's orthodoxy. Bede says they both brought much light and learning to the country. Certainly Theodore, in spite of his age, did a splendid piece of organization. As a Greek he was used to the closest co-operation between the ecclesiastical and civil authorities. When, therefore, he divided the country more thoroughly into dioceses he did not follow any arbitrary pattern, nor repeat the Roman custom of sticking to the great towns. He approximated much more closely to the Celtic custom of making the tribe the unit, so that the local king could have a bishop by his side. The boundaries of the dioceses were adapted to suit the tribal limits,[9] and the tribal headquarters became the see town. Thus Lichfield became the centre for the Mercians, Lindsey for the Middle Angles, Winchester for the West Saxons and Selsey for the South. It is, of course, to be noted that Theodore did not adopt the full Celtic system, but the plan he did adopt shows an interesting readiness to effect a compromise and use just as much of either system as seemed best for his purpose.

It would be fascinating to pursue further the story of the consolidation of this amalgam. It is important in secular history inasmuch as it enabled England to realize the ideal of national unity earlier than any of the continental countries. We must hasten, however, to what may be described as the final stage in our origins, the Norman invasion. This is important from the ecclesiastical point of view because it drew us still more firmly within the orbit of the Roman Church. This, indeed, was one of the purposes Pope Alexander II had in mind when he gave his blessing to William's expedition. William faithfully fulfilled, as he thought, his part of the bargain. In making England practically a part of France, he laid it open to the full force of the papal reform movement, bringing diocesan centres into the great cities, easing the entry into England of the new Cistercian monasticism, encouraging stricter discipline of the clergy, paying up arrears of financial dues.

But the Norman invasion is also important as giving official expression to the decided independence of spirit that characterized England, or at least its rulers, in ecclesiastical matters. William, in spite of the fact that he recognized his obligation to the papacy, refused to do homage to the Pope or to allow any canon to become effective or any citizen to be excommunicated without his consent. The letter that he dictated to the redoubtable Gregory VII (Hildebrand) on the point is so illuminating, and even amusing, that it deserves to be quoted:

'Gregory, the most noble Shepherd of the Holy Church. William, by the Grace of God renowned king of the English and duke of the Normans, greetings with amity. Hubert your Legate, Holy Father, coming to me on your behalf, bade me do fealty to you and your successors, and to think better in the matter of the money which my predecessors were wont to send to the Roman Church: the one point I agree to, the other I do not agree to. I refuse to do fealty, nor will I, because neither have I promised it nor do I find my predecessors did it to your predecessors. The money for nearly three years whilst I was in Gaul has been carelessly collected but now that I am back to my kingdom, by God's mercy, what has been collected is sent by the aforesaid Legate, and what remains shall be despatched when opportunity serves by the legate of Lanfranc, our faithful Archbishop. Pray for us and for the good estate of our realm for we have loved your predecessors and desire to love you sincerely and to hear you obediently before all.'[10]

There, then, is a letter offering the filial obedience of William to the chief Bishop of Christendom, and yet, at the same time, asserting in the strongest terms that he will not acknowledge him as his overlord or do fealty for his realm. It is representative of the independence of spirit that was characteristic of England during the medieval period. The Pope may well have wondered whether he had gained much except hard cash from the accession of William. Certainly the Saxon church, however lax it may have become, had done much through its missionaries to enhance the papal power on the continent. 'Willibrord and Boniface, consciously looking back to the days of Augustine, deliberately sought papal approval and guidance. Under the leadership of Boniface (*legatus Germanicus sedis apostolicae*), the Anglo-Saxons gained for the Pope power over the Frankish church such as he had never before enjoyed. England thus appears to have played a considerable part in the evolution of the machinery by which, in later times, the papacy maintained control over the West.'[11]

It is true that the great missionaries were emissaries of the Church, while William was most concerned about his kingdom. But in spite of the fact that William had for the first time in English history separated the ecclesiastical from the civil councils* and the ecclesiastical from the civil courts, yet the King still held himself to be supreme in all causes, ecclesiastical as well as civil. This inevitably made for a definite unity of state and church under the person of the monarch. The attitude of the King in regard to the one was bound to affect the other. The independent spirit of the state was generally reflected in the church. The exceptions occurred when the state and the church were at loggerheads and each was playing for the support of the Pope.

The infusion of Norman blood into the body corporate of the English Church showed itself in the incursion of new and lordly prelates, the reorganization of the monasteries, and the glorious great romanesque churches. While it implied a formal tightening of the bonds with the papacy, it did not involve a meek submission to Rome. This third stage in our origins set the character of the church in this country for the next five hundred years.

It was at the end of the Middle Ages that a decisive change took place and it is to that point that we must direct our attention. Before doing so, however, it may be well to notice how the pattern of relations set at the Conquest was worked out during the rest of the medieval period.

There was, of course, one humiliating moment in 1213 when King

---

*Today the Convocations are still summoned simultaneously with Parliament but sit apart from it. The first approximation to this custom occurred in 1085 when Primate and clergy sat on after the Witan had dispersed.

John surrendered his crown and the two kingdoms of England and Ireland to Pope Innocent III, receiving them back on his promise to hold them as the Pope's vassal and to pay to him, in addition to the usual Peter's Pence, an annual tribute of 700 marks for England and 300 for Ireland. This, however, was a momentary lapse in fear of an imminent French invasion. By 1236 the Council of London was actually barring the Papal Legate, Otto, from its discussions while it debated the demands he had brought from Rome. A little later, in 1281, Bishop Peckham is found assuring the Council of Lambeth that England has its own special and peculiar customs which it is prepared to maintain. If this was the attitude of the clergy, that of the laity was far more stiff. In 1377 the Commons asserted that no statute should be made on the petition of the clergy without their consent. This was an unconstitutional interference with the Convocations' right of direct access to the Crown, but it was done in order to make doubly sure of a firm check on Rome.[12]

Perhaps more important than these specific events, as showing the independence of the English spirit, is the series of continuous causes that operated to keep Rome and Canterbury apart. It is significant that England was never a part of the Holy Roman Empire, and was, therefore, not affected by the general atmosphere in which continental affairs were conducted. Again when Pope Gregory IX in 1232 allowed the Dominicans to found the Inquisition, England was not included in its sphere of operations and, in point of fact, it never did operate in this country.

The Papacy became quite accustomed during the Middle Ages to receiving rebukes from the more virtuous and masterful of its suffragans, but there can be few bishops who belaboured the Pope for his shortcomings so soundly as did Grosseteste, Bishop of Lincoln. It was small wonder that people of less distinction in the hierarchy, like Wycliffe, should be even less restrained in their language. If Wycliffe failed to produce a religious revolution at home in the fourteenth century, his teaching produced the revolt of Huss and his followers on the continent in the fifteenth, and that in its turn prepared the way for the more general Reformation in the sixteenth.

That kings should take an independent line was perhaps more natural. Henry V, in fact, went further and, under the stress of the French war, suppressed a number of the foreign monasteries in England, although they were under the special protection of the Papacy. He thus unwittingly prepared the way for the wholesale dissolution of the monasteries at the Reformation.

Too much should not be made of the fact that England had a number of liturgical models of her own. Important as was the Use of Sarum, it was paralleled by other uses on the continent and elsewhere. We must not conclude, therefore, that England had her own liturgy distinct from the rest of the Catholic world. The same should be said of the canons and customs governing the ecclesiastical society. The once popular view that England was a law to itself has given way before the researches of Maitland and his followers.[13] That there were some distinctive features from the time of Theodore to Lingard is natural enough, but by and large Englishmen throughout the Middle Ages lived by the same ecclesiastical law as their fellow churchmen on the continent. Whatever might be the effect of local idiosyncrasies the international unity of the Church was throughout the Middle Ages regarded as fundamental.

Separation

We seem to have travelled rather far from our first point, which was our origin, but at least we have been brought to the second, which is our separation. The most important turning-point in our history was the Reformation. Modern scholars in search of new ideas and controversialists trying to bolster up a position have, in these latter days, sought to belittle its effect. Certainly, if we were writing a history, we should have to place beside it other movements, like that of the early nineteenth century, to enable us to strike a proper balance.[14] But there has been nothing that went so deep, and that affected our character so strongly for good or evil, from the period of our origins to the present day as the Reformation of the sixteenth century. This is all the more true inasmuch as the English Reformation was *sui generis*; there was nothing else quite like it in the whole of Christendom. All the more, therefore, does it stamp us with a special and peculiar character. 'The Key to a right understanding of the modern Church of England,' says Hensley Henson, 'lies in a just appreciation of the unique character of the English Reformation.'[15] He goes on to point out that there are two elements in that uniqueness: one is the assertion of national independence, which includes the repudiation of the papacy; and the other is the subordination of the Church to the State, which is involved in the Royal Supremacy. To them we must add a third: the determination to secure at all costs the historical continuity of the church of this country.

The sources of all three elements are deeply rooted in our history. It is important to get them clear, otherwise one cannot hope to understand the distinctive character of Anglicanism. If disappointment is felt because none of them suggests a great spiritual or intellectual force, it must be remembered that what there was of religious impulse in the movement England shared with all other affected lands. For instance, the sudden demand for religious freedom, that is for a religion of the spirit as distinct from a religion of law and works, which was first sounded by Luther in a voice that brooked no delay, echoed in all the countries of northern Europe no less than in England. No explanation of the Reformation is adequate that does not recognize this cataclysmic upsurge of human emotion. Even nationalism was by no means confined to this country. 'Within the splendid hollow framework of the Western Church by 1500 the national churches had already developed and were ready to break with that control which for centuries had been becoming more and more nominal.'[16] But in this country the nationalist temper was over-heated by the special circumstances in which the King was placed.

Henry VIII's need of an heir was, of course, the occasion rather than the cause of the Reformation. It was this that made necessary the break with the Pope. But even if it had not been for this paramount necessity, it is conceivable that there might have been a religious and theological movement within the existing framework of the Church. However, since the Pope would not, or could not, annul his marriage with Katherine, Henry had to find some other authority that would.

The path to the Royal Supremacy had been made surprisingly easy by Wolsey. Unfortunately for him he did not realize the true trend of affairs until too late to save himself. However, he had in all innocence shown the way to success by gathering all the reins of power into his own hands. Under the indulgence of his sovereign he had become supreme in both Church and State. As Lord Chancellor he was head of the legislature and judiciary: as the Pope's *legatus a latere* he was effective head of the church, taking precedence even over the Archbishop of Canterbury. It was the first time in English history that one person had been all-powerful in both spheres.[17] A relic of the combination is seen even today in the House of Lords, which claims that it owes its red-covered benches to Wolsey's cardinalate. When the crisis came it seemed the easiest thing in the world for Henry to get rid of Wolsey and to take over the double power he had allowed his chief minister to assume.

It is unlikely that at the outset Henry intended to do more than solve his immediate problem. But once the decisive step had been taken and the Pope's authority abolished in 1534, the temptation to enrich himself and to buy support by the creation of a new aristocracy proved too strong. The monasteries were dissolved. No one today who sees the ruins of Glastonbury and Fountains or any one of a host of other relics, whatever his theological opinions, can look back upon this wholesale spoliation without regret. But at least it should be remembered to Henry's credit that he treated such monks as yielded with much greater respect than has been generally conceded by partisan historians, and that he formed out of the proceeds of the suppression six new bishoprics.

Be that as it may, it is certain that Henry, who was himself something of a theologian (and might have been Archbishop of Canterbury if he had not become heir to the throne), had not the slightest intention of changing the religion of his people. In this he was at one with his Parliament. Had it not, in the Act cutting off supplies for the Papacy, denied that 'your grace, your nobles and subjects intend by the same to decline or vary from the congregation of Christ's Church in any thing concerning the very articles of the Catholic Faith of Christendom'?[18] Indeed, Henry showed no mercy to those who tried to change the religion of the country. The King's Book, or to quote its full title 'A Necessary Doctrine and Erudition for any Christian Man; set forth by the King's Majesty of England', was definitely intended to stem the tide of change and to fix religious faith and observance in the old channels. Not for nothing was Henry Defender of the Faith and champion of Christendom. Already, in his time, we see the rise of a Catholic as distinct from a Papalist party. Catholicism without the Pope was Henry's aim. In fact, he has been, not altogether facetiously, described as the first Anglo-Catholic. Temporary as we may think this position to have been, it was to have important effects later upon Elizabeth and her settlement. Nevertheless Henry was often accused even in his own time of Lutheranism. There is this, at least, to be said in favour of the charge that the King thoroughly approved of the revived importance given to the Old Testament with its emphasis on the sacrosanct position of 'the Lord's Anointed' and that he fully appreciated the Lutheran defence of the monarch's right to dictate the religion of his subjects. Perhaps the best description of the King's position would be to say that he was Lutheran in politics and Catholic in theology.

The stand taken by Henry VIII at the outset of the Reformation in England was of special importance, since it was instrumental in preserving the continuity of the English Church. The lawyers saw to it that the break with Rome meant little change in the constitutional framework, apart from the handing over of Papal powers to the King and the Archbishop of Canterbury. There was no doctrinal change and very little change in the form of worship. Consequently the average congregation was not much affected.

The dam so carefully erected by Henry was breached in the reign of his youthful successor. Edward VI's uncles were rapacious men, who, having tasted the sweets of spoliation, were only too happy at the opportunity to carry on the work of devastation a little further. They gladly seized on the intellectual revolution on the continent to provide a rationale for their scheme. They thus used the opinions of more honourable men. Cranmer was honestly affected by the theological revolution and the young King himself was in ardent sympathy with the new thought.

The main struggle in the doctrinal reform was over the Presence of Christ in the Eucharist. Unfortunately the reformers bundled together the doctrines they did not like, such as those of sacrifice and transubstantiation, and linked them with the term Mass, which in itself is an entirely colourless word taken from the *Missa est* or formula of dismissal at the end of the Latin service. This misappropriation has led many English people to think that there was some essential difference between the Mass and the Lord's Supper, forgetful of the fact that they are merely variant names for the same service. Actually in the Lutheran countries of Scandinavia the name Mass is still preserved for the service, even when there is no consecration of the elements and, consequently, no question of sacrifice or of transubstantiation.

The change in doctrinal emphasis can be perceived in the titles given to the service in the two Prayer Books of Edward's reign. In that of 1549 the title reads, 'The Supper of the Lord, and the Holy Communion, commonly called the Mass'. In that of 1552 it reads 'The Order for the Administration of the Lord's Supper, or Holy Communion'. Obviously if the service thus variously designated was the Mass in 1549, it was still the same in 1552. It is undeniable, however, that there was a change in emphasis, and this change was reinforced, and indeed made glaringly obvious to the congregation, not only by the use of the vulgar tongue already introduced and some rearrangement of the service, but by the shedding of some of the old vestments and ceremonies. The effect has been vividly described by Miss Ady. 'When the new liturgy was first used in St Paul's Cathedral on All Saints' Day 1552 the choir was dispersed, the organ silenced, and the officiants, according to the directions of a new rubric, wore neither alb, vestment, nor cope. Protestantism was enthroned in all its starkness at the heart of England's religious life. Just over eight months later Edward VI was dead and the brief career of his second Prayer Book was ended.'[19]

It is very questionable, in view of the slow communications and the usual delay over effecting such changes, whether the second Prayer Book of Edward VI was ever used at all in many of the parishes. In any case the accession of Mary and the consequent reversion to the Latin liturgy, prevented people from becoming accustomed to it. Nevertheless, the brief interlude of Edward's reign was a period of reform that left a lasting mark on the church in England. Mary's reign, bitter as it seems to us in retrospect, by a merciful dispensation of Providence performed two services for Anglicanism: it prevented continental protestantism from running riot in the land, and at the same time, by the very violence of its reaction, it so disgusted the nation with the type of catholicism the Queen represented that papalism lost for ever its chance of capturing or re-capturing the heart of the people.

It is paradoxical that Mary was able to establish what must now be called Roman Catholicism only under the doctrine of the Divine Right of Kings and of the Royal Supremacy, which had been asserted by Henry VIII. During her reign the reformers were hoist with their own petard. Their tragedy lay in the fact that it was so difficult to see how far the duty of obedience to the crown should be allowed to carry them against their own conscientious views. This difficulty comes out clearly in the contrasted attitudes of Ridley and Cranmer. The former under Edward VI tried hard to induce Hooper to wear the episcopal vestments required by law, because they were, he said, 'things indifferent'. On the other hand he made a fierce attack on images, and wherever he could he turned 'altars' into 'tables'. He went to greet Mary on her accession, but as he had already recognized Lady Jane Grey's title to the throne and declared both Mary and Elizabeth illegitimate, he was sent straightway to the Tower. He showed no inclination to recant, but maintained a stiff attitude to the end. Cranmer, as is well known, did recant, and has often been regarded as a coward for that reason. This judgment is hardly fair to one who felt in conscience bound to do his utmost to obey his sovereign's wishes. His decision would have been more difficult, if she had treated him more leniently. In her efforts to discredit him, she pushed him too far. When he finally realized that she was determined on his execution, he felt that he could not die with a lie on his lips; and so he spoilt her designs by withdrawing his recantations and proclaiming for the benefit of the public his real beliefs.

If Edward's reign had made the nation disgusted with Puritanism and Mary's with Papalism, it was clear that Elizabeth must look for a settlement to some other interpretation of Christianity. She found the *tertium quid* in her father's non-papal Catholicism. It is often suggested that this choice arose from mere policy. In spite of the general conclusion of historians on the subject there seems no need to doubt Elizabeth's sincere religious conviction. It is adduced against her that during Mary's reign she attended Mass. But only those should blame her on that score who think that the Mass is some idolatrous service quite different from the Lord's Supper. In any case, by her conformity at that time she saved her own life and the Reformation. For once policy and conscience seem to have been in agreement. It is in line with the religion she inherited from her father and confirmed by her own reading. She had an individual dislike of Puritanism, a masculine taste for good order, a feminine appreciation of appropriate adjuncts to worship, and above all a strong belief in England (including England's Church) for the English.

It is well thus to understand the Queen's personal religion or we can never grasp the nature of her settlement. It was meant to be inclusive, embracing as far as possible the whole population of the country. At first all except the incipient parties of extreme puritans on the one hand and committed papalists on the other appeared to agree. In the result it was only the Queen's personal influence that contrived to keep the balance. Sir J. E. Neale's researches[20] have shown us that the majority in both church and state was against her. Because of the strength of the opposition, she could not get all that she wanted. But she induced her chosen Archbishop Parker to exercise a measure of discipline and her Prayer Book of 1559 won back a good deal of the ground lost in 1552. Episcopacy was retained and presbyterianism excluded; the Black Rubric of 1552, which denied the real presence of Christ in the Holy Communion, was dropped; the reference to his Body and Blood in the words of administration was renewed; the old vestments and ornaments were restored.* Actually this went further than the prevailing temper would allow, and not much use seems to have been made of the order to restore the eucharistic vestments; the surplice in parish churches and the cope in Cathedrals was all that could be generally enforced. It was sufficient, however, to conciliate not only the middle core of the population but also a number of Catholics, who might have become recusants, and of Lutherans whose co-religionists in Northern Europe were still wearing the old vestments.

It was from this background that Anglicanism emerged as a distinct tradition. First had come the separation, arising out of the practical difficulties of Henry's reign; then had come certain developments in

---

*To the level of the second year of Edward VI, i.e. *before* the Prayer Book of 1549.

doctrine and worship owing largely to the pressure of the new thought from the continent; now came the effort to provide a rationale of what had happened and to set the new attitude in a coherent system of thought. As we have already seen this attitude was recognized from the outset to be an Anglican, as distinct from a Roman, Catholicism. That did not prevent an equal recognition of the fact that Anglicanism was a protestant version of Christianity. In that immediate context, however, Protestantism meant little more than freedom from the shackles of Rome. The opposite of 'protestant' was not 'catholic' but 'papal'. Roman Catholicism as distinct from Anglican is generally dated by Anglican historians from the Council of Trent.

The sixteenth century was a great period for composing confessions of faith. In view of the current changes and the need for defining its position it was inevitable that the Church of England should follow the fashion. Since, however, it claimed to represent a continuity of the age-long historic church, it did not find it necessary, as some churches on the continent did, to formulate its whole scheme of Christianity afresh from the beginning. All it needed to do was to make clear its attitude towards Rome and towards the more important changes induced by the revolt against her. This it did in a series of sets of Articles, in which we can see the fluctuations of opinion before a final position was reached. The first, known as the Ten Articles, published under Henry in 1536 showed no change in doctrine but substituted the royal for the Papal supremacy. Two years later Cranmer drew up the Thirteen Articles, which never saw the light of day, but are important as introducing Lutheran influence into the series. By 1553 Lutheran pressure had been replaced by Calvinist, and the latter influence can be seen in the Forty-two Articles published in that year. Even so, neither of the two extreme doctrinal positions, Justification by Faith alone nor Pre-destination, managed to get itself accepted. Such protestant influence as did infiltrate was toned down still further, ten years later, when the Queen gave her sanction to the Thirty-nine Articles in roughly the same form in which they appear today. They hold the balance so very carefully that they have been regarded as susceptible both of a catholic and a calvinist interpretation.

The intellectual protagonist of emergent Anglicanism was Richard Hooker (1553–1600), author of the *Ecclesiastical Polity*, a book which won the praise of Pope Clement VIII and which Hallam reckoned 'the first great original prose work in our language'. He emphasized the nature of God as the Eternal Reason, expressing itself in the laws of the universe. Our own reason is the main instrument by which we gain practical knowledge of Him. By this reason also we are able to understand the revelation He has given of Himself in the Scriptures. The Bible is not an end in itself, as the Puritans implied. Much is left to the judgment and interpretation of the Church, which has been divinely guided to speak its mind in the Ecumenical Councils and with which the Church of England is historically continuous. While he rebutted the calvinistic view that the original polity of the church was presbyterian, he did not go so far as to hold that episcopacy was essential or necessary—thus differing from a number of other champions of Anglicanism who clung firmly to the view that bishops were not only of the *bene esse* but of the *esse* of the Church. Later generations have found something specially ambivalent in his doctrine of the Eucharist. Nevertheless, he seems to have adopted a teaching of the Real Presence. He thus drew the line firmly dividing Anglicans from both Romanism and Puritanism. From the outset he, therefore, established a characteristic Anglican position, a position that received official affirmation under James I in the Hampton Court Conference of 1604, and that later was to be strengthened and confirmed by the great Caroline divines such as Andrewes and Laud.

Expansion

The Anglicanism thus established was peculiar to the English. This was no disadvantage in the eyes of its members. Some of its leaders realized the mischief and the danger risked by dissecting 'the body of Christ', and tried to preserve relations with other bodies of Christians. But during the period of fervid nationalism, when Englishmen quite seriously thought themselves better than any foreigners, it seemed no disadvantage to have a church whose superiority was extolled above all others and whose liturgy was soon to be regarded as 'incomparable'. The insularity of the church matched the insularity of the nation. Both might easily have stagnated if it had not been for the great new expansion overseas. As the nation developed first into an empire and then into a commonwealth, so the Church of England developed into the almost world-wide Anglican Communion.

Close at hand the omens did not seem particularly propitious. In Ireland and Scotland, which could be regarded as more definitely the heirs of the Celtic tradition than England, the bulk of the population followed lines which, though contradictory to each other, were equally opposed to Anglicanism. In Scotland the Puritan revolution had succeeded, and after the failure of efforts to find a middle way the country had become calvinist, supplanting the episcopalians and reducing them to the position of a small sect. Presbyterianism became the established religion. It was not until the Toleration Act of 1792 that clergy ordained by Scottish bishops were allowed to officiate in Scotland itself. The reason was that the Jacobite sympathies of the episcopalian clergy were well known. They had close ties with the Non-jurors in England, and some had even participated in the dynastic struggle. Consequently full toleration was only granted to them by the Act of 1792 after the death of Charles Edward. However, it was of great importance that the bishops, though few and weak, were still there, for they were able in due course, as we shall see, to supply English deficiencies and consecrate a bishop for America.

It is sometimes said that the episcopalian cause could have triumphed in Scotland if the English had been more forthcoming. The harm done by English aloofness in Scotland was matched in Ireland by English readiness to interfere. There the bulk of the population developed a cordial dislike, not wholly undeserved, for both the Scots and the English. Consequently in ecclesiastical matters they followed their own line; they opted for the unreformed religion and in 1614 set up their own Roman Catholic hierarchy. Anglicanism, although a minority religion, was still the established church of the country and was later united by the Act of Union (1800) with the Church of England. It had far too many dioceses for the size of its membership, but the action of the state in suppressing two out of the four archbishoprics and eight out of the eighteen bishoprics in 1833 was largely responsible for starting the Tractarian Movement in England. The Church of Ireland was disestablished in 1869.

The life of Wales was much more closely integrated with that of England. But even there the Celtic temperament showed itself in a determination to follow no clearly marked line of traditional development. Both church and state might have done a good deal more for the people in their remote valleys than they did. The emotional nature of the Welsh craved for something more exciting than was offered by the traditional and somewhat formal worship of the Church in the eighteenth and nineteenth centuries and found it in the warm atmosphere of the newly built conventicles of the evangelical movement. Non-conformity grew until, as a whole, it outnumbered Anglicanism. It seemed to many an act of belated justice when Lloyd George succeeded in disestablishing the Welsh Church in 1920. Its remarkable progress since that date has often been used as an argument for universal disestablishment.

But this is to anticipate. We have only followed the story so far in order to show how the home church was split up into definite national churches and how in the majority of its branches Anglicanism was freed from its connection with the state. We must now return to the story of expansion, remembering that it was not the Church of England only but also the episcopal churches of Scotland and Ireland—the nucleus of the Anglican Communion—that took part in this development.

Already expansion had begun in the early seventeenth century. The Church accompanied the merchants as they went from the British Isles to various parts of the world. There were three main centres of their settlements: India, America and the great trading cities of Europe. Laud, who was Archbishop of Canterbury from 1633 to 1645, was very missionary-hearted as well as pastorally-minded. He wished all these centres to receive Christian ministrations. Also he was a disciplinarian, and he was anxious to send a bishop to America to 'keep the Puritans in order'. (It will be remembered that the Pilgrim Fathers had sailed on their great adventure in 1620 and had proved a somewhat disturbing influence.) However, this was more easily said than done. A bishop was a great state official who sat in the House of Lords. How to create bishops who would have no state rights? No solution offered itself and in default of anything better Laud persuaded King Charles to put all the overseas work under the Bishop of London. It is interesting that one fragment of that vast undertaking, the chaplaincies of North and Central Europe, still remains under the jurisdiction of that bishop today.

Bishops of London such as Compton and Gibson had the interests of the American colonies much at heart, and did everything they could both for the emigrants and for the natives, though all the time urging the need for a bishop to live and work on the spot. Had Queen Anne survived a little longer Dean Swift of St Patrick's Dublin might have been consecrated as Bishop of Virginia, but she died before the proposal could be carried through. It is time to get rid of the legend that the Church of England was unwilling to consecrate bishops for America. The Society for the Propagation of the Gospel (SPG) indeed put forward a scheme for four bishops. The responsibility for the failure of the various efforts rested solely with the ministers of state.[21] Even their unwillingness can be understood when it is realized that, over and above the constitutional difficulty, opinion on the American side was by no means universally favourable. The general dislike of prelacy, the fear of discipline, the jealousy of governors, the independence of the vestries, the nervousness of slave-owners, the shrinking from financial obligation—all these moods combined to make the introduction of bishops to

America far from a safe bid from the political point of view.

Happily some Americans persisted. Failing to obtain satisfaction in England they were on the point of seeking a nominee in Denmark, when Dr Routh, the President of Magdalen, advised them to try Scotland. In 1784, the year succeeding the peace that ended the War of Independence, Seabury was consecrated in Aberdeen by three Scottish bishops as Bishop of Connecticut. The ice once broken, the Church of England was quick to take advantage. In 1786 an act was passed to allow the archbishops to consecrate, as bishops, citizens of countries outside the King's dominions and for office beyond the shores of Great Britain. The very next year advantage was taken of the act: an American citizen, William White, was consecrated by English bishops for Pennsylvania, and another, Samuel Provoost, for New York, in the Archbishop's Palace at Lambeth. A third consecration, that of James Madison for Virginia, followed in 1790. This was tardy recognition of the needs of the Church overseas. It was too late to repair all the damage done by past neglect, particularly in the embittered atmosphere caused by the War of Independence. Nevertheless, the difficulty of attempting to organize an episcopalian church without bishops was ended; America could now consecrate bishops for itself. From that time the story of the Protestant Episcopal Church in America has been one of continual increase and advance.

Anglican expansion in India can be dated from 1614 when the East India Company began to employ chaplains there. From fear of violent reaction the policy of the Company was against any attempt to convert native Indians. Such reaction indeed did occur in the Vellore Mutiny of 1806, owing to the mistaken belief that the British meant to put down the native religion by force. In the interval, however, mission work had been spread first by German Lutherans supported by the Society for the Promotion of Christian Knowledge (SPCK) and then by a succession of English priests sent out by the Church Missionary Society (CMS founded in 1799). The missionaries worked at a great disadvantage because they were representatives of a conquering power and yet were manifestly not supported by their own government. Here, as so often, English officialdom leant over backwards to avoid any appearance of religious favouritism and, consequently, was a good deal less than fair to its national church. Nevertheless, under the combined efforts of missionaries and chaplains the word advanced sufficiently to warrant the appointment of a bishop (T. F. Middleton) in 1814. His jurisdiction was held to be limited to the chaplains and their European congregations and not to extend to the missions; it was only gradually that the missionaries with their flocks were brought under full episcopal control.[22]

Canada, as a separate colony after the War of Independence, had already received a bishop for Nova Scotia in 1787. Other sections of the new British Empire soon followed. This brings us to the fresh and even more important period of expansion in the nineteenth century. The West Indies received a bishop for Jamaica and Barbados in 1824. A bishop was consecrated for Australia in 1836, and for New Zealand in 1841. South Africa had its Bishop of Cape Town in 1847; West Africa saw its see of Sierra Leone created in 1852; and Eastern Equatorial Africa welcomed Bishop Hannington in 1884 (Mauritius and Madagascar having received a bishop in 1854 and 1874 respectively). In addition to the churches in countries which have or have had a vital connection with the British Empire or Commonwealth there are considerable branches of the Anglican communion in China,* where the diocese of Hong Kong was established in 1849 and in Japan where a see of South Tokyo was created in 1883. As a result of this expansion the Anglican Communion now consists of some 260 dioceses overseas in addition to the 70 in the home churches of the United Kingdom and Ireland (England 43, Wales 6, Scotland 7, Ireland 14). The United States (Protestant Episcopal Church of America) has now 75 dioceses together with 28 missionary districts.

We thus see that the Anglican Communion today consists of a considerable congeries of some 330 dioceses scattered over a very considerable portion of the globe. Within these dioceses practically all its forty million members are contained. Although there is no visible head on earth of the Anglican Communion all these dioceses recognize the Archbishop of Canterbury as their senior bishop and all are invited by him to send their diocesan bishop to a decennial conference at Lambeth.

As there is no head on earth of the Anglican Communion, so there is no body that can legislate for it. Each national or provincial church legislates within strict limits for its own dioceses. Outside these limits each diocese legislates for itself under its own diocesan bishop, who is the fount of jurisdiction in his own area. This means that the Lambeth Conference is essentially a deliberative body of equals. No doubt the size and importance of an individual bishop's see will add some weight to his opinion, as will also his personal character and prestige. But fundamentally, the bishops meet on a level of absolute equality and the

*What has happened to the Church in China since the Communist revolution is not yet clear.

fact that the Archbishop of Canterbury is in the Chair gives him no more authority than is usually accorded in the courtesy of debate to one who is both host and chairman.

Nor have the findings of the Conference any more authority than is lent to them by the standing of those responsible for them. Naturally, in fact, tremendous weight is attached to the solemn recommendations of so many fathers-in-God, who have gathered so much experience in so many quarters of the world. News of their resolutions is eagerly awaited by the Press and by the Church throughout the world. When their report is published the points requiring legislation are taken to the provinces and dioceses, and there the necessary decisions are taken or not as seems fit to the local church. In most cases the recommendations of the Conference provide what the lawyers call persuasive precedents, but the local churches are not obliged to accept the recommendations of Lambeth and sometimes do not.

In recent times the Conference has threatened to become too big for smooth and efficient working. Until 1958 all bishops in active episcopal work, whether diocesans, coadjutors, suffragans, or assistants, had expected to receive an invitation. This meant that, although by no means all were able to come, there was an attendance of well over 300. Some attempt was made in 1958 to reduce the numbers but even so there were 310 bishops present. It is likely that in future some care will be taken to see that each diocese is represented by no more than one bishop. Such a step may prevent the numbers from becoming too unwieldy.

There is thus no central government in the Anglican Communion. The effective unit of government is the diocese. This arrangement is in accordance with the pattern of the early Church, where the bishop, surrounded by his presbyters, was responsible for the management of his 'home affairs' and also acted as the 'liaison officer' between his own and other dioceses. At first sight it may look as if the bishop has almost autocratic powers, but closer inspection shows that, within his own diocese, he has to work with a number of committees which effectively check any undue tendency to autocracy, while in the larger world outside he is continually meeting his fellow-bishops from a larger or smaller circle and their influence generally checks the development of too marked an idiosyncrasy.

It might be wondered how so loosely constructed an organization can be kept together. The unity, however, is surprisingly strong. It is sometimes alleged that the Church of England is so divided against itself that only the establishment holds it together. But here we see that these dioceses, in almost all of which the same differences are to be found as in England, keep together perfectly well without any 'establishment' to support them. The various individual expressions of their unity, their common worship and ethos, we shall have to discuss at length in the following pages. But here, already, we can clearly see that combination of independence and loyalty which we had occasion to notice as a marked characteristic of the Church in England from its early days. No doubt it is helped by an interchange of clergy that tends to increase as the years go by and means of communication become easier. There is now a sort of shadowy staff-college at St Augustine's, Canterbury, which includes priest-students from every land. There is also an American bishop who has taken up residence at Lambeth and acts as a kind of adjutant to the Archbishop in the handling of inter-provincial affairs. He is known as the Executive Officer.

Most important of all, the clergy of any part of the Anglican communion are capable, under proper permission, of exercising their ministry in any other part. If they sometimes find to their surprise that as visitors in some national Anglican church other than their own they are not permitted to celebrate a wedding, it is not because of any ecclesiastical regulation, but because the state has its own views as to who shall officiate at a ceremony which is civic as well as religious and which is, therefore, very much the concern of the secular authority. But such civic statutes apart, the unity of the Anglican communion throughout the world is manifest by the interchangeability of its clergy. To the discerning eye it is also recognizable in the peculiar ethos of the Anglican clergy, an ethos compounded of elements from their Roman, Celtic, English, Norman ancestry and including a love of independence and adventure which can only be understood by continual reference to their common history.

CHAPTER TWO

ITS SISTER CHURCHES

Protestant Episcopal Church of the USA: Consecration of Seabury, White and Provoost—Philadelphia Convention of 1789—The Episcopal Church in modern times—Canada—Australia—New Zealand—South Africa—India—Foundation of Church of South India—China—Japan—South-East Asia—Jerusalem—Africa—West Indies

HAVING SKETCHED the development of Anglicanism as an organization it would now be proper for us to give some attention to the component churches. We have already dealt with the British Isles; we now add a note on the rise of the greater national churches overseas.

United States of America

The largest is the Protestant Episcopal Church of the United States, with three and a half million baptized members, 7,485 parishes and 8,785 clergy. Its progress in modern times has been quite astounding. After the War of Independence, when Anglicanism was, not unnaturally, associated in the minds of many with loyalty to the British Crown, there was only a small proportion of the population that maintained its adherence to the national church of the old country. It is true that what we now know as Anglicanism had already had a not ignoble history in the States. It was, indeed, the original Christianity of the area. It had been 'established' by the first English colonists of Virginia who held their first service at Jamestown in 1607. It had been introduced into New York after the Dutch surrender in 1664 and had there grown apace. It had entered Massachusetts with a first service at Boston in 1686. By 1692 the Roman Catholic dominance had been replaced by episcopalian establishment even in Maryland. The Puritan stronghold of Connecticut received episcopalianism somewhat later in 1722. Everyone knows under what mixed religious auspices the American colonies began their existence. It says much for the vitality of Anglicanism that, without any resident bishop, it was able to maintain itself so strongly up to the time of the separation.

One reason for this steadiness was that it did not, like Congregationalism and Presbyterianism, allow its own unity to be broken as a result of the 'Great Awakening', brought about by the revivalist methods of Frelinghuysen, Edwards and Whitefield. That division into Old Light and New Light had even affected the universities, Harvard and Yale remaining in the old fashion while Princeton was created to follow the

29

New Light. In any case, the revival, with all its excitement and enthusiasm, was lost in the struggle for independence and the war with England (1775–83). The sufferings of the clergy in that war were naturally severe. They can best be described in the words of an American historian:

'The majority of them outside the South were Loyalists, a result of their political conservatism and, in some cases, their English birth and education. Many in the North were missionaries of the SPG, and for most of these men their ordination oath of allegiance to the Crown was an insuperable obstacle to their support of the cause of independence. Reviled as Tories, branded as traitors by the news sheets and broadsides that stirred up popular indignation and mob violence against them, repudiated by many of the laity by whom the problem of conscientious loyalty was not so keenly felt, the Anglican clergy were treated with a cruel harshness that forms one of the least attractive chapters in American history. Mistreated, their property confiscated, their churches wrecked, they were silenced, imprisoned, and banished. Many of them accompanied the Loyalists to the Canadian maritime provinces or to the West Indies.'[1]

We have remarked that in the very year when the war was concluded Seabury was sent to England to seek consecration as bishop. As legal considerations prevented the English bishops from consecrating one who could not take the oath of allegiance, he obtained consecration at the hands of three Non-juring bishops in Scotland. His first duty on his return was to exercise his right of ordination and fill up the depleted ranks of the ministry. Presently, however, doubts were raised about the regularity of these ordinations. To set the matter at rest two other priests were sent to England to be consecrated. By this time English scruples had been overcome, and White and Provoost were consecrated at Lambeth in 1787.

This marks an important change in the position of Anglicanism in the States. The consecration of Seabury had been the result of efforts made by the church in the state of Connecticut alone. That the request for it should have been so partial was evidence of the lack of organizational unity among the Anglicans of the various states, each of which was accustomed to go its own separate way. It was clearly necessary that something should be done to knit together the whole body of church people in the new nation. It was William White, then rector of Christ Church, Philadelphia, who took the initiative in this effort. It would take too long to trace the full story here. A number of the states sent representatives to a convention at Philadelphia in 1785 which requested the English Archbishop to consecrate chosen men from the states. The Englishmen got a suitable act passed through Parliament, and that is how White and Provoost came to be consecrated in England. In the end a General Convention was held in Philadelphia in 1789 which adopted a constitution, a body of canons, and a Prayer Book for the whole national Church. It is interesting to notice that the liturgy adopted followed the canon of the Scottish Episcopal Church rather than that of the Church of England. This choice was made not merely because the Scottish liturgy was intrinsically better, but as an expression of gratitude to the church that had given America its first bishop. Seabury, indeed, had agreed to try to get this choice effected before he was made bishop. The same sentiment was revealed in the style and title which the new organization adopted for itself, namely the Protestant Episcopal Church of the United States of America.

The result of the war, combined with a doctrinal declension in the direction of Unitarianism, brought organized religion in America to its nadir. It has been said that after the war no more than 7 per cent of the population were willing to admit affiliation to any religious body. Today the recorded church membership has reached its record peak of 63 per cent. The turn of the tide began with the Second Awakening, associated with the famous camp meetings of the beginning of the nineteenth century. This movement proliferated in new sects; and the fissiparous tendency was extended by sharp differences of view on the question of slavery. Some of the largest denominations were split into different organizations over this question. The episcopalians maintained their cohesion, and although one bishop (Louisiana) was actually fighting as a combatant on the side of the south, they refused to excommunicate each other. When peace was declared in 1865 the southern bishops resumed their seats in General Convention. As an American onlooker says, 'The incident reflects the genius of Anglicanism for tolerating differences of opinion and conviction within the framework of its corporate life.'[2]

The same writer thinks that the Anglican Book of Common Prayer with its implicit pledge that services shall be conducted decently and in order is Anglicanism's greatest single source of attraction for non-episcopalians in his country. It would, no doubt, have come to occupy a still greater place in the nation's life if episcopalians had not been somewhat laggard in the great trek to the west. As things are, the Protestant Episcopal Church comes only seventh in the grading of denominations in USA according to size of membership. But it is generally agreed that its influence, particularly in the towns, is far greater than one might expect from its numbers. The fact is that to be an Episcopalian carries a certain social prestige. Although the Episcopal Church does particularly fine work among the Indians and Puerto Ricans, to say nothing of

the down-and-outs, it is accused of running all the dangers that
commonly attend the possession of wealth. At the same time it is
generally conceded that the Episcopal Church is the only religious
organization that can offer the use of cathedrals such as Washington
and St John the Divine, New York, for worship that can be called in any
approximate sense national.

Another point in which the organization of the American Episcopal
Church agrees with the Scottish is that it has no archbishops. The
bishop who is elected as senior over the whole Anglican community in
that country is known as Presiding Bishop. He has no diocese of his own
but exercises a general oversight of the whole church. It is true that the
church is divided into provinces, but even they have no archbishops;
however, one of the diocesan bishops who takes the chair at provincial
gatherings is recognized as 'President'. The consequence is that the
individual provinces have no very great consciousness of themselves as
corporate entities. This has its good side, in that it enables great stress to
be laid on national duty and privilege, especially in respect of missions.
Missionary enthusiasm is not broken up among societies as in England.
But there may be some disadvantage in the system through loss of local
interest.

If it is true, as it undoubtedly is, that the modern tightening of the
bonds that draw the constituent churches of the Anglican Communion
together has enabled each of those churches to make a larger contribution to the life of the whole, there has been no instance in which this
development has been more obvious than the Church of the United
States. Its very numbers and the enormous prestige enjoyed by its
country throughout the world together give it a quite special importance. Such influence as it owes to those causes is enhanced by the
vigour and originality of its way of life.

The special contribution the American Church has made to the
common life of Anglicanism is threefold: democratic organization,
employment of the laity, and business capacity. Owing to the peculiar
circumstances of its early history, passed among so many Independents
and Congregationalists and deprived of the unifying influences of the
episcopate, stress was inevitably laid on local drive and initiative. Once
the help of SPG and various state aids had been lost there was otherwise
no hope of survival. Parishes and dioceses had to fend for themselves or
they would have disappeared. Something of that local vigour thus
generated still remains and has been learnt by other branches of the
Anglican Communion. Even the conservative church of the home
country has been shamed into recognizing how much a mere handful

of church folk can do for themselves if they are sufficiently devoted.

It followed almost inevitably from such a situation that a large part of the power in American ecclesiastical affairs passed into the hands of the laity. Even the Roman Catholic Church felt this pressure and Rome had to recognize in its exaggeration a new heresy. Anglicans on the whole welcomed the change. Certainly, in the various provinces of the Commonwealth it was realized that progress was likely to be very slow unless the laity could be taken into full co-operation. And again even the English Church has found it necessary to reorganize its whole governmental procedure in order to meet the same need. In doing so it has been happy to have the experience of its overseas partners to provide a model.

Nowhere has the English Church been more ready to admire the American than in the sphere of business administration. The idea of incorporating up-to-date business methods into financial and parochial administration was quite foreign to the minds of English clergy, and consequently suspect, until the beginning of the present century. Recently, however, the ice has been broken. If American methods cannot be precisely duplicated in the English parish they can at least be taken as a guide to efficiency. Particularly is this influence seen in the new attitude to the Christian stewardship of money. It is safe to say that the condition of many an English parish has already been revolutionized by this west wind from the other side of the Atlantic. The three influences taken together have produced something like a revolution in English Church life.

Thus we are compelled to recognize the reciprocal influence exercised by the constituent Anglican churches upon each other and the Mother Church. The American side of this influence is well summarized in the following private communication from Dr Stephen Bayne, formerly Bishop of Olympia, USA, and now Anglican Executive Officer for the whole Anglican Communion:

'The most characteristic contribution of the American Church to Anglicanism is doubtless in the part that the laity play in the life and government of the church. The Colonial Church in Virginia had to deal with the vacuum revolving around Parson's Freehold, Advowson, etc., created by the absence of almost all the normal machinery of the Church of England. The response of the Colonial Church was to pick up and develop the idea of the select vestry which became the characteristic "rector, church wardens, and vestry" of our current usage. It was the vestry which held title to the parish property and administered parish funds. Although our American clergy are still irremovable and some fragments of the parson's freehold still remain, in effect the vestry took over the freehold and also the rights of patronage.

33

'Thus in colonial America the laity took a dominant part in parish affairs from the very outset. When the General Convention was established following the revolution, the laity were unquestionably accepted as a constituent part of the Convention, in equal numbers with the clergy (although the right to a vote by orders has always been preserved). This has also been followed in diocesan affairs: so all through the American Church from its colonial days to the present day the place of the laity in the full life of the Church has been clear. I think it was this sense of wholeness in the Church which Selwyn wanted to reproduce in New Zealand.'

We need only add that Selwyn's efforts bore abundant fruit both in New Zealand and in England, and indeed throughout the whole Anglican Communion.

Something of the size and importance of the Episcopal Church in USA has been seen from the fact that it now consists of eight provinces divided into seventy-five dioceses. There are also no fewer than twenty-eight missionary districts. Early missionary activity was naturally centred in the work among the Indians in North America. It soon spread to areas especially open to United States influence such as Mexico, Central America, Cuba, Colombia, Brazil, Haiti, Puerto Rico, Hawaii and Honolulu. In the last named island the British had already prepared the ground, and the friendship of Queen Victoria for the reigning monarch of the time had secured an admirable grant of land where a fine cathedral with its ancillary building now stands. It is an intriguing thought that the Union Jack is still quartered in the flag of the island.

In addition to all this independent work, the Episcopal Church shows its solidarity with the whole Church by contributing largely in men and money to the work of other branches of the Anglican Communion. Its priests can be found working in the dioceses of Hong Kong, Singapore, Cape Town and the Upper Nile as well as in India and Japan. One American bishop presides over the diocese of Nassau and another over that of Damaraland. As often happens, missionary work has also in this instance paved the way towards unity. In the Philippines there is an Independent Church of about two million members, formed at the beginning of the twentieth century by a secession from the Roman Church. This Philippino Church formed cordial relations with the American mission, sending many of its ordinands for training to the Anglican seminary and inviting Anglican bishops to share in its consecrations. It was natural that such intimate relations should lead to full communion. In this development a parallel can be seen with the mutual *rapprochement* between the Episcopal Church in America and the Polish National Church on that continent.

Canada

When the American War of Independence was over, the colonies to the north which did not secede received a flood of United Empire Loyalists from the south, who had emigrated rather than lose their British connection. Some settled in Nova Scotia and the maritime areas; others pushed up the St Lawrence into Upper Canada and founded cities like Kingston. Many of them were Anglicans, and they found themselves members of a state church, which indeed remained established in Canada until 1832. There were, however, many who followed Presbyterian and other faiths. There was also the very strong Roman Catholic body in Quebec. That city had been taken by Wolfe in 1759 but had been allowed to retain both its French and its religious ethos. As in the States, both Romans and Anglicans suffered from failure to seize their opportunities in the rush to the west. Nevertheless, the Anglicans shared in the general development and they did particularly fine work among the Indians and the Esquimaux. Today the Canadian Church is divided into four provinces, Canada, Ontario, Rupertsland and British Columbia, each with its own Archbishop and with twenty-eight dioceses in all.

Here again, in spite of the debt owed to SPG and CMS in the past, the societies have not been allowed to pursue their missionary aims down separate paths. They have been absorbed into one central organization, which makes itself responsible for the missionary work of the whole Canadian Church. Far and away the most important organization for the support of every kind of activity is the Women's Auxiliary which provides interest and work for so many women volunteers that there is little place in Canada for any other religious organization for women.

Life and work in the larger Canadian towns are very similar to life and work in cities all the world over. But the towns are comparatively few and far between. An interesting experiment made necessary by the vastness of the country and the sparseness of its dwellings is the Sunday School caravan, by means of which a modicum of religious education is provided for children in the most remote regions. Another interesting feature of Canadian work is illustrated by reliable pictures of fur-clad clergymen driving their dog-teams in the frozen wastes of the north to bring the gospel and medical help to the Esquimaux. The romance was not lessened by the resounding title of the first bishop to hold the northernmost see, 'Archibald the Arctic'.

As is naturally to be expected there is a fair amount of exchange between the two churches of the United States and Canada. One finds men trained on either side of the border crossing the boundary to occupy new charges. The situation is not unlike that between Wales and England. USA with its unrivalled set of seminaries has been able to offer facilities for theological education which Canada is only now beginning to rival. Toronto is, at least, comparable with General or Seabury-Western, and Canada has had at least one considerable theologian in the person of Archbishop Carrington of Quebec besides providing two notable scholars to be successive Deans of Christ Church, Oxford. The leaders of both churches have taken a not inconsiderable part in the ecumenical movement, although the name of Bishop Brent and the remembrance of the Chicago-Lambeth Quadrilateral will always preserve a special respect for the part played by the Church of USA. As far as size of membership goes, USA's three and a half million are being balanced by the two million on the Canadian side of the border. As far as comparison with other local churches is concerned, the latter figure is rather less than one third of the number of Roman Catholics in Canada, and it is also exceeded by the two and a half million of the Canadian United Church.

Australia
On the other side of the Pacific, the Church of England in Australia (no inducements have so far been strong enough to make Australian churchmen change the name) embraces not only the island continent but also Tasmania to the south and New Guinea to the north. This vast territory is divided into provinces in accordance with the boundaries of the separate states, only Tasmania and the dioceses of Willochra and Adelaide remaining outside the provincial organization. The diocese of New Guinea is attached to the province of Queensland. This means that there are four archbishops in Australia, of whom one is Primate, presiding over twenty-two dioceses in almost incredibly extensive areas very sparsely inhabited except in the cities. The fact that the population is congregated for the most part in four or five coastal towns, leaving the rest of the townships comparatively small and the farms or stations widely separated, constitutes, as can well be imagined, a very special problem in the way of pastoral care. The Church has consistently pursued the policy of seeking out the people wherever they are and ministering to them, if need be, in their own homes. No other body has been so consistently faithful to this principle, and the question is now sometimes raised whether it would not have been better to have set up central churches and let the people come into them instead of pursuing them to their own stations. Whatever may be the answer to that question, the result of the policy has been to make the Church of England the church

of the bushdweller as no other church is, and to set up an intimacy between priest and people such as is hardly enjoyed in any other part of the Anglican communion. In this result the Bush Brotherhoods (small groups of clergy dedicated under temporary vows to the task of taking the Church's ministrations to the more lonely dwellers in the out-back) have played a noble and conspicuous part. In fact, it is a joke of the country that some of its more remote highways must have been laid down for the exclusive use of the Bush Brother and the mail-man.

There is no established church in Australia, but if the trait just described does not give the Anglicans the right to call themselves the 'national' church, they might perhaps draw an argument from their relative numbers. The law does not require householders to state their religious allegiance, but from the census returns of the 80 per cent who do so voluntarily a sufficiently close estimate can be made. The proportions vary from state to state, but in the country as a whole round about 45 per cent of the total population declare themselves Anglican.

This is a considerable achievement for a church that was founded almost by accident. It was only at the last moment, just before the first fleet, bringing a thousand convicts and soldiers, set sail from England that William Wilberforce found that no provision had been made for their spiritual welfare, and secured the appointment of Richard Johnson as chaplain. This was in 1788, and it was not until three years later that Johnson received any clerical help. During the early years the work of the Church was under the remote superintendence of the Bishop of London, but when a diocese of Calcutta was formed to cover the area of the East India Company, Australia was made part of it. The first and last 'Bishop of Australia' was William Grant Broughton (1836–54). He was so successful as to be able to found new sees of New Zealand (1841), Tasmania (1842) Newcastle (1847), Melbourne (1847), becoming Primate of Australasia in the latter year, and retaining for himself the see of Sydney.

Hitherto both provinces and dioceses have displayed a more than usually strong spirit of independence. As a national church of the whole country their legislative needs have been met to some extent by their reliance on the church in England. It is true that there is a General Synod to which representatives are sent every five years from the whole church in Australia and of which the president is the Primate of Australia. But while the Australian church had no constitution of its own, the power exercised by the General Synod was extremely vague. After many years of anxious discussion and of repeated failures a constitution was at last accepted in 1959, and there is now good prospect

37

of an even more rapid advance in ordered life and effective evangelization.

It is well that it should be so, for the Anglican community with its 45 per cent of the Christian population of the country, far outnumbering any other single denomination, may be able to exert a valuable unifying influence in the nation. It is true that the church in Australia illustrates vividly the varying shades of ecclesiastical colour characteristic of Anglicanism and it is not altogether free from the rivalry between states which is a special feature of Australian life. But it has overcome these differences to a marked degree in arriving at a common constitution, and it is likely that it may help in future to bridge the difference between Scots and Irish, Conservative and Labour, and even between Presbyterians and Roman Catholics, differences which, since they so often coincide, produce deeper cleavages than they do in countries where racial, religious and political divisions cross each other.

New Zealand

The Anglican Communion in this country consists of a single province incorporating five dioceses. Out of a white population of under two million a third are Anglican, and they constitute much the largest single denomination. Out of a Maori population of roughly 100,000 only a quarter are Anglican, but they again form by far the strongest of the native Christian bodies. The Maori Anglicans are organized as a distinct diocese under their own bishop. This is not due to any colour bar, which in fact does not exist, but is a matter of cultural convenience. The missionary diocese, Melanesia, scene of the martyrdom of the saintly Bishop Patteson in 1872, is also associated with the province of New Zealand.

The first mission to New Zealand came from Sydney, Australia, in the person of the Reverend Samuel Marsden, who arrived, accompanied by a schoolmaster, a carpenter, and a shoemaker, in 1814. Twenty years later the work was so flourishing as to earn the congratulations of Charles Darwin. The first bishop of New Zealand was George Augustus Selwyn who was consecrated in 1841. He was one of the really great missionary pioneers. In a quarter of a century of arduous work and wise administration he established firm foundations for a truly national church. In the process he learnt valuable lessons about ecclesiastical management, which he took back with him when he returned to England to become Bishop of Lichfield in 1867, lessons from which the church in the old country still benefits.

In New Zealand the English churchman feels particularly at home.

There is much the same variety of churchmanship, and nowadays, since Selwyn's influence in both countries, much the same democratic type of church government. If the great wooden cathedral at Wellington seems a trifle odd, the Victorian Gothic cathedral at Christchurch, built right at the centre of the city with everything flowing around it, seems exactly right. Actually the Wellington Cathedral is being replaced by a modern building in reinforced concrete on the most commanding site in the neighbourhood. Concrete seems the best material with which to build in the neighbourhood of an earthquake area. Many of the country churches are now constructed in that material. But that does not mean that they have forsaken the traditional Gothic design. The visitor might find in them replicas of many an English village church, true in every detail to the general pattern, even to the niche over the south porch with the figure of the patron saint comfortably ensconced within it. So strong is the tendency of Anglicanism to reproduce itself in similar forms wherever it penetrates.

South Africa

Anglicanism in this area is represented by what is officially known as the Church of the Province of South Africa. It is an independent province of the Anglican Communion under its own metropolitan, whose archiepiscopal see is that of Cape Town. There are altogether fourteen dioceses in the province.

The English took over the Dutch colony at the Cape in 1795. From the first the situation presented difficult features. Not only was there a preponderance of native people, but the white population was soon divided between those of Dutch and those of British stock. The Dutch (although separated from their mother country) stuck to their language, their religion and their cultural ethos. Friction with the British led to the Great Trek and the formation of the semi-independent Transvaal and Orange Free State.

From the early years of the occupation, Anglican chaplains ministered to the troops. When British immigrants began to arrive, SPG made itself largely responsible for their spiritual welfare and from 1820 supplemented the Government's grant of financial aid. Jurisdiction was at first vested in the Bishop of Calcutta.

Independent church life began in 1847 with the arrival of the first resident bishop Robert Gray. He was an indefatigable worker. In three years he had increased the number of clergy to fifty, and in three years more he had divided his see by the creation of the two new dioceses of Grahamstown and Natal. This gave the opportunity to convert the

39

church in South Africa into a province with himself as the first metropolitan (1853).

Gray was a child of the Oxford Movement, and his own views lent
their particular ecclesiastical colour to the whole province, which has
remained ever since consistently 'high church'. One effect of this bent
has been to afford great opportunity for the work of the religious communities, of which a notably large number have founded branches in
South Africa. There are today probably more monks and nuns in
proportion to the size of the church membership than in any other part
of the Anglican Communion. But Gray was not a mere traditionalist.
In his ideas of administration he was quite advanced. He realized that
as the ties with the state were gradually loosened the Church must
develop a strong organization of its own. In 1857 he convened a synod
which gave the Church an effective voice in the management of its own
affairs.[3]

Unfortunately, both these influences brought him into violent
conflict with Colenso, Bishop of Natal, a great friend to the natives,
but a low-churchman and a somewhat extravagant believer in the new
science of Biblical criticism. His views both on Baptism and on the
Bible seemed to be heretical, and Gray procured his conviction and
deposition in the church courts. Colenso turned to the civil power; and
ultimately won his appeal to the Judicial Committee of the Privy
Council, which left the church property in his hands. Gray, however,
refused to admit any over-ruling of the spiritual powers of the Church.
In 1869, although Colenso was still alive, a new bishop was appointed
to succeed him. That threw Colenso and his followers into schism.
Unfortunately, the schism, calling itself the Church of England in South
Africa, although small still persists.[4]

In spite of the creation of the new states, friction between the Boers
(farmers) and the people of British stock continued to mount until it
resulted in the Boer War (1899–1902). The war revealed the inadequacy
of the British military machine, but it ended in the uniting of the
Transvaal and Orange Free State with the other provinces to form the
Union of South Africa. The peace was arranged on such liberal terms
as to allow the ultimate preponderance of Dutch, or Afrikander,
influence.

In the meantime the Church had launched at least one unique
experiment. In 1892 was started the South African Church Railway
Mission. The vast distances between townships meant that large
numbers of railway employees were widely scattered and out of touch
with regular parochial ministrations. The mission catered for their needs,

and by its romantic character attracted a specially fine class of workers both from South Africa and from Britain. Inevitably as the country became more closely settled the need for it decreased.

The recent history of the Church in South Africa has been largely taken up with the struggle to maintain a fully Christian service for the native population. The government policy of *apartheid*, with its severe separation between black and white, has appeared to the church leaders a negation of the Gospel and they have felt bound to resist it. This is not the place in which to enter upon a discussion of this heart-rending problem. Whatever may be the rights and wrongs of the question, it is safe to say that there is no present field of church work in which Anglicans have more reason to be proud of the witness of their Communion.

India

In the last few pages mention has been made more than once of the Bishop of Calcutta. We must now consider the church of which he is metropolitan, although in order of precedence it should have been mentioned earlier.

Anglicanism was first introduced into India when five chaplains were appointed to the East India Company in 1614. Their duty was to minister to the servants of the Company rather than to convert the Indians. No actual missionary seems to have been sent out until 1789, when SPG secured the services of a Cambridge graduate for a short period before he became a chaplain of the Company. This does not mean that English churchmen were not interested. For a long time SPCK had been assisting the work of the Danish missionaries at Tranquebar; and when the Lutherans began work in British territory the venerable society took on their financial support. This was the beginning of a long association between the English Church and the Lutherans. The Danish and German missionaries were quite ready to use the Book of Common Prayer and at first the English made no complaint of their lack of episcopal ordination.

It was not until 1814 that a bishopric was founded for India. In that year Middleton was consecrated as Bishop of Calcutta. He was faced with formidable difficulties, arising not only out of the vast size of his diocese but also from the fact that the existing clergy were so little under his control; the missionaries were under the societies and the chaplains were under the Company. In the circumstances the bishop did not raise the question of episcopal ordination for the Lutherans.

His successor Bishop Heber took a different line. He proceeded to license the missionaries, thus bringing them under his jurisdiction. He also admitted four of the Lutheran pastors to deacons' orders. However, he did not press the latter device universally, but in certain areas left the Lutheran missionaries to get on with their work undisturbed by the question of a fresh ordination. After Heber's death SPG continued to maintain the Lutheran missionaries, but the society did not actually send out any missionaries to work as clergymen who had not been episcopally ordained. CMS encountered a still greater difficulty when a Lutheran, working under its direction, wished himself to ordain some of his catechists. The society not only refused to countenance such a step but laid it down that all future ordinations must be according to the Anglican rite. It maintained this decision although it led to a small and temporary schism. By 1861 no non-episcopally ordained ministers were left working in the Anglican missions.

In the meantime new bishoprics had been founded in Madras (1835), Bombay (1837), Colombo (1845)—until they reached the number of fourteen, all under the Bishop of Calcutta as metropolitan, retaining that title rather than adopting that of archbishop. The Church in India remained, in effect, part of the Church of England, subject to many of the hampering clauses of the Act of Uniformity. Bishop Copleston of Colombo (1875–1903) struggled with difficulties created by the divided allegiance of his clergy and the often conflicting interests of soldiers, permanent or temporary European residents, Eurasians, and Indians. In spite of them, he began to lead the way towards some sort of self-government. Colombo had a voluntary diocesan synod and on its model the bishops devised a constitution for the whole Church in India, a Provincial Council meeting for the first time in 1922. At length an Indian Church Measure, having passed through both Houses of Parliament, received the royal assent in 1928, and was actually acted upon two years later, when the Council of the Church of India, Burma, and Ceylon met in Calcutta and formally adopted a constitution, rules and a body of canons.

It was the hope and expectation of those who framed the constitution that the church thus organized would be able to lend its own particular racial and national colour to the local expression of Anglicanism. Certainly, the effect of it has been felt not only in the religious but also in the secular sphere. It would be true to say that a large measure of the training of the Indian peoples in the democratic way of life has been due to the patience and good sense of Anglican teachers, who, learning by experience elsewhere, have seen to it that the laity should be encouraged to take the fullest possible share in church government.

This is not to suggest that the bishops have in any sense abrogated their own specific rights and duties. Indeed more legal rights belong to the Episcopal Synod meeting alone than is the custom elsewhere in the Anglican Communion. This is an advantage in a country of such vast size and poor communications. It means that business is expedited, and long delays, while the greater numbers of the other houses are assembled, are avoided. One has the impression that Anglican Christianity in India has been mainly a village movement and that its adherents are mostly from the depressed classes. A fresh factor of some importance seems to be the rise of a professional middle class in which Christian teaching has made considerable headway.[5] In any case, the practice of religious worship is far from being an affair for Sundays only. In the villages the devout Christians will attend evensong in the church most days of the week, and religious observance is much more closely intertwined with social life than it is today in our semi-paganized west.

The year 1947 was a fateful one for Indian Christians. That year British rule in the country came to an end, and Pakistan was separated. If there was some loss in the resultant confusion, at least the incubus of the imperial connection was removed and the church reaped the benefit of its previous Indianization. The other important event of that year was the inauguration of the Church of South India, to assist in which four dioceses left the Anglican Communion. This quite unprecedented step was taken with general goodwill, in the hope that it might lead to a wider-than-Anglican fellowship and ultimately to the re-union of the separated churches throughout the world. At the moment there are fourteen dioceses in the Church of India, Pakistan, Burma, and Ceylon. Before 1947 its membership amounted to 800,000, but about half that number went to help form the newly united Church of South India. It is probable that in the fresh lease of life since independence Christianity will make great strides. The ground has been well prepared. The universities of Oxford and Cambridge and Trinity College, Dublin, have poured some of their best men into the India mission. Out of such skill and devotion much good must assuredly come.

Other Anglican Churches
We can do little more than mention the remaining provinces of the Anglican Communion. Some of them have suffered heavily from the catastrophe of war; others are in a condition of rapidly changing development. The church in China, Chung Hua Sheng Kung Hui, which had fourteen dioceses, is now so cut off that it is not easy to know

what is happening there. Communication was made all the more difficult because the bishops were not allowed by the communist government to attend the Lambeth Conference of 1958. The very fact, however, that Chinese Christians are thrown on their own resources* and are made to face so much opposition in welding the faithful nucleus into a solid strength will ultimately assist greatly in the spread of the gospel. The neighbouring Church of Japan, Nippon Sei Ko Kwai,† is materially in much better case. How far it may have been psychologically affected by association with the post-war American occupation is not yet clear, but the sense of unity in Christ is more likely than any other sentiment to break down racial and national barriers and even the inevitable mistrust betweenconquerors and conquered.

The churches of South-East Asia, including the dioceses of Hong Kong, Rangoon, Korea, Singapore, Malaya, Borneo, and the Philippines have formed themselves into a council in the hope of becoming a duly constituted province. They have already held more than one meeting together with the Executive Officer for the Anglican Communion, Bishop Bayne, and there is every prospect that their ambition will one day be fulfilled.

That ambition has already been achieved in the Near East where Jerusalem has now the status of an Archbishopric exercising metropolitan rights over the Anglican dioceses in Egypt and Libya; in the Sudan; in Jordan, Lebanon and Syria; and in Iran. The Archbishop in Jerusalem maintains close relations with the Patriarchs and Bishops of the ancient churches in these regions and this friendly relationship is proving of the greatest assistance in the progress towards the reunion of the Church.

Nowhere has the constitutional development of Anglicanism been more marked than in Africa. Indeed it is probable that here something like a record has been set up. In a single decade no fewer than four different provinces have been inaugurated: West Africa (1951), Central Africa (1955), East Africa (1960), and Uganda (1961). Such a record would alone have been sufficient to make Geoffrey Fisher's tenure of the chair of St Augustine (1945–61) of outstanding importance in the long history of the Anglican Communion.

---

*All their bishops are now Chinese, and they no longer receive any financial aid from the west.

†Anglican missions were first started in Japan by American missionaries in 1859 and one of them, C. M. Williams, became the first bishop. English missionaries entered later, the two missions being united under a common constitution by the first General Synod in 1887. The Church has made a great revival after the sufferings of the war years. There are ten dioceses under a Presiding Bishop.

In this he followed the excellent example of one of his predecessors, Tait, who in 1880 was instrumental in forming a province of the West Indies. Here, as in Africa, ecclesiastical development has ante-dated the progress of the civil constitution. It is to be hoped that experience of the benefits of closer ecclesiastical co-operation will remove the prejudices against political federation. It is noteworthy that in most of the modern provinces ecclesiastical autonomy preceded political. In this respect Anglicanism returns to the pattern of its beginnings for it was the unity of the Church in England that led to the unity of the Kingdom.

CHAPTER THREE

FAITH

Comprehensiveness—Continuity—Biblicism—Nationalism

IF ITS organization is the most obvious feature of any church, the most important must assuredly be its faith. All Christians are distinguished by their belief from the rest of the world, for all hold basically the same view of God and his revelation through Christ. Unfortunately, in the present divided state of Christendom, some groups of Christians are also distinguished from each other by particular doctrines that are held by them exclusively. Thus the Roman Catholic is easily discernible by his acceptance of Papal Infallibility, the Congregationalist by his doctrine of Independency, the Seventh Day Adventist by his observance of Saturday as the weekly holy day. It is the boast of the Anglican that he holds no such exclusive or distinctive doctrine. He claims that his faith is essentially that which was held by the early Christian Church in the days before the divisions. He would begin to feel that there was something wrong if it could be shown that he affirmed some dogma that was denied by every other Christian body.

At the same time it must be recognized that churches are not always marked out by exclusiveness of doctrine. The fact that the great fundamental teachings, such as those of the Incarnation and the Trinity, are held in common at least by all those who belong to the main stream of historic Christianity should be sufficient to clarify the point. What distinguishes the separate churches within that main stream is not so much their distinctive beliefs as the balance in which they hold the common doctrine. Differences between Christians generally arise from variations of emphasis rather than from the assertion of new or strange articles of a creed. This fact received interesting illustration at the time of the debate on the revised Book of Common Prayer in 1927–8. It was possible for Archbishop Davidson to meet one of the main objections to that book quite honestly by assuring Parliament that in the new book there was no change of doctrine. But one imagines that everyone would be prepared to admit a shift of emphasis in the new book. That, in fact, is what in the end defeated it. It is thus the balance or emphasis and not only the exclusively held doctrine that is important. After all we are familiar with the same truth in regard to human physiognomy. The nose is a common feature, but the addition of a mere fraction of an inch to Helen of Troy's would have prevented the launching of a thousand ships. If, therefore, we select certain traits as distinctive of Anglicanism, it is not because we deny their possession by other Christian communions, but because they are held by Anglicans in a peculiar balance which makes of Anglicanism a distinct type of Christianity.

Comprehensiveness

We begin, then, somewhat daringly, with the trait of comprehensiveness. This is to grasp the nettle, for there are many today both within and without the borders of Anglicanism who regard its alleged comprehensiveness as a reprehensible trait and would bid us get rid of it at all costs. Its critics have long taunted it with its apparent inconsistencies. It does not present the nice, tidy appearance of a clear-cut dogmatic scheme, reflecting itself consistently in every aspect of life and worship. We have, we are told, a Catholic liturgy, a Calvinistic set of articles, and an Erastian clergy. There is just enough truth in the aphorism to make it sting. Modern study, however, has revealed the qualifications to which it must be submitted and by which its sting is removed.

Today the attack has shifted a little. The form it now takes is the allegation that Anglicanism is trying to hold together two opposed religions, one Catholic and the other Evangelical. It is suggested that these two types of Christianity have no natural cohesion and that they would fall apart if 'the establishment' did not exist to hold them together. The latter part of this argument at least needs no refuting. Its falsity is shown by the obvious facts. Anglicanism, in every country of its adoption, shows just the same divergencies as in England. In those countries there is no establishment to hold it together, yet it appears to cohere without any difficulty whatsoever.

Nevertheless, apart from the external critic, there are some even within the ranks of Anglicanism who feel acutely the disadvantages of its comprehensiveness. It prevents dogmatic precision. It leads to the view that the articles of faith should be the fewest and the simplest possible. It means that many questions must remain without a decisive answer. It encourages pious opinion at the expense of authoritative dogma. And it often leaves the faithful floundering in doubt. It is a field for the amateur rather than a bastion for the professional theologian.

A good deal of this must be admitted and even acclaimed as true. Whether we find the picture attractive or not will depend upon our *a priori* ideas of what a religion is intended to be. If it is meant to put us in some strait-jacket of spiritual and intellectual authority, then Anglicanism is hardly likely to be pleasing. But if it is meant to give us help and guidance in the effort to think for ourselves, then we shall probably be happy to notice that the limits of comprehension are kept as wide as possible. We shall make a virtue of what others think a defect.

In any case it should be clearly understood that, whether for good or ill, comprehensiveness is an essential trait of Anglicanism. If we did not possess it, there would scarcely be justification for our separate existence. We have seen how mixed was the Church in England from its beginning. Inclusiveness was meant to be a strong feature at the time of its separation. Elizabeth tried hard to unite all men of good will within the bounds of the national church, and the desire affected the form both of her ecclesiastical policy and her Prayer Book. She was not, however, prepared, in order to attain her end, to allow the character of the national Church to be disrupted. Nonconformist Papalists and Puritans alike were deliberately excluded.

Curiously enough, when the next attempt was made to extend to an intolerable degree the limits of comprehension, it was again the crown that refused to give way. James I's experience of presbyterians in Scotland had confirmed him in the view 'No bishop no King', and at the Hampton Court Conference of 1604 he disappointed the expectations of the Puritan divines. Later, however, the crown would have given away the distinctive character of the church had it not been for the stubborn stand of clergy and people. Charles II at the Savoy Conference of 1661 was quite prepared to temporize, but the country, rejoicing in its defeat of a grim Independency, was determined that the church as they had known it should share fully in the benefits of Restoration. Later still, when William III would have welcomed a greater inclusiveness in favour of his pan-protestant schemes, it was Beveridge ('the reviver and restorer of primitive piety', the theologian who refused to allow himself to be intruded into Ken's see of Bath and Wells and was later made Bishop of St Asaph) who led the opposition and finally defeated him.

Nevertheless, in spite of these official defeats Puritanism left a strain of Calvinism in the Church of England, which has never, perhaps happily, been eradicated. This influence showed itself not in polity but in theology and in a certain austerity of worship. Actually the strict Calvinistic theology is implicitly excluded by Article IX which speaks of man being 'very far gone from original righteousness' instead of 'totally gone', as well as in the very cautious Article XVII on Predestination. But many Anglican theologians managed to combine a semi-Calvinist doctrine of grace and worship with a somewhat advanced doctrine of the Church and ministry. Of that number Beveridge was himself an example, as was also George Morley, Bishop of Worcester, who had been one of the leading figures at the Savoy Conference. Later, however, a good deal of this churchly feeling hived off with the Non-jurors while the Calvinistic strain was strengthened by the evangelical preaching of George Whitefield. It was left to the Tractarians of the early nineteenth century to revive the strong interest in Church and sacraments.

It might have been expected that the liberalizing tendencies of the Latitudinarian and Modernist schools would have proved a solvent of both these rival strains. That, however, has not proved to be the case. For a time it meant only the formation of a third party of 'broad churchmen', but that party did its work in assisting all schools alike to accept the methods, if not the conclusions, of modern critical study. Today there are only small groups of Anglican ultramontanes at the one extreme and of Puritan fundamentalists at the other, who appear to be totally unaffected by historical criticism. For the rest Anglicans are divided into two main groups of catholics and evangelicals. Even those who claim to be 'central' and acknowledge no allegiance to either party are inevitably judged by the laity and by clergy alike as they lean to the one side or the other. But the important thing is that all alike are still included in the same Church. Even the two extreme wings prefer the unity of the comprehensive body to the alternative of seeking elsewhere the more uncompromising expression of their respective theologies.

That there has been a good deal of recrimination between the two parties representing these diverse views it would be idle to deny. Indeed, the nineteenth century saw a continuous feud develop, which recourse to the law and even to the Judicial Committee of the Privy Council failed to appease. Consequently, condemnation of the party spirit became a constant theme in the pulpit and on the platform. No doubt it deserved castigation when each group endeavoured to deny to the other any rightful place in the Church. During the twentieth century, however, wiser thoughts have prevailed. It is not that the respective points of view have been surrendered; in all probability they are more strongly held than ever. But it is more readily recognized that each represents a valuable element in the common gospel and that the full strength of each is most likely to be preserved if it is fostered by a school of thought particularly devoted to it. At any rate it might justifiably be said that, however much the party spirit has been decried, its parties have provided the main strength of Anglicanism.

In any case, it is difficult to see why as schools of thought there should be any internecine conflict between the two. The psychological, biblical approach of the evangelical with its emphasis on faith, conversion and the atonement need not exclude the ontological, sacramental approach of the catholic with its emphasis on grace, authority and the incarnation. St Paul certainly held both the psychological and biological elements together without any sense of incongruity. If our scientific age with its love of analysis helps us to discern more clearly the differences, it is still true that Christianity is intended to appeal to the *whole* man and that a complete faith must satisfy the needs of every part of our complex human nature.

The difficulty between the different attitudes becomes acute when the two types of thought lead to markedly different types of worship. It was this test that was found most trying during the nineteenth century. To it also some solution has since been found, but our description of this situation must wait for a later chapter. In the meantime it is worth remembering that Christianity has never in the whole course of its history presented a completely homogeneous aspect to the world. In the New Testament itself there are as many 'views' as there are writers. And even from the more practical consideration of liturgical usage one imagines that there must have been considerable differences between the conservative staidness of Jerusalem and the somewhat corybantic worship of Corinth.

How important it is that there should be a church in Christendom which does deliberately endeavour to combine the two contrasting points of view is shown by the close interest in Anglicanism displayed in recent years by the churches of the continent. The ecumenical movement in bringing Christians of almost every kind into closer touch with each other has made possible a general reconsideration both of their similarities and their divergencies. In all the discussions it is interesting to note how soon the general attitude resolves itself into an encounter between catholic and evangelical. It is between these two points of view that the dividing line runs right through the whole length of Christendom. Sometimes, as in the cases of Sweden and England, the difference is clearly seen within the national Church itself. Of these two England is, perhaps, in one respect at least the more fortunate. Unlike the Lutheran church of Sweden it is not tied to the prescription of any one great theologian. Anglicanism has no Luther or Calvin or even a Thomas Aquinas to set the standard of its teaching. It is, therefore, more free to follow the argument where it leads.

For the rest it may even be possible to see a divine ordering in the fact that in the midst of divided Christendom there are churches that straddle the dividing line. It may give hope that other churches on either side of the line may ultimately find it possible to unite even though the line remain. Christians may be of the same mind even though they are not of the same opinion.

As for the situation within Anglicanism, renewed satisfaction with its comprehensiveness is not likely to lead to complacency with respect to its divisions. Always its best minds will be seeking for a more satisfactory synthesis of the two opposed theses. There was a time when the synthesis devised by Hooker was presumably found satisfactory by all but comparatively few. Today, however, the two terms of the synthesis have been pushed a good deal farther than Hooker himself contemplated. What is now needed is a new synthesis at a higher level. If *per impossibile* it could not be found and Anglicanism split up, the clock would be put back four hundred years. Thus hopes for reunion would be dashed and Christendom would suffer a grave disaster. It is inconceivable that such a thing should happen, but knowledge of the consequences should help Anglicans to treasure the comprehensive character of their church at its true value and to refrain from speaking lightly of it.

Continuity

The second trait on which Anglicanism prides itself is its continuity. The greatest insult you can offer to the Anglican is to tell him that his church was founded by Henry VIII. The resentment will not be due to any popular prejudice against that monarch, but to the implied suggestion that the Church of England was something new in the sixteenth century and had no roots in the historic past. Our consideration of the development of its organization has shown us that, once it is granted that the papacy is not essential to the Church, then we must agree that everything possible was done to maintain the constitutional structure of the Church in England through the change-over from the medieval to the post-Reformation period and that, as far as external signs are concerned, the attempt was successful. The position of Anglican apologists is that their ministry is a continuous one and can be traced from the beginning of Christianity to the present time without a break.

This was the position already taken by that very delightful person, Sir Thomas Browne of *Religio Medici* fame, whose life covered nearly the whole of the seventeenth century, 'I am of the Reformed newcast Religion, wherein I dislike nothing but the Name,* of the same belief

*i.e. 'Protestant'.

our Saviour taught, the Apostles disseminated, the Fathers authorized, and the Martyrs confirmed.'[1] It is true that the emphasis here is on faith rather than order, and that the continuity of doctrine was regarded as even more important than that of the ministry. It is, in effect, an assertion that the Church of England possessed the apostolic tradition, but the greatest help to the preservation of that tradition was the apostolic ministry. It is to that double continuity that the Anglican Communion has stuck with the utmost tenacity. At a time when one type of Christian people seemed to be adding both to the grades of the ministry and to the articles of the faith while others were subtracting from both and claiming to have restored a biblical simplicity, the Anglicans refused to take any leap either forwards or backwards but were content quietly to continue what they believed to be the ministry and doctrine of the undivided Church.

It may well be asked why it should be thought necessary to lay so much stress on the outward form; would it not be enough to preserve the inward life? The answer is that the outward form is itself the best guarantee of the preservation of the inward life. It is the shell that preserves the kernel from harm. This is in conformity with the general sacramental principle by which the existence of the Church is governed. The physical continuity is the outward and visible sign of the inward and spiritual grace. Just as in the sacraments of the Eucharist and of Baptism we are always careful of the outward elements, so in the continuous life of the Church one would naturally be anxious to preserve intact the outward succession by which the inward life is symbolized and conveyed.

The continuity between Anglicans and the early Fathers was vehemently asserted by no less a person than the monarch, James I. In his *Premonition to All Most Mighty Monarchs*, published in 1609, he affirms, 'I am such a CATHOLIC CHRISTIAN as believeth the three Creeds, that of the Apostles, that of the Council of Nice, and that of Athanasius, the two latter being paraphrases to the former. And I believe them in that sense as the ancient Fathers and Councils that made them did understand them, to which three Creeds all the ministers of England do subscribe at their Ordination. . . . I admit the Four First General Councils as Catholic and Orthodox. And the said Four General Councils are acknowledged by our Acts of Parliament, and received for orthodox by our Church.' James's main contention here is that English Churchmen have preserved the *depositum fidei*, but he was perspicacious enough to recognize the close connection between the maintenance of doctrine and that of polity. Also he recognized that, for the time being at least, the fate of the crown was bound up with that of episcopacy. Motives of policy as well as of faith combined to enforce the idea that continuity of doctrine and ministry was a consistent whole that should not be divided. This goes far to explain his attitude at the Hampton Court Conference.

It also helps to explain the tremendous, and perhaps unique, emphasis that Anglicans place on episcopacy. If it had not been for this precise historical situation England might have followed the example of the Lutheran churches in exalting purity of doctrine over questions of ministerial order. Not even in Sweden, which did retain its episcopal succession, does the bishop loom so large as in Anglican circles. The long struggle with Puritanism and the presbyterian polity gave episcopacy an overwhelmingly important place in Anglican theology. The importance of the bishops in political circles during later centuries served to emphasize their prelatic character, and in so doing (as we have seen) spoilt their chance of quick and easy acceptance in the church overseas.

It was not only against the new churches of the Reformation that Anglicanism developed its doctrine of episcopacy but also against Rome, where one might have expected that most help in this respect would have been given. The truth is that if Lutheranism had developed a doctrine of *sola fides* and Calvinism a doctrine of *solum verbum*, Romanism was fast developing a doctrine of *solus papa*. The counter-Reformation, in its efforts to defend Rome against the corrosive influences of the new thought, had contrived a comprehensive measure of centralization in constitution, liturgy and doctrine, culminating in the supreme authority of the Pope. This had confirmed an already existent tendency to minimize the office and semi-independence of the individual bishop. Whereas Anglicans held the orders of the sacred ministry to be deacon, priest and bishop, Romans held the three major orders to comprise the sub-diaconate, diaconate, and priesthood, the last named including both presbyter and bishop. Although elevation to the episcopate required a separate act of consecration and although only the bishop had the power to ordain, it can easily be seen that this type of enumeration, combined with the new centralizing emphasis on the Papacy assisted in reducing the episcopal status.

Anglicans had no doubt that the bishop belonged to a separate order, and affirmed in their ordinal that this had been so since the Apostles' time. They were, therefore, quite sure that as far as they themselves were concerned they must regard episcopal ordination as essential for all who would enter their ministry. But what of the churches on the continent that had entered upon their separate and independent life without preserving the episcopal continuity? Anglicans were not prepared to unchurch them just on that account. After all they were their close allies. On the continent Christianity had been cut clean in half by the dividing line between Roman and Protestant, and in the contemporary conflict Anglicans were clearly on the Protestant side of the line. They were naturally disposed to take the best possible view of their friends' situation. They, therefore, said that inasmuch as it had been impossible for those churches to obtain episcopal ordination they must be recognized as true churches without it. Inevitably such a concession made the Anglican position on episcopacy less than logically water-tight. It led to many compromises in special instances where non-episcopal ministries were concerned. The official attitude has never, even now, been completely defined. Theologians argue over the respective merits of *esse*, *bene esse*, and *plene esse*. But since the Oxford Movement, popular opinion has hardened in favour of the strict view that apostolic succession of the ministry through episcopacy is necessary to the proper constitution of a church.* That is always made a *sine qua non* in Anglican negotiations for reunion with other Christian bodies, and forms indeed, together with Bible, Creed, and Sacraments, a part of the famous 'quadrilateral' or four-fold basis for ecclesiastical reunion.

It must be emphasized that in any discussion of this subject we should be losing the essential point if we did not recognize that the fundamental issue is whether Christianity is or is not a sacramental religion. By sacramental in this connection we mean sacramental *au fond*, through and through, accepting sacraments not as mere picturesque excrescences upon the worship of the Church, but as belonging to its very essence. If, as William Temple is often quoted as saying, Christianity is the most material of all the great religions, then it must be essentially a sacramental religion, and one must expect to find in every aspect of it outward signs acting as the symbols and vehicles of inward grace. What may seem, at first sight, to be a merely mechanical continuity will wear a different aspect when it is seen as part of the outward sign by which the grace of ordination is conveyed to the candidate for the ministry. In this, as in other sacraments, one will naturally exercise care and reverence in regard to the outward sign, not thinking it all-important in itself but honouring it for the treasure it conveys.

It was their satisfaction in the knowledge that they had preserved the

*The two most important books on this controversy in its modern aspect are Sykes, *Old Priest and New Presbyter* (CUP, 1956) and Peck, *Anglicanism and Episcopacy* (Faith Press, 1958), in which the two distinguished authors, using the same evidence, come to opposite conclusions.

continuity of the primitive ministry that enabled the English divines of the classical period to emphasize other elements in the continuity. Thus Jeremy Taylor,[2] consecrated Bishop of Down and Connor in 1661, writes to defend his church against Roman charges:

'What can be supposed wanting [in the Church of England] in order to salvation? We have the Word of God, the Faith of the Apostles, the Creeds of the Primitive Church, the Articles of the four first General Councils, a holy liturgy, excellent prayers, perfect Sacraments, faith and repentance, the Ten Commandments, and the sermons of Christ, and all the precepts and counsels of the Gospel. We teach the necessity of good works, and require and strictly exact the severity of a holy life. We live in obedience to God, and are ready to die for Him, and do so when He requires us so to do. We speak honourably of His most Holy Name. We worship Him at the mention of His Name. We confess His attributes. We love His servants. We pray for all men. We love all Christians, even our most erring brethren. We confess our sins to God and to our brethren whom we have offended, and to God's ministers in cases of scandal or of a troubled conscience. We communicate often. We are enjoined to receive the Holy Sacrament thrice every year at least. Our priests absolve the penitent. Our Bishops ordain priests, and confirm baptized persons, and bless their people and intercede for them. And what could here be wanting to salvation?'

This comprehensive statement by one of its standard divines may be taken as typical of Anglican defence at all stages of its history.

One ought not to leave this section of our subject without reflecting what a burden the Anglican emphasis on episcopacy lays upon the shoulders of those who bear this office. Often a diocesan bishop is appointed without having had any opportunity of serving an apprenticeship to his task. If he has been a parish priest, a school-master or a don he has had little experience of the kind of administration for which he has now become responsible. His position is not made any easier by the fact that he is generally regarded, even by some of his clergy, as exercising a quite despotic power. That is very far from being true. It is true, of course, that in most spheres of Church government he still retains a power of veto, but with regard to the more positive side of the organization, in spite of what is often said to the contrary, he is hedged about with so many committees, each of which has its own statutory power and authority, that it becomes increasingly difficult for him to guide policy or even to move at all. He may, therefore, to his surprise find himself incurring all the blame of an autocrat without the power to become one.

What is worse, much worse, is that he may now find himself quite suddenly, for the first time, launched on the stage of national affairs. He has become fair game for a news-hungry press. He may be asked for his opinion on subjects about which he has never entertained any views until now. He is expected to take part in the symposium. He is one of the people from whom hard-pressed newspaper men expect to get a story. He will often be surprised at the strange appearance borne by his expressed views when he meets them in print. The quick witticism of the common-room, the harmless irony of the pulpit, the magisterial pronouncement to the fourth form look very different when they have passed through the hands of a sub-editor eager for a headline. It is not easy for him, at first, to realize that in this strangely assorted situation lies perhaps his greatest opportunity. If the great problem of our time is communication, then a sympathetic understanding of the press and its needs is one of the surest ways of solving the problem.

This may seem a trivial illustration of the practical results flowing from the exaltation of the bishop's office. And so from the point of view of high theology it undoubtedly is. But it is certainly not trivial to the new diocesan, nor may it seem trivial to the thousands who devour the daily news and judge God and his Church by the reports they read therein. In any case, it is a faithful translation into the terms of modern life of the Anglican stress on the doctrine of episcopacy.

Biblicism

If Anglicanism is somewhat peculiar in the interpretation it applies to the concept of continuity, it is remarkable also in its use of the Bible. Its attitude to the scriptures is here described by the term 'Biblicism' in full consciousness that it is a word with a sinister meaning; it implies an undue deference to, and an exaggerated use of, the Bible. It is not intended to suggest that the Anglican regard for the Bible is at all disproportionate, but rather to forestall any complaint that we are making Anglicans appear superior to all others in their appreciation of the Bible. So to avoid appearance of boasting we use 'Biblicism' in the German fashion as a term implying a certain element of disparagement.

That leaves us free to recognize, merely as a matter of fact, that Anglicans do in their public worship use the Bible more than any other body of Christians. This does not, unfortunately, apply to private use in the home, where in modern times members of the Free Churches have probably passed the standard set by the average Anglican. But as far as public worship is concerned there can be no doubt. Anglicans do read the Bible in church more than other Christians. This, of course, is the effect of our liturgical rubrics. At each of the statutory daily services of Mattins and Evensong there is a lesson from both the Old and New Testament. In this same daily office the Psalter is recited completely every month. Also, in many churches there is a daily celebration of the Holy Communion, which involves the reading of Epistle and Gospel. Thus in the ordinary routine of the Church's daily worship six sizeable passages of scripture are read every day. There can be little doubt, therefore, that as far as public reading is concerned the Bible is more used in Anglican Churches than in any other. In fact, apart from anything that may happen at special services, the Old Testament is read through once every year and the New Testament twice.

If this is the practical attitude to the Bible, the theoretical is no less impressive. It is regarded as foundation document, charter, and trust deed. The more intelligent Anglicans, of course, recognize that it post-dates the Church. The Church was, in fact, responsible for the selection of the books that make up the authoritative list, or canon, of scripture, to say nothing of producing the authors and editors by whom the constituent books were composed. At the same time, it is also recognized that the anthology as a whole represents a consolidation or precipitation of the apostolic tradition. It brings us as near as we are ever likely to get to the actual words and teaching of Jesus and his immediate followers. What it inculcates is, therefore, accepted as in the highest degree authoritative.

It would be difficult to express this view more strongly and at the same time more accurately than in the words of Article VI:

'Holy Scripture containeth all things necessary to salvation: so that whatsoever is not read therein, nor may be proved thereby, is not to be required of any man, that it should be believed as an article of the Faith, or be thought requisite or necessary to salvation.'

This statement established a principle of the greatest importance, and one thoroughly characteristic of Anglicanism. It does not take up the ridiculous position of some extremists that nothing can be legitimately thought, said, or done by the Christian that is not in the Bible, nor does it assert the 'infallibility' of the Bible, but it does affirm, most emphatically, that subscription cannot be demanded to any doctrine as an article of necessary faith if it is not contained directly in the Bible or clearly provable from it.

The article then goes on to state what are the books it receives as making up the Bible. Somewhat optimistically it affirms, 'In the name of the Holy Scripture we do understand those Canonical Books of the Old and New Testament, of whose authority was never any doubt in the Church'. This, although it recognizes the part played by the Church in compiling the list of authorized books, appears to forget the long-fought struggle against the inclusion of II Peter and Revelation to say nothing of long lingering doubts about the Johannine epistles. It does, however, explain the Anglican position in regard to the Old Testament Apocrypha, consisting of the books included in the canon accepted by Greek-speaking Jews of the Dispersion but excluded from the canon of the Hebrew-speaking Jews of Palestine: 'The other Books (as Jerome saith) the Church doth read for example of life and instruction of manners; but yet doth it not apply them to establish any doctrine.' Actually, the Old Testament Apocrypha remains largely unknown to a proportion of the Anglican laity because the British and Foreign Bible Society, which publishes the cheapest bibles, does not print it in any of its editions. Selected portions, however, are read in the course of the daily and Sunday lections in church, where their unfamiliarity gives occasion for many expository sermons.

This public use of the Bible is closely bound up with Anglican history. During the medieval period it had become chiefly known through the stories of the Golden Legend and the pictures in murals and stained glass windows. Except for the few who could read and afford to buy expensive Latin books, it was mostly a matter of second-hand knowledge. Still, as is evident, from the moralities and miracle plays, there was a considerable familiarity with Bible stories and their import. The medieval churchman was not wholly ignorant of the scriptures.

Nevertheless, the open Bible was the greatest gift of the Reformation. The invention of the printing press made possible its wide and speedy dissemination. Cranmer saw its importance and tried unsuccessfully to get a suitable authorized English translation. Thomas Cromwell, with the State at his back, ordered the 'Great Bible'* to be set up in the churches, so giving an opportunity for all, who could get anyone to read it for them, to obtain a direct knowledge of its contents. Of course, the knowledge went to their heads; it seemed so unlike the pre-digested version of its teaching served out by the historic church. Everyone began to interpret it for himself and many made fine nonsense of it, just as the Kikuyu and other African tribesmen have done today. In the end, James I stopped the practice of putting tendentious comments in the margin. He brought together the best scholars of his day, regardless of their churchmanship, and they produced the Authorized Version of 1611. It was allowed to be read in churches and became also the private reading of the people for many generations. There is more than a little truth in the statement that the English

*Coverdale's translation. Later revised and issued with preface by Cranmer and thereafter known as 'Bishop's Bible'. From a version of Jer. 8 22 sometimes known as 'Treacle Bible'.

became the 'people of a book and that book the Bible'. It set the standard both in literature and religion for English-speaking people both at home and overseas. It was largely responsible for the moral standards accepted by the people, and continued to be read and used as a fetish even when it was not understood. Indeed, it was only in recent times, when people began at last to realize that they did not understand it, that it became less regularly read. But it still remains the best seller in English literature.

William Chillingworth, an Anglican divine of the first half of the seventeenth century, who was converted to Rome but returned to become a chaplain in the Royalist army, gave birth to a famous aphorism when he proclaimed that 'the Bible and the Bible only is the religion of Protestants'.[3] The rhetorical statement is often taken at its face value both by those who agree with it and those who do not. Both sides are inclined to forget that in its context it was intended to meet the Tridentine argument that tradition and scripture are co-equal means of revelation. The point made is that tradition speaks with many voices, Pope against Pope and council against council; whereas the Bible speaks with one voice only. Happily, perhaps, at that time the mysteries of modern scholarship had not been revealed to Papist or Protestant, and neither would have dared to say that the Bible too spoke with many voices. It was taken for granted that there was only one way of salvation set forth in scripture. It was the claim of each side to the exclusive possession of knowledge of the right way that made their controversies so bitter. In any case, belief in the sufficiency and inerrancy of scripture led many Protestants to try to establish that the Bible alone was their religion, but ultimately, as men began to take wider historical views, the attempt broke down.

Anglicans as a whole held a mediating position. They recognized, as a result of the Reformation experience, that even if the Bible spoke with only one voice, there were many different ways of interpreting it. Who was to decide among the many claimants to possession of the right understanding? The dissidence of dissent was already making itself felt in the creation of many sects. At the same time, bibliolatry was mounting to the point of the Helvetic 'Consensus' in 1675 which declared that the Swiss reformed churches accepted the Hebrew text of the Old Testament not only in its substance but in its words, both the consonants and the vowel points.[4] Who then was to judge between the rival interpretations? The second epistle of Peter had said that no scripture was 'of private interpretation'. The Church itself, then, must be allowed to be the judge.

This was the line taken by William Beveridge, the hard-working Rector of St Peter-upon-Cornhill*

' . . . The Scripture itself cannot decide the controversy, for the controversy is concerning itself: the parties engaged in the controversy cannot decide it, for either of them thinks his own opinion to be grounded upon Scripture. Now how can this question be decided better or otherways, than by the whole Church's exposition of the Scripture, which side of the controversy it is for, and which side it is against? . . .'[5]

The argument was carried further by Daniel Whitby who was Rector of St Edmund's, Salisbury, and defended Bishop Hoadly in the Bangorian Controversy. In his *Answer* to some Roman controversialists published in 1666 he maintains that, where there is doubt of the meaning of Scripture, the interpretation of any particular passage must be determined (a) by principles of faith, (b) by tradition (so long as it is not a forgery), and (c) by reason. We have, thus, arrived at the classical description of Anglican authority in matters of faith: the Scriptures, the Creeds, the first four General Councils, and Reason. Thus interpreted the Bible as a whole is seen to be the record of God's plan for salvation. It is the *Heilsgeschichte*, the religious explanation of the history of the Jewish people culminating in the life of Jesus and looking forward to the end of the world. Of these events it is the authoritative interpretation given by inspiration of God.

As God thus speaks generally through the whole Bible, so in any part of it he may speak directly to the individual soul. It is both a light to lighten the nations and a lantern to guide the feet of the single believer. It shows how the eternal Word of God speaking through the whole cosmic order was 'made flesh' in Christ and how Christ is the Saviour of each one who puts his trust in him.

This does not mean that the Bible is to be treated as some sort of extended magical formula. It is not to be used as a sacred Old Moore's Almanac. Reason, as Hooker saw and Anglican divines have always emphasized, must play its part in our efforts to understand it. The mind as well as the heart and will must be engaged. Nor does it mean that the Bible is the primary source of our religion. As we have seen, both historically and logically the Church comes before the Bible. Most of us, in point of fact, learnt our religion at our mother's knee; it was only later that we began to read the Bible and try to understand it for ourselves. Even then the Church is at hand to provide us with a compass through those seas, which she has already charted for us. Hence the typically Anglican aphorism: The Church to teach and the

*See p. 48.

Bible to prove. It is hardly to be expected that the new explorer would be able to find for himself, without assistance, the precise creed of Christendom as it is contained within the Bible. Nor indeed is he expected to. The Church gave to the world the creed and the canon of scripture at roughly the same time and they were always expected to be taken together.

Today it requires a good deal of exact scholarship to show how the two fit in together. It is mostly out of this scholarly study of the sacred scriptures, to which they have given such whole-hearted attention, that the clergy of England earned their reputation for learning. It was Creighton who said that the appeal to sound learning was the formula most justly expressive of the position of the Church of England. *Clerus Anglicanus stupor mundi* was an old encomium upon English attainment in the field of patristic as well as biblical learning, but it was justified by Pope Clement VIII's praise of Bull,* which latter was endorsed by a formal vote of thanks from the French clergy assembled in synod at St Germain in 1686.

In more recent times the influence of Anglican learning has been directed towards showing that retention of the traditional creed is quite compatible with the modern methods of scientific study of the scriptures. Since the death of the Cambridge trio, Lightfoot, Westcott and Hort, Anglicans have not shown the brilliance of discovery nor the massiveness of scholarship displayed by the Germans, but there has been a steadiness and a magisterial judgment in their learning which has carried great weight not only in academic circles but also among the rank and file of simple believers. The Anglican scholar's researches have never led him altogether outside the range of pastoral responsibilities. He has, therefore, been quick to see the practical relevance of his academic conclusions. He has been kept in touch with actual life and has been less tempted to follow every change in academic fashion.

The progress of Anglican studies in the New Testament has been greatly facilitated by the classical training most theological teachers have received in their schools and in the ancient universities. Unfortunately, in quite recent times the intensification of specialization has meant a steady decline in the study of Hebrew and the ancient Semitic languages. That decline has led to a comparative neglect of Old Testament studies which is much to be deplored. However, some of the more modern universities have shown themselves aware of the difficulty, and places like King's College, London, may yet fill for Anglicans in

* Bishop of St David's 1705. The work so highly praised was his *Judicium Ecclesiae Catholicae* (1694).

England the gap now left by Oxford and Cambridge. In overseas provinces of the Anglican Communion this particular disability does not apply in the same manner or degree.

We cannot leave the subject of Biblicism without referring to the fact that in recent years, in spite of the tremendous advance made in biblical studies, there has been a surprising resurgence of something very like fundamentalism. Those who belong to that general school of thought do not like the term; they prefer to be known as conservative evangelicals. This means apparently that, while they are not prepared to fight for the full fundamentalist position, they are anxious to retain the old belief in Bible inerrancy as completely as possible. It suggests that they are prepared to accept the lower or textual criticism, but are not prepared to accept either the methods or the results of the higher or source criticism. Once the correct text has been established, it must be accepted in whole, and in part, as the word of God. It is extremely difficult to see how this attitude can be reconciled with scientific approaches in other fields of study, but it cannot be denied that those who hold this view must be numbered among the most devoted and zealous Christians of our generation. They are, however, comparatively few in number, and their influence has hardly affected the typical Anglican attitude to the scriptures which remains humane, scientific and devotional.

Nationalism

The fourth main characteristic of the Anglican ideology is its emphasis on nationalism. In an age when we are blaming so much of the unrest in Africa and the East on the 'upsurge of nationalism' it may seem a pity that such a characteristic should be encouraged in the sphere of religion. Would not something unashamedly international, global, and ecumenical be more appropriate? As far as Christianity is concerned, we have to recognize that one of its avowed aims is to break down the barriers between nation and nation, class and class. St Paul at least saw the culminating point of all history in the establishment of such unity of mankind in Christ, where there is neither Greek nor Jew, circumcision nor uncircumcision, barbarian, Scythian, bond nor free, but Christ is all and in all.[6]

Nevertheless, it seems part of the natural constitution of the human race that men should be born in families, and the nation is little else than the family writ large. As each family appears to have its own common traits and idiosyncrasies, so the nation develops its own idiom and culture. It would seem natural that this difference should express itself in religion, and that even if the nation shares a religion in common with other nations it should give to it a form and expression derived from and expressing its own particular genius. So at least it seems to the typical Anglican, and so far from apologizing for this view he makes it especially his own. It will not be forgotten how the Lambeth Fathers described the churches of the Anglican Communion in the Conference of 1930: 'They are particular or national churches, and as such, promote within each of their territories a national expression of Christian faith, life and worship.' Thus each of these churches is encouraged to form for instance its own edition of the liturgy, its own hymn-book, its own style of church architecture. As it develops, it is expected that it will produce its own modification of typical Anglican polity and theology.

It must be confessed that this special trait of Anglicanism has been so strongly developed largely through the circumstances of its own particular history. But it has a far more venerable ancestry than that. When Henry VIII took over the headship of the national church from the Pope, he was able to rely on the new knowledge of the Bible and especially of the Old Testament. In Israel, it was generally recognized, Church and State were just two sides of the same shield, and the King, as the Lord's anointed, was the head of both. After the Exile, when the effort was made to re-build the Jewish nation on the lines of a church-state, there was a period in which the ecclesiastical and secular heads ruled side by side. That, at least, seems to be the meaning of Zechariah's mysterious prophecy about the two 'sons of oil'.[7] Later still, by the time the sect responsible for the Dead Sea Scrolls had developed their peculiar organization at Qumran, an effort was made to reverse the traditional positions, and in their ideal State as depicted in their writings the King must give precedence to the Priest, must allow him to give the blessing at the banquet, and never even take his seat until the Priest had already done so. But that may have been a reaction against the Hasmonean system in which the head of state had succeeded in arrogating to himself in reality the position and prestige of the High Priest. By New Testament times the position had entirely altered. The High Priest had become the sole official head of the Jewish Church. Herod, in any case, was regarded as a foreigner, and not even his magnificent gift of a restored temple could win him any place either in the people's affection or in their religious organization.

The Christian Church, born in the cradle of Judaism, was quite accustomed from the outset to being at odds with the state. In any case Christianity claimed to be a universal religion. In breaking the bonds of Judaism, it broke free from all national ties. For a time, indeed, it enjoyed the toleration that was accorded by their Roman conquerors to the national religion of the Jews. But once the Romans had learned to distinguish between Christian and Jew and had begun to understand the universalism of Christianity, the Church was regarded as a rival to the Empire and was made to suffer accordingly.

After three centuries of spasmodic persecution, during which the Church had been made to appear an alien element in the Roman Empire, Constantine determined on a change of policy. In the hope of using the Christian religion as a cement to bind together his vast territories, he first tolerated and then favoured the Church. He took a close interest both in its faith and in its organization. He protected its property by law and brought the bishops together from the four corners of the world to decide on one authoritative creed. He proclaimed himself as 'the bishop of those without', and at the same time allowed the professional bishops compensating influence in the administration of justice. It was not a very long step to the establishment of the Church as the only legal religion of the Empire by Theodosius I in 381.

Here began the close association between the religious institution and the state that characterized the life of Europe down to the period of the Reformation and beyond. Indeed, when complaints were made in modern England about the influence exercised by the Crown in episcopal appointments, the reply was that monarchs had insisted on their share in the appointment of bishops ever since the time of Constantine. The Church, in fact, became a nationalized institution. This was most evident in eastern Europe, where the Byzantine Emperors took a leading part in the management of church affairs such as their opposite number was seldom able to do in the West. Recently strong objection has been taken to the term Cesaro-papism, which was held to describe the relation between Church and State in Constantinople. It has been pointed out that if the Emperor had great influence in church affairs, it was balanced by the great influence exercised by the patriarch in state affairs. The peculiar part played by Archbishop Makarios in the civic affairs of Cyprus has opened the eyes of western Europeans to a situation very unlike that to which they are accustomed in their own lands.

In the West during the period of the barbaric invasions and the decline of the secular powers, the Church was the one stable element in public life and the Pope the one great personage who was capable of showing powers of leadership. It was largely under the guidance of the Church that the barbarians settled down as good Europeans. It was perhaps natural, therefore, that the Papacy should learn to expect, as of right, a homage and an obedience that had originally been granted it as the due recognition of its desert. Strong rulers, of course, knew how to protect their own rights. Charlemagne in 800 took up much the same position as Constantine had done in the fourth century. We have already seen how sharp a line was drawn by William the Conqueror between the civil and the ecclesiastical claims of the Pope after the 1066 invasion. Nevertheless William himself kept a close watch on church affairs; and the relation between secular and ecclesiastical government in England was exceedingly close throughout the Middle Ages.

It was made even closer after the Reformation in those lands that accepted the Lutheran principle of *cujus regio ejus religio*. This was to hark back to the Old Testament and the principle of 'the Lord's anointed'. It suited Henry VIII's book exactly and lent an air of religious respectability to the extraordinary steps he took. What is more important from our present point of view is that it stamped Anglicanism with the character of nationalism that it has never lost. The submission of the clergy may have been somewhat sullen in the first instance but there was surprisingly little open rebellion; the abuses of the old system were too evident, and the rising tide of nationalism in the secular sphere made the English laity less averse to the idea of having a church of their own.

The new patriotism had its disadvantages when the rapid changes on the throne and the diverse views of the monarchs meant that the leading clergy must veer like weather-cocks to keep pace with them. Under Mary the loyalty of people like Cranmer and Ridley was strained to breaking-point. Under Elizabeth loyalty to Church and Queen became synonymous. The Queen's own determination prevented it from taking a completely Erastian form. Her attachment to the religion of her father and her determination to make Parker exercise his constitutional powers kept the faith and order of the Church intact, in spite of Parliament's efforts to remould religion after the continental model. Hooker's figure of the triangle with the Church at one end of the base and the state at the other with the monarch at the apex represents, not unfairly, the position of the Elizabethan settlement.

With the arrival of the Stuarts and the doctrines of divine right and passive obedience the nationalism of the Church took on a still more personal form. The final responsibility for the governance of the Church rested with the sovereign and could not be delegated to any other body. This was laid down by Laud in his answer to Lord Saye and Sele, touching the Liturgy:[8]

'I meddle not here with the King's power. For he may be present in Convocation when he pleases, and take or leave any canons as he pleases, which are for the peace and well ordering of the Church; as well as in Parliament, take or leave any laws made ready for him, for the good and quiet of his people. But if it come to be matter of faith, though in his absolute power he may do what he will, and answer God for it after; yet he cannot commit the ordering of that to any lay assembly, Parliament or other, for them to determine that which God hath entrusted into the hands of His priests. Though, if he will do this, the clergy must do their duty to inform him and help that dangerous error if they can; but if they cannot, they must suffer an unjust violence how far soever it proceed; but they may not break the duty of their allegiance. . . .'

The tragedy of this highly personalized form of nationalism was that it led to the schism and sufferings of the Non-jurors, perhaps the most vital section of the Church of their day. They felt themselves so bound by their oath of allegiance to James II that they could not accept William and Mary. They regarded the oath as absolute, and not qualified by any such concession as 'according to law' or 'in accordance with the Canons'. Since the oath was absolute it allowed for no trans-ference of allegiance; and their bishops and clergy suffered deprivation rather than break it. They recognized the difficulties in which they and the Church were landed but saw no way out of the *impasse*. They even went so far as to describe the terrible illogicality in which they were involved as the doctrine of the Cross. The situation is clearly set forth by one of them, John Lake, Bishop of Chichester, who refused to take the oath but died before he could be deprived, in a profession of faith dictated on his death-bed to his chaplain:[9]

'Being called by a sick and I think a dying bed, and the good hand of God upon me in it, to take the last and best Viaticum, the Sacrament of my dear Lord's Body and Blood, I take myself obliged to make this short recognition and profession.

'That whereas I was baptized into the Religion of the Church of England, and sucked it in with my milk, I have constantly adhered to it through the whole course of my life, and now, if so be the Will of God, shall die in it; and I had resolved, through God's grace assisting me, to have died so, though at a stake.

'And whereas that Religion of the Church of England taught me the doctrine of Non-Resistance and Passive Obedience, which I have accordingly inculcated upon others, and which I took to be the distinguishing character of the Church of England, I adhere no less firmly and steadfastly to that, and in consequence of it have incurred a suspension from the exercise of my office and expected a deprivation. I find in so doing much inward satisfaction, and if the Oath had been tendered at the peril of my life, I could only have obeyed by suffering.'

The same point is brought out in the famous will of the most saintly of the Non-jurors, Bishop Ken, who was deprived of his see of Bath and

Wells but later resigned in order to allow a successor the full rights of the appointment in conscience as well as in law. 'I die,' he says, 'in the communion of the Church of England, as it stands distinguished from all papal and puritan innovations and as it adheres to the doctrine of the cross'[10]—the doctrine of the cross being, in this instance, the doctrine of non-resistance and passive obedience, the doctrine that one must accept the will of the sovereign as supreme governor both in church and state, according to Lake 'the distinguishing character of the Church of England'.

Although the Church as a whole did not follow the Non-jurors but accepted the constitutional position of the monarch as it developed from the change of 1689, such views were sufficiently widespread to emphasize the character of Anglicanism as a national religion. This national character gave the clergy a privileged position and involved them in duties not always regarded as ecclesiastical. Indeed, they are still agents of the state in the conduct of marriages, and the registers they keep in that respect are state documents. But also, until comparatively recent times, many of them were expected to take an official part in the administration of the law. A paragraph in *The Church Magazine* for September 1840 under the heading 'Clerical Magistrates' reads:

'A return to the House of Commons has been published, of the names, addresses and residences of justices of the peace, being ministers of the Established Church, which makes the total number above 2,000. In Norfolk there are 102 reverend justices of the peace, and in Suffolk not less than 111. These counties are the best conducted in England.'

Two consequences of considerable importance followed from this official connection of church and state. It meant that the Church took its full share in the expansion overseas that began in the sixteenth century. As chaplains in the armed services, or to the great trading companies, or to the penal settlements, the clergy had a recognized right to participate. If the missionary followed the flag, the flag also followed the missionary. The Church took a full share in the national expansion. It was part and parcel of the state organization, and if this was sometimes a source of embarrassment to both parties, there can be no doubt that it was also the means of bringing the consolations of religion to many who were in sore need of them. The Church was, as a consequence, an important instrument in the development of civilization and culture in the English colonies during the formative part of their history.

A further and still important consequence of this national character of the Church of England is that every portion of the land is divided into parishes each with its own parson or official representative of God and his Church. This carries with it a reciprocal relation between clergy and people; the people have certain rights in their own parish church and can demand the services of their own clergy. The clergy have a right and duty to minister to the whole of their flock. It follows that there is not a soul in the country for whom some clergyman is not responsible. It is, therefore, natural that when individuals are asked to state their religion and have no particular denominational affiliation, they should write themselves down as C. of E. This custom has given rise to the derisive jest that 'the Church of England is the church people stay away from', which has enough truth in it to make it hurt. But if it is an undoubted weakness to have so large a fringe of uncommitted members, there is also the glorious opportunity of effective evangelization among the many thousands who have accepted the name of Anglican and therefore opened wide the door to spiritual ministrations.

But the Anglican trait of nationalism is not dependent on the establishment of the Church of England. Indeed, it is sometimes said that in England the church has so far lost its national character that it has no right to be established. That is not true. Even on statistical grounds its claim still holds good. It still conducts half the marriages celebrated in the country and it still baptizes nearly 70 per cent of the children. In other words, it has more right to be called national than the actual government of the country. And many people would maintain that in the traits already mentioned it displays more adequately than any other type of Christianity the peculiarities of the English character. But what is interesting from the point of view of Anglicanism as a whole is that this close connection between church and state in England has stamped a national character even on its daughter churches in countries where there is no establishment. It has given its members a wide humanitarian outlook, an interest in civic affairs, an impulse to associate the gospel with every aspect of social life which cause its membership to acquire a national interest and outlook. Nowhere does Anglicanism wear the appearance of a sect; it never could be in the idiomatic sense a 'gathered' church. Like its Saviour on the cross it opens its arms wide to the whole nation.

These then are the four traits that seem most characteristic of the Anglican ethos: comprehensiveness, belief in continuity, emphasis on the Bible, and a clinging to nationality. These traits, of course, in no way form a creed, but they give some indication of the special way in which the common creed of Christendom is held in Anglicanism.

Individually, of course, they are not the exclusive possession of the Anglican Communion, but in their combination and in the peculiar balance in which they are held they are more truly descriptive of Anglicanism than of any other church in Christendom.

CHAPTER FOUR

A WAY OF LIFE

Humanism: The effect of the Cambridge Platonists—Moralism: Moderation—tradition— reason—consistency of character—appeal to conscience—Pelagian influence—Piety: Sobriety— sincerity—practicality—Worship: Historical development of present day forms of worship— Cranmer's Prayer Books—Influence of Laud—Tractarian and evangelical controversy—Future liturgical development

WE HAVE tried to trace the development of Anglicanism as an organization and a doctrine; we must now consider it as a way of life. That is, of course, a very comprehensive heading. An attempt at analysis shows at least four points that will have to be brought under special consideration: the typical Anglican attitude to life, its expression in a moral code, its characteristic piety, and its form of worship.

Humanism
First then we ask what is the Anglican's attitude to life, his *weltan-schauung*? This question, of course, is frequently asked of Christianity itself; and it is always possible that there may be room for different answers within the one general Christian ethos. Inasmuch as Anglicanism claims to reflect the whole gospel we may expect to find any such variations faithfully reflected, even if not emphasized, within the comprehensive limits of the Anglican communion.

Dr Richard Niebuhr,[1] in his interesting and illuminating book *Christ and Culture*, has taught us that there are many possible interpretations of the attitude of Christ to contemporary civilization. In the ultimate resort it might seem, however, that there can be only two sharply contrasted and mutually exclusive attitudes, that of total acceptance and that of total rejection. The great religions of the world have often been divided as they appeared to fall under one or the other of these heads, world-accepting or world-renouncing. A moment's reflection shows that, however possible such a choice may appear in theory, in actual practice it is quite impossible to stand wholly by the one or the other. We can totally reject our environment only by refusing to live at all; and we can totally accept it only at the expense of being pulled every way at once and ending in a mental hospital. There must be some choice and some principle by which to direct the choice.

Actually, there is a third principle beyond that of mere acceptance or rejection which is generally agreed to be more specifically Christian than either. It is that of transformation. The Christian's duty in this world is to co-operate with the divine purpose and transform that which has been subjected to the corrupting influence of sin into what it was intended to be in the 'determinate counsel and foreknowledge of God'. This is thoroughly in line with the incarnational and sacramental teaching of the Fourth Gospel. Even the material elements of this lower world are intended to become the vehicles of life and truth; and it is man's business so to use them. In this process they may legitimately be said to be transformed. We are reminded of St Paul's use of this idea in connection with human personality. 'Be not conformed to this world, but be ye transformed (or transfigured) by the renewing of your minds.'

Of course, the application of this principle may be differently distributed. If it implies an essential element of both acceptance and rejection—for you cannot transform without first accepting, and you would not need to transform if you did not first reject—the respective extent of acceptance and rejection need not be evenly proportioned. Actually, throughout the major part of its history Christianity has not sought to distribute them evenly. A good deal has been left to the will or the conscience of the individual. Monasticism has attracted those who have felt the call in a literal sense to 'leave all and follow' Christ, while Puritanism has sought to make a large area of rejection incumbent upon all faithful Christians. Perhaps differing extensions of the principle of rejection appeal to Christians at different periods of their spiritual growth. At least it seems the universal experience that some element of deliberate self-denial must enter at some stage into all true religion. Monasticism defines a clear-cut area for repression and leaves to the individual the decision whether, by leaving 'the world', to choose it for himself or not. Puritanism stakes out a less well-defined area within the world and seeks to make the observance of its limits an obligation for all. Neither emphasizes adequately that it is the bounden duty of every Christian to surrender his all into the hand of God and then to use thankfully whatever God gives him back.

It is clear that Christianity, with its hope for the ultimate 'restoration of all things', engenders a much more optimistic frame of mind than the more nihilistic religions. To that extent, in spite of its pessimistic view of the present state of the world corrupted by original and actual sin, it must be put on the side of the 'accepting' rather than on that of the 'rejecting' faiths.

Certainly that is the prevailing attitude of mind in Anglicanism. It has been so ever since such questions were canvassed at the time of the

Reformation. It has sometimes been said that the aim of Luther, Calvin, and Zwingli was to destroy the idea of a double standard in Christianity and to bring the height of monastic spirituality into every home. It may have been so, though in view of what they thought of monastic piety the contention requires some careful explanation. But it can hardly be maintained that they succeeded. The probability is that they condemned too much. Certainly Calvin's regime in Geneva was far too austere. In England the Puritans got a bad name, not merely for what was commonly esteemed their hypocrisy, but also because they too often gave the impression that 'whatever was nice was bad'. This stricture applied not only to such sensuous pleasures as were indulged in by the Restoration court, but also to the intellectual adventures undertaken by men of science and philosophy. All was to be decided on the basis of revelation. Hooker put up a magnificent defence of the place of reason in determining our whole attitude to life, and it became one of the most important planks in the Anglican's platform. It was natural, therefore, that when Descartes and the New Philosophy came along, Anglicans should be found among their notable defenders. The new discoveries of science, said Robert Boyle, actually helped the enquirer to understand the great Artificer of the universe. Francis Bacon said that, while a *little* philosophy may induce atheism, *much* of it strengthens our assurance of God. Nor, he continued, need we pin our faith to miracles; the ordinary works of God are sufficient to assure us of His handiwork.

Anglicans thus refused to accept the Puritan rejection of the good things in life whether in the physical or the intellectual sphere. Sanderson, Tillotson, Isaac Newton all assert the value of Natural Theology. They are not averse to the idea of a revelation, but they think that while a good many doubtful items have been grouped under the protective assertion of 'revealed truth', reason has surer evidence in the works of creation. The so-called Deists were not deistic in the sense that they held God to be a kind of absentee landlord who had no present dealings with his property or with his tenants. On the contrary, they were Deists in the sense that they believed God manifested himself in the works of his own hands, and that the very laws by which the universe was sustained were the declaration of his will.

> 'The spacious firmament on high
> With all the blue ethereal sky
> And spangled heavens, a shining frame,
> Their great Original proclaim. . . .
> In reason's ear they all rejoice

And utter forth a glorious voice
For ever singing as they shine
"The hand that made us is divine".'[2]

Of course, such a point of view can easily degenerate into a merely naturalistic religion or a philosophy of religion, implying a rejection of all special revelation. As far as Anglicanism is concerned that fate was avoided, partly through the continued strength of creed and liturgy and partly through the high spirituality of the school of thinkers known as the Cambridge Platonists.

The tradition of Platonism has always been strong in Anglicanism. This tradition has generally accounted for the definite vein of intellectualism in its teaching. The philosophy of Plato has never, it is true, been so clearly formative of Anglican theology as Aristotle's teaching has of Roman Catholicism. The one has influenced many students and thinkers; the other, through Thomas Aquinas, has given an official and authoritative form to doctrine. The former with its characteristic teaching of the reality of the ideal and its belief that whatever we see of goodness, truth, and beauty in this finite sphere must be a kind of effulgence from those absolute qualities in the infinite, has seemed to lend itself to a generally diffused notion of an Incarnation with its consequent sacraments, while being far less susceptible of precise formulation in the form of dogma than its rival.

At the same time it must be admitted that it was less in the realm of material sacraments than in that of mystical thought that the influence showed itself most markedly among the Cambridge Platonists (1633–88). Whether in the aphorisms of Benjamin Whichcote or the poetry of Henry Vaughan, there is a sense of community with the eternal that implies spirituality of a high order. Mysticism of this kind did not lead those who professed it to neglect the sacramental teaching of the Church, still less to doubt the Incarnation (in spite of the fact that some of them were confused with the Deists), but it prevented them from manifesting any desire to multiply either sacraments or dogmas. They thought it wise to keep the doctrines of the Church to the fewest and the simplest. Nevertheless, their Platonism did enable them to surmount the scandal of particularity. With them time and eternity touched and intermingled, but it was time that derived its importance from eternity. They were called 'latitude men', and have been hailed as the progenitors of the school of Broadchurchmen. But they were not Latitudinarians in the sense of Hoadly, who according to his great antagonist, William Law, would have left the Church without sacrament, creed or ministry and would indeed have sacrificed religion for the sake of philosophy.

73

The Cambridge men were very far from all that. They were determined to baptize everything into Christ, to bring every thought into captivity to Him. They wished to take the whole world of thought for their parish. *Nihil humani alienum*. They believed that their religion had given them a key to unlock the doors of all knowledge and they were totally unwilling to minimize their claims. In other words they were humanists. Not the modern kind of scientific humanist, who thinks that science can solve all human problems and is, therefore, a substitute for religion. Nor the flamboyant, Nietzschean laudator of omnipotent man: Glory to Man in the highest! for man is the Master of things.[3] But the Christian humanist, who stretches to the utmost the principle of world-acceptance precisely because he wishes to re-create the whole world through the gospel and is unwilling to leave anything outside the sphere of salvation. In thus devising their own particular brand of humanism the Cambridge Platonists set an indelible mark on Anglicanism.

That mark *has* persisted in spite of all efforts to delete it. In our own generation, under the leadership of the continental theologian Karl Barth, an attempt has been made in the Theology of Crisis to obliterate all traces of Natural Theology from Christian teaching and to assert the strongest possible dualism between Christ and the world. Indeed, the tangential touch of Christ on the perimeter of the world is so infinitesimal in this teaching that one wonders how there can have been any Incarnation at all. Such a view of God is coupled with a teaching of the depravity of man that is reminiscent of the old Calvinism at its most extreme. This is 'world-rejection' in the intellectual sphere. Now it is quite true that Barth, with his strong reminder of the 'otherness' of God and his general assertion of a duality in the universe, did assist us to break free from a type of humanism that had degenerated into a mere evolutionary monism. Yet in 1948 when, at the Lambeth Conference, the Bishops composed their report on the Nature of Man, they quite consciously and firmly remained true to the Anglican tradition, rejecting the Barthian view and developing their thesis along the familiar lines of Anglican humanism.

There are, of course, a number of reasons in the peculiar circumstances of Anglicanism for clinging to this humanist view. There is the strongly developed activism of countries like America and Australasia. This becomes particularly important at the Lambeth Conferences, where a large proportion of the bishops come from overseas. There is also the profound effect of a lay opinion in England which always remains in favour of the broadest possible views whatever the clergy may say. There is further the traditional influence of the establishment in England, on the one hand making it imperative for the Church to be as inclusive as possible and on the other preventing, through its courts, the clergy from pushing doctrinal differences to the point of mutual exclusion. Far more important than all this is the fact that, up till now, the education of the section of Anglicans most capable of coherent philosophical thought has been in schools where the Greek and Latin classics have formed the basis of education. A Christian who through the formative period of his life has had to do his thinking against that kind of background would be a peculiar person not to develop some kind of humanist tendency. The poverty of the religion presupposed in that literature may cause him to reflect on the splendour of his own. But the clarity of thought, the beauty of diction, and the width of interest must make him feel an heir of the world as well as a son of God. Anglican humanism has done a great deal to enable its adherents to retain both sides of its inheritance. There seems no reason why science, if properly taught, should cause any change in this outlook in the coming period when, we are told, science will exclude the classics from the schools. Science is no less humanistic than literature.

Moralism

For our second trait in the Anglican way of life we choose moralism or ethicism. Both words suggest a certain exaggerated emphasis, and it is for that reason that we choose the terms—not because we are suggesting that a proper regard for moral standards is not to be found in other types of Christianity, but because the emphasis typically laid by Anglicans upon the qualities they represent may, in point of fact, become something of an exaggeration.

This can be realized at once if it is remembered what strong approval is generally given by Anglicans to the aphorism, 'It is character and character alone that can truly save us'; or what especially close attention used to be given in the education of the young to that section of the catechism which includes 'my duty towards my neighbour'; or how ready is the typical Anglican to say 'it does not matter what a person believes so long as he does what is right'. To such rough and ready tests we shall return presently. In the meantime it may be interesting to try to effect an analysis of Anglican moralism with the aid of teachers of the classical period.

In their characteristic description of the moral attitude proper to the Christian one is able to distinguish five elements. The first is that of moderation. The Anglican does not desire to be righteous overmuch.

He does not like extremes either in morals or in anything else. Paradoxically it is the very emphasis on moderation, on good form, on merging with one's environment, on refusing to stand out as being singular or conspicuous that he exaggerates. He is as conscious of the virtue of the *via media* in moral conduct as in everything else. By him Christian virtue is not normally regarded as something *sui generis* but as the extension, to a slightly higher degree, of the virtues common in pagan society. Indeed, he is apt to extol the common pagan virtues with greater sincerity than those that are specifically Christian. A thoroughly utilitarian flavour is given to this view of virtue by Isaac Barrow:*

' . . . In fine, the precepts of religion are no other than such as physicians would prescribe for the health of our bodies, as politicians would avow needful for the peace of the state, as Epicurean philosophers do recommend for the tranquillity of our mind and pleasure of our lives; such as common reason dictateth and daily trial sheweth conducible to our welfare in all respects; which consequently, were there no law exacting them of us, we should in wisdom choose to observe, and voluntarily impose on ourselves, confessing them to be fit matters of law, as most advantageous and requisite to the good (general and particular) of mankind. . . .'[4]

This point of view may not unfairly be described as typical of the Anglican layman. It requires a special effort on the part of his theologians to persuade him of the uniqueness of Christian morals.

The second strand we unravel in this analysis of virtue is the stress laid upon what is traditional. The Anglican's fondness for history has already been pointed out in other connections. It is no less conspicuous in the sphere of morals. He is apt to be puzzled by the people who are morally adventurous, and is inclined to be contemptuous of them when they have made ship-wreck of their lives. They should have attached a proper importance to the experience of their elders. After all, man has been living a long time and there must be some point in the conventions he has established. They do at least mark out the route for the traveller who wishes to arrive safe. What is found good and right in one age is likely to be good in another. So Thomas Browne warns us against the view that morality is 'ambulatory' and encourages us to stand in the old, fixed ways:

'Live by old ethics and the classical rules of honesty. Put no new names or notions upon authentic virtues and vices. Think not that morality is ambulatory; that vices in one age are not vices in another, or that virtues, which

---

*Son of Charles I's linen-draper. Became Professor of Greek at Cambridge and then Professor of Mathematics, which latter post he resigned in favour of Isaac Newton.

are under the everlasting seal of right reason, may be stamped by opinion. And therefore, though vicious times invert the opinions of things, and set up new ethics against virtue, yet hold thou unto old morality; and rather than follow a multitude to do evil, stand like Pompey's pillar conspicuous by thyself, and single in integrity.'[5]

Here, amusingly enough, the one reason that will justify the layman in standing out alone is his adherence to the old ways!

A third strand in the Anglican type of virtue is reasonableness. Here, as in his theology, he regards reason as one of the basic elements. Henry More the cabalist (a Grantham boy who became one of the best known Platonists and died in Cambridge in 1687 at the age of seventy-three having consistently refused every preferment offered to him), divided living existences into three classes, of which he named man as the middle term, marked out distinctly by his gift of reason:

'We have now competently set out the nature of the *Animal Life*. But before we pass to the *Divine*, it will be needful to us to take notice of a *Middle Life*, or faculty of the soul of man betwixt the Divine and Animal which, if we might name by the general principle or common root thereof, we may call it Reason. . . .'[6]

Reason would induce the acceptance of the four cardinal virtues—prudence, temperance, fortitude, justice—which had commended themselves alike to the old teachers of the Greco-Roman world as well as to the medieval scholastics. What happens to the three theological virtues of faith, hope and love is not quite so clear, but they seem to be merged in the three 'deduced' virtues of charity, humility, and purity. Here it seems that emphasis on reason leads to some exploitation of pagan standards at the expense of Christian.

Again it is held that staunchness of character is best based upon a rule. Flexibility and resilience were not much praised in the stolid society of the seventeenth century. The ideal of the times was, no doubt, thoroughly 'bourgeois' as we should say in our patronizing way today, but people did like to know where they stood and what to expect. So they demanded consistency and were rather shocked by flippancy or undue lightheartedness. To quote Isaac Barrow again:

'It is a fair ornament of a man, and a grand convenience both to himself and to others with whom he converseth or dealeth, to act *regularly, uniformly, and consistently;* freeing a man's self from distraction and irresolution in his mind, from change and confusion in his proceedings; securing others from delusion and disappointment in their transactions with him. Even a bad rule constantly observed is therefore better than none.'[7]

Consistency, staunchness, reliability, solidity may be recognized as

English rather than Anglican ideals. But this shows how great has been the influence of the Church in forming the national character.

The last strand we shall disentangle from this description of the typical Anglican character is the appeal to the conscience. This again is, of course, a received convention of the English in any case; we all believe that in the last resort we must not act contrary to conscience. Our national playwright noted our universal shrinking from its condemnation: 'Conscience doth make cowards of us all.' But there are varieties, of course, in conscience. The Anglican is not so obtrusive as the Non-conformist conscience. The Anglican expects the conscience to be more under control, more subject to authority and reason. The paradox of conscience, its absoluteness and its need for right guidance, were stated as long ago as the seventeenth century by Joseph Hall, who had been one of King James's representatives at the Synod of Dort:

'If [conscience] condemn us, in vain shall the world beside acquit us; and, if that clear us, the doom which the world passeth upon us is frivolous and ineffectual. I grant this judge is sometimes corrupted with the bribes of hope, with the weak fears of loss, with an undue respect of persons, with powerful importunities, with false witnesses, with forged evidences, to pass a wrong sentence upon the person or cause, for which he shall be answerable to Him, that is higher than the highest; but yet this doom, though reversible by the tribunal of Heaven, is still obligatory on earth. So as it is my fault, that my conscience is misled; but it is not my fault to follow my conscience. How much need have I therefore, O my God, to pray that Thou wouldst guide my conscience aright, and keep this great judge in my bosom from corruption and error!'[8]

It is not often that in homiletic literature one finds so clear a statement that, if conscience is to be accepted as a guide, it needs education.

It seemed desirable thus to sum up the main features of the Anglican moralism in the words of historical authorities in order to make our study as objective as possible. If the analysis here reached is generally accepted, the way is left open for a consideration of the way in which this standard has imposed itself throughout the generations. We can then conclude the point by asking whether it provides us with a recognizable portrait of Anglican moralism today.

Of course, it is a well known fact that moral questions have always had a special attraction for the British. In the sphere of philosophy we have produced no great names to compare with those of the Greeks or the Germans as far as metaphysics are concerned. But we can claim a special eminence in the sphere of ethics. Not only did we produce in early days the heretic Pelagius, but we were responsible in more recent times for the production of the important school of Utilitarianism.

The fact consorts well with the practical bent of the British mind. In this respect English religion has on the whole displayed a faithful reflection of the British character.

Pelagius, as we have seen, denied the need of special grace from God, but thought that men ought to be able to lead a good life by the exertion of their own will, aided by the general grace with which God had endowed every man at birth. In developing this teaching he started a world-shaking controversy with the great Augustine who leaned strongly to the determinist side. Indeed it was the latter's epigrammatic prayer, 'Give what thou commandest, and command what thou wilt,' that caused the original protest on the part of Pelagius. It is often contended that, in spite of all their official acceptance of authoritative doctrine on the matter, the English have always retained a sneaking fondness for the emphasis on free-will and the self-assured morality which Augustine repudiated.

Certainly an emphasis on moral character, Pelagian or not, was strongly stamped upon English religion at the crisis of the Reformation. The opening up of the Bible and particularly of the Old Testament seemed to reveal a hitherto unrealized demand for moral goodness, especially on its negative side. 'Touch not the accursed thing' was a phrase that echoed continuously in the mind. The regulations drawn from the Old Testament were often uncritically received. The Ten Commandments were set up in all the churches and recited at the beginning of every celebration of the Lord's Supper. After all, the Reformation itself was in large measure a revolt against what was conceived to be the lack of moral goodness in the medieval church. And prohibitions can generally be more easily grasped than affirmative injunctions.

Anglicans, *more suo*, managed to keep the pursuit of goodness from getting out of hand. But by the time of the Commonwealth a cult of holiness was firmly established in the sects, especially among the Independents and Quakers. It even led to the Rule of the Saints in the Nominated or Barebones Parliament. But, like Prohibition in America, extreme Puritanism defeated its own ends. At the Restoration there was a reaction that made the Caroline court and its theatre a by-word for licentiousness. It was the influence of the Cambridge Platonists and some of the Latitudinarians that restored the balance, and set the tone, which is truly characteristic of Anglicanism, of a steady, if somewhat unemotional, pursuit of common goodness.

It would be a mistake to think that this ideal, if it lacked emotion, lacked spirituality and depth. It was the real goal of the Anglican pilgrim. In the temper of the times he was allowed no elaboration of worship or of creed; so his religious energies were spent upon the pursuit of virtue. In this respect Bishop Butler is typical. His balance between extremes, and his aphorism that 'probability is the guide of life', suggest the earnestness with which the *via media* was followed in ethics as elsewhere. Even William Law, whose *Serious Call* is perhaps the most eloquent and persuasive appeal for whole-hearted devotion that we have in the English language, did not favour extravagance or 'enthusiasm'. The longing for something more than ordinary goodness, the passion for utter holiness, that characterized Wesley and Newman, Simeon and Pusey, are not, even if we have to say it shamefacedly, typically Anglican. We are proud to have had such men in our ranks and we strive to follow them—but at a distance. Perhaps we are not prepared to pay the price of their complete self-dedication.

The dangers inherent both in the special emphasis on goodness and in the acceptance of a standard less than the highest have not been altogether escaped. In one social stratum it has led to 'Public School' religion with its picture of the 'Christian gentleman', in which the features of the Christian have been often obscured by those of the gentleman. Frequently the rules for conduct in school and in the world have been drawn from sport rather than bible or creed. The example of Christ has been there, but it has been kept somewhat in the background. The result is that even the educated Englishman is in religious matters little more than an adolescent, sheepish and tongue-tied in any spiritual crisis.

In a different social stratum the effect has been almost equally devastating. If the object of religion is to make people good, then the normal adult considers that he himself knows all about goodness, at least within the terms of his own station. He wants his children to know all about it too. For that reason he will send them to church or Sunday school because that is where they learn these things. But for one who has already learnt the lesson there is surely no need to go: therefore he and his wife can stay away. That is the reasoning, sub-consciously argued no doubt, for the small attendance at many churches.

It is possible that the extension of Anglicanism over many lands, and the ease with which its leaders of different races may now communicate with each other from continent to continent, will one day redress the balance of our moralism. People less profoundly affected by centuries of Pelagian influence may help us to realize that the primary object of religion is not goodness but God. The Presbyterians put it well: 'The chief end of man is to glorify God and enjoy him for ever.'

It is because He whom we love is good that we become good, as we are made more and more like Him. He is utter goodness and the consistent Christian can never be content with any half-way house.

Piety

No one would describe piety as a quality peculiar to the Anglican. The peculiarity lies in the quality, the special brand, of the piety. There is nothing in the whole range of our subject so difficult to analyse and describe as the peculiar character of Anglican piety. It has few of the obvious characteristics that mark devotion in other churches and faiths. It has none of the cold intellectualism of the French or the fervent emotionalism of the Italian. It would be as ill at ease amidst the excitement of revivalism as amidst the fervent ejaculations of the old-fashioned Salvationist. If it was aware of them it would be just as aghast at the extravagances of a St Francis as at those of Madame Guyon. It is made as uncomfortable by the emaciation of El Greco figures as by the rolling eyes of a Goya saint. Its atmosphere would have been quite alien to the ecstatic worship of Pauline Corinth, and it is doubtful whether the dramatic scene of Pentecost could ever have been enacted in a typical Anglican setting.

The shrinking from outward manifestations of piety becomes, sometimes, almost pathological. The effect of the great modern movements, both Evangelical and Catholic, has been to break down this extreme reserve to some extent. But it is still observable. Whether one is sharing in the worship of high or low church, or discoursing privately with some quite faithful individual member, there is almost always some inhibition that represses any display of emotion. Probably every parish priest could give instances of members of his flock who, having suffered a bereavement, promptly absent themselves from attendance at church, not out of any rebellion against the dealings of Providence, but simply from fear of displaying emotion in public. This may seem an extreme instance of reserve, but it is indicative of a very general attitude of mind.

It is also indicative of a truth that is sometimes missed. Anglican piety does not avoid violent expression because it is too shallow, but often because it is so deep. It is none the less heartfelt for being modest and gentle in its expression. 'Still waters', according to a favourite motto, 'run deep'. It is the shallow brooks that make most noise. The Anglican is by nature reserved and inarticulate. He does not take kindly to forms of piety that seem to him extravagant and exotic. The modern efforts to 'limber him up' by introducing him to extraneous devotions, whether they come from American evangelism or from post-

Tridentine Catholicism, leave him too often unmoved and colder than ever.

It may be that some of this chilliness comes not so much from the national character but from historical circumstances, such as the resistance that had to be exerted against the excesses of the prophesyings in the reign of the first Elizabeth, and the extravagances of the Quakers and Anabaptists. It was still the same dislike of emotionalism that in the eighteenth century brought out Bishop Butler's famous retort against the 'enthusiasm' of John Wesley. 'Sir, the pretending to extraordinary gifts and revelations of the Spirit is a horrid thing, a *very* horrid thing.' The mentality that cultivated a modest *via media*, even in the realm of ethics, was likely to exercise a similar restraint in the realm of piety.

It would, however, be a great mistake to think that there was no strong positive element in this subdued piety. It carries with it all the characteristic English genius for understatement, and still exhibits it, even in lands where over-statement has become part of the secular vocabulary. For its most typical example we may go, perhaps, to Keble's *Christian Year*, first published in 1827 before the Oxford Movement got under way and rapidly re-issued in a series of editions whose number* reveals how exactly the book spoke for the religion of the day. It is a churchly book, following the round of the ecclesiastical seasons, but linking them almost without fail to the seasons of the natural year. It is redolent of the English countryside. There are no great heights or abysmal depths, no tempestuous rages. All is quiet, gentle—but never, except to the jaundiced eye, flat, dull or uninteresting. For a century it sold widely and formed the devotional reading of thousands. Today it scarcely suits the more strident mood of the current generation. Lord David Cecil, a great authority, has even said that he can see no poetry in it. But it is possible he is mistaken and that *The Christian Year* will come back into some kind of favour when the 'still, small voice' has once again been recognized as a proper vehicle for religious truth.

Beside the *Christian Year* one would like to set the earlier *Serious Call* of William Law, if it were not objected that, since Law was a Nonjuror, he can hardly be accepted as a typical Anglican. The objection will not hold, for Law remained an Anglican to the end of his life and his piety was certainly of the typical variety. It was far from typical, however, in its intensity. It was not, like Keble's verse, an expression of the general piety, but a deliberate and well-conceived attempt to deepen devotion. It was, as its title announces, a call to a devout and holy life. And it was a serious call. It was an effort to make the ordinary

* In 1867, a year after his death, it had mounted to 109.

believer regard religion as an important business. The religious man must not treat his religion as if it were a matter for his leisure hours only, or as if its needs were satisfied if he threw it a few crumbs of time each day. It was not something apart from the work and pleasure of everyday life; it was part and parcel of that life and should be engaged in with at least as much earnestness as we accord to ordinary affairs. That is Law's case, and he presents it with a grace and a wit that have seldom, if ever, been equalled in English literature. Its nearest equivalent is, perhaps, to be found in François de Sales, though there is an illuminating contrast between the aristocratic elegance of the Frenchman and the bourgeois solidity of the Englishman.

If we wished for an example of this kind of piety in practice we could not do better than study the history of the 'Arminian Nunnery' at Little Gidding, which was found so very attractive by King Charles I. There Nicholas Ferrar and his family occupied themselves in prayer, in copying manuscripts, and in the relief of distress. The community was not exactly a reversion to type of the old mixed monasteries of monks and nuns, because the old vows were not taken, family life was continued, and all members of the family were included, children as well as adults. But it was a genuine attempt to bring the old spiritual values of community life into Anglicanism, while avoiding such 'extremes' as had led to breakdown in the old system. It was above everything else an attempt to give *practical* expression to the true ideal of piety. As such, Izaak Walton tells us, it afforded a welcome refuge from time to time to many of the clergy who were wearied of the controversies of the day:

'It is fit to tell the reader that many of the clergy that were more inclined to practical piety and devotion than to doubtful and needless disputations, did often come to Gidding Hall, and make themselves a part of that happy society, and stay a week or more, and then join with Mr Ferrar and the family in these devotions, and assist and ease him or them in their watch by night.'[9]

It is clear that, generally speaking, the same ideals were shared by the clergy and their flocks. It was not, and never has been, a case of the clergy cultivating one kind of piety and their people another; although, inevitably and properly, the clergy have generally tried to precede along the way they wished their people to tread. To the disparaging this may simply seem to mean that the piety, even of the clergy, has always been pedestrian. It does not, however, necessarily imply that it has been dull or uninspiring.

Spiritual directors have always been inclined to distrust the fickleness of moods. They have, therefore, tended to order their own life by rule

G   83

and to encourage their people to do the same. The clergy have, indeed, been given their own basic rule in the recitation of the daily office. One does not often see them doing it in public, except of course in church, but it is a rule and is widely observed. A religion that lives by rule may not seem the most exciting kind of piety, but it at least ensures that observance will not drop below a certain level. And it can hold a position until the tides of emotion begin to flow again and encourage one to pass beyond the rule. George Herbert, the friend of Izaak Walton and Nicholas Ferrar, saw that long ago and recorded it in his description of the Country Parson:

'He therefore thinks it not enough for him to observe the fasting days of the Church and the daily prayers enjoined him by authority, which he observeth out of humble conformity and obedience; but adds to them, out of choice and devotion, some other days for fasting and hours for prayers; and by these he keeps his body tame, serviceable and healthful; and his soul fervent, active, *young and lusty as an eagle.*'[10]

If this severely practical element is to be found in the parson's piety, it is to be found also in his preaching, which he himself would have been the first to regard as part of his piety. Here there is the same anxiety to eschew all suspicion of anything like extravagance. In the preaching of the sects there has been many an example of a perfervid eloquence that began to sound hollow once the first fine rapture had evaporated out of it. Anglickn congregations have always tried to avoid this experience and have asved for 'practical' sermons. John Earle, Bishop of Salisbury in the seveneteenth century, showed how the contemporary parson met the need:

'He shoots all his meditations at one butt; and beats upon his text, not the cushion, making his hearers, not the pulpit, groan.'

If moderation and practicality were, and are, twin notes of Anglican piety we must not forget that sometimes a deeper note is struck. Normally it can be done only by someone who has himself been through the abyss of anguished experience. Anglicanism had no St Paul, Augustine of Hippo, or Kierkegaard. But, at least, it had John Donne who became Dean of St Paul's in 1621 and whose effigy carved in his shroud still adorns the wall of the church he served. His range of feeling includes a consciousness of evil which has done a good deal, combined (it must be confessed) with the difficulty of his cramped metaphysical poetry, to endear him to the present sophisticated generation. His lines on the Cross, in spite of their studied epigrammatic form, convey a real depth of feeling for the material cross itself and its meaning, for the sign and pictures that bring it to our mind, and for the individual suffering we are called upon to endure as part of our bearing of that selfsame cross.

> 'Be covetous of Crosses, let none fall.
> Cross no man else, but cross thyself in all.
> Then doth the Cross of Christ work fruitfully
> Within our hearts, when we love harmlessly
> That Cross's pictures much, and with more care
> That Cross's children, which our Crosses are.'[11]

Worship

The most important element in any religious way of life is its distinctive method of worship. If the aim of all religion is to bring the worshipper in contact with God, then it is clearly important *how* he should worship. Consequently, not only does Christianity differ from all other religions in the way it worships, but the different sections of the Christian Church have each developed its own distinctive type of worship expressing its own particular ethos and marking it out from all the rest. Anglicanism is no exception.

Two contrasting traits in Anglican worship would immediately strike the most casual observer who was at all knowledgeable in these matters: the first that it is in the vernacular, and the second that it follows ancient forms. The two traits are not universally found together. Churches that worship in the common tongue generally do so according to modern forms, while, conversely, those that use ancient forms are inclined also to use ancient tongues. The combination of these two traits is not the only uncommon feature in Anglican worship. The enquiring visitor may be a little disconcerted at the variety of services. He cannot always be sure that he will get the same kind of service at the same hour in different churches. In one he may find that the choir office is being sung, and at another the Eucharist. Even if he finds the Eucharist at two different churches he may be puzzled at the stark simplicity with which it is celebrated in one and at the solemn elaboration with which it is celebrated in the other. Fascinated or repelled, he will be, at least, further intrigued if he learns that this variety stems from a Book of Common Prayer imposed on the English people by Act of Parliament in order to ensure universal uniformity in worship. If he concludes that this is merely another peculiarity of the English, he will be surprised to hear that much the same phenomenon is in evidence throughout the length and breadth of the Anglican Communion, even where there is no Establishment and no Act of Uniformity to dictate

85

how people shall worship. He will then probably guess that in this, as in most things Anglican, some recourse must be had to history in order to understand the precise nature of the present situation.

The outcome of her own particular Reformation struggle was that the Church of England tried to make the best of both worlds, ancient and modern. The two were divided by a fairly sharp difference in their attitude to worship. In the former the manifest aim had been the honour of God; in the latter the effective aim was the edification of man. The former was characterized by stress on the ministry of the sacraments; the latter by stress on the ministry of the word. The former elaborated its services; the latter translated and re-translated the Bible. The former emphasized the role of the priest; the latter the role of the preacher. All this is, of course, a grotesquely crude generalization, and it would be manifestly absurd to suppose that the two aims were altogether contradictory and mutually exclusive.

Nevertheless, there is a great deal of truth in the opposition. It was the business of Anglicanism to see that the gulf did not widen and to provide a bridge. This is what in his Prayer Books Cranmer deliberately tried to do. He refused to abandon the ancient liturgical forms as urged by the extreme reformers, and tried to put the old offices into a shape that would express the new teaching and make it popular with the laity. He retained the essential structure of the Mass, while suppressing the idea of sacrifice in favour of that of communion. He simplified the order of service and adopted the language understood by the people. Above all, he brought in a vast amount of Bible-reading. It would be difficult to see how any service-book could more clearly declare its intention of combining the best of both new and old. That intention was indeed plainly stated in the preface. It was hoped that by this means the people would receive a balanced ministry of both word and sacraments. For a time some embargo had to be put on preaching. But when things had settled down and there was less fear of disruption, the Anglican clergy were given licence to preach; and then the balance between the glorification of God and the edification of man was at last made even.

But as so often happens after such upheavals, when an effort has been made to reconcile conflicting elements, it is more easy to state a concordat than to put it into effect in practical life. Varying emphasis was laid by one side or the other on sermon or sacrament, and some efforts were made to discard the liturgy altogether. It was probably not until the time of Charles I and Laud that the country saw a really determined effort to live by the Prayer Book as a whole. Then one did get a regular recitation of the Daily Office combined with frequent communion. Beveridge at St Peter's upon Cornhill later had morning and evening prayer and a weekly communion, and although such faithfulness to Prayer Book standards could not yet be described as general, it set a pattern to which future generations were to aspire.

Laud with his disciplinarian qualities was able to work towards the ideal of uniformity stated by Sanderson, Bishop of Lincoln, of Savoy Conference fame, in his preface to the 1662 revision of the Prayer Book:

'It hath been the wisdom of the Church of England, ever since the first compiling of her Public Liturgy, to keep the mean between the two extremes, of too much stiffness in refusing, and of too much easiness in admitting any variation from it.'

Laud was also able to work for a general restoration of dilapidated churches and for the establishment of some decency in furnishing. He was also anxious to achieve some adequate solemnity in the conduct of services after all the devastation and dishonour that had resulted from secular greed and Puritan pressure during the previous period. As far as externals go he was not able to do much more than insist upon the retention of the surplice with the additional use of the cope in cathedrals and collegiate churches, though some of his supporters, like Cosin at Durham, were able to set a higher standard. Elizabeth, it is true, had tried to ensure the use of the eucharistic vestments that belonged to the ancient tradition, but the rubric ordering them had never been much more than a dead letter.

The benefit of the Laudian impulse was seen after the Restoration when Anglicanism achieved the height of its popularity, although the politicians, then as always, were only too anxious to use it for their own ends and exercised a devastating effect on its influence and policies. It may be wondered why no serious attempt was made until the Non-jurors to turn back to the standard set by the original book of 1549. The answer lies not only in the relations with the state, but also in the general dislike and fear of Rome. Suspicion engendered a desire not to be found doing things as Rome did them. Added to this inhibition was the growing insularity of the English church and people, which deepened the popular ignorance of liturgical matters. Even the bishops and clergy had little knowledge of Prayer Books other than their own. Belief in 'our incomparable liturgy' certainly did not spring out of a studied comparison of it with the classical models or out of any deep learning in the science of liturgiology, but merely out of a blissful content with the rite as it was known and used.

Nevertheless, there was something to be said for Englishmen's complacency about their Prayer Book. It probably was the best of its time. It was certainly well calculated to meet their needs, and it was used far more than is generally realized.* The eighteenth century is generally given a bad name for churchmanship, but that disparagement was at least not deserved in the first half of the century. It is on record that already in 1692 nearly all the churches in the cities of London and Westminster had two services daily and in some of them matins had to be duplicated, being said at an early hour for the workers and in the middle of the morning for the elderly and well-to-do. The habit of weekday church attendance extended into the most exalted circles. George III for instance, when in residence at Windsor, always walked over to the chapel for morning prayer before breakfast.

The daily services seem to have been well attended until the middle of the eighteenth century, when there was a rapid falling off. By 1824 only nine parish churches in the cities of London and Westminster had even one daily service. It is a singular comment on the shortness of human memory that a few years later, when the Tractarians began to re-introduce them, they were denounced as an indication of Popery. This misunderstanding is all the more surprising since in the interval had come the Evangelical revival, one of whose early characteristics had been an emphasis on just this type of thing. It is well known that John Wesley was himself a precisionist in these matters and that the name 'Methodist' was given to his followers because of the meticulous care with which they kept the rules of the Church. What is less well known is that it was at the present-day Mecca of evangelicalism, St Mary's Islington, that the regular recitation of the litany on Wednesdays and Fridays and early morning celebrations of the Holy Communion were first restored.

There seemed, therefore, no reason in the nature of things why Tractarians and Evangelicals should not have met together in their efforts to improve the programme of worship. What made such cooperation difficult was the insistence by the successors of the original Tractarians on their right to use the old vestments and ceremonies in their celebration of the Eucharist and to celebrate it (preferably without communicants) in the most elaborate manner possible at the chief service-hour of the week. That insistence at least had the effect of bringing before the public mind, in the most clear and vivid manner, the

* We are told that Elizabeth's Lord Burghley never failed to attend Morning and Evening Prayer, and the same is said of Jeremy Taylor's Lady Carbery, in spite of her great household and ten children. (G. J. Stranks *Anglican Devotion* (1961) pp. 26, 71.)

different doctrine and ideology lying behind the Catholic way of performing the rite. It shocked some Englishmen into a first realization
that such views could legitimately be held in the Anglican Communion
and others into a stout denial that they could properly be held anywhere at all. After the first surprise was over, a certain number of
Anglicans found that this was the way they wished to worship, while
many others preferred to remain in what were to them the old and
familiar ways. The difference, starting in England, has spread into
every province of the Anglican Communion. The heat of controversy
has now died down; we recognize that this contrast is the penalty for
trying to reconcile in one communion and fellowship the two main
schools of Christian interpretation, and we abide the relaxation of the
tension. But it has left us with the uncomfortable realization that if one
attends a strange church in the middle of a Sunday morning one will
have no idea what type of worship one will find.

In either case it appears from the remarks of his friendly rivals that
the Anglican excels in the quiet and ordered dignity with which he
offers his worship. On occasions of great national importance he is
often told: 'Of course no one can do this kind of thing like you
Anglicans.' Salisbury people cherish the story of the way in which their
Bishop Ridgeway drove out to offer his felicitations to Thomas Hardy
on the occasion of that great novelist's eightieth birthday, only to find
him away from home. The next day the Bishop received a charming
note from his agnostic neighbour excusing himself for his absence on
the ground that he had given himself his usual birthday treat, and gone
in to Salisbury to hear evensong in his Lordship's Cathedral. It is not
only from the great cathedrals that worshippers have drawn the sense
of the numinous. We are told, in an oft repeated passage of Izaak
Walton, that when George Herbert's bell in the little church at
Bemerton rang for prayers even the ploughman would pause at his
work. More surprising, perhaps, is the nostalgic eloquence with which
Cardinal Manning speaks of the village church where in his Anglican
days he used to lead the worship: 'The little church under a green hill-
side, where the morning and evening prayers, and the music of the
English Bible for seventeen years became a part of my soul. Nothing is
more beautiful in the natural order, and if there were no eternal world,
I could have made it my home.'[12] The question of language received
even clearer recognition from another Roman Catholic priest, a
chaplain in the First World War. He had been asked by his Anglican
colleague why he always stopped by, after having said his own Mass, to
listen to the English service. 'Ah, padre,' he replied, 'you will never

understand how wonderful it is to hear Mass in your own language.'

At the moment it seems likely that changing social customs and advancing liturgical knowledge may help to bridge the gulf between the varying practices of Anglican schools of thought. Radio and television are making it possible for everyone to learn how other people conduct their services, and to that extent are reducing the fear of the unknown. In new towns and freshly built up areas, where the organization of church services starts *de novo*, it is the custom to arrange for a service of Holy Communion with music and sermon at some time between nine and ten in the morning. This hour appeals to the modern housewife and such worship can easily become the family service and a rallying point for the whole parish. In some parishes it is found that awkward questions of ceremonial, which have hitherto proved a divisive influence, can be avoided by the adoption of the so-called Byzantine rite with the celebrant standing behind the altar facing west. It is held that this method appeals to evangelical and catholic alike as being reminiscent of the Last Supper and as following ancient precedent. Further, since some of the Anglican Ultramontanes have begun to follow the example of the Pope and celebrate High Mass in the evening, they find themselves not far removed from the practice of extreme evangelicals for whom Evening Communion has long been a party badge.

Perhaps the happiest element in all these suggestions is that people are thinking, and thinking intelligently, about the best way of offering their worship to God. There is probably more earnest thought being given to the subject of liturgy today than at any time since the Reformation. The fact that the revival of interest coincides with the liturgical reform movement on the Continent and in the Roman Church means that the debate is likely to be carried on with the utmost skill and learning. Under current proposals it seems that Anglicans may have the opportunity of making experiments by bits and pieces, rather than by trying to adopt a whole new Prayer Book at once. This means that liturgical scholarship may once more become a live instead of a static thing. Too much change, of course, would destroy its own end; people must become thoroughly habituated to a form before it can serve as an adequate instrument for the expression of their feelings. But recent experience has shown us that worship, like water, will find its own channel, and it is much better that it should be helped to do so officially for the benefit of all, rather than burst its barriers and run to waste.

In this connection it appears that there are two conflicting needs that will require attention, if we are to fill adequately our pastoral and evangelistic tasks. The first is for variety, and the second for simplicity.

Our present Book of Common Prayer is adapted to the purposes of the instructed churchman. A certain amount of *expertise* is required before it can be used efficiently. But such a churchman, when he has begun to use it to the full, may well find that he would be glad of more variety than it affords. A richer calendar would give him more changes in the Eucharist and perhaps illuminate still further the Daily Office. In any case, it is time that we came to some conclusion about the enrichments proposed in the 1928 book.[13] At the same time, while one section of church people would be glad of more variety, there are others for whom we need a form of service much simpler than anything we have already. There are thousands who are being attracted to the church but have no knowledge of liturgical worship. We badly need some form of service that can be used in connection with evangelistic efforts, a kind of mission service that does not involve turning over many pages to find scattered parts, but will bear its scheme plain upon the surface. It should be sufficiently liturgical to introduce the new-comer to that type of worship, but it should not be so complicated as to cause the tyro to lose his way in it; and it should leave plenty of room for the initiative of the minister or missioner. If the needs for variety and simplicity conflict, there is no alternative but to provide for their satisfaction in different services. No least common multiple will do; that way neither need would be satisfied. But if both can be met within the pages of the one book, then the Book of Common Prayer will be even more valuable than it is.

It is a shame to end our discussion of Anglican worship by pointing out a deficiency. But nothing is perfect. Time, which makes ancient good uncouth, has been kind to our Anglican liturgy, which still raises the hearts and illuminates the minds of millions. But there are millions of others to whom its spirituality is inaccessible because its language is no longer comprehensible. (The astonished face of an American Rhodes Scholar the first time he heard it used in College Chapel was sufficient evidence of that.) Somehow we must find a way of reaching the understanding of the unlearned without surrendering the beauty of our heritage.*

---

*Evelyn Underhill, *Worship*, p. 327, draws attention to the part played by books of private devotion, which in their attitude to the sacrament of the altar were hardly distinguishable from the Catholic literature of the Continent, and of which there was no lack between the Elizabethan settlement and the Tractarian revival. 'It is chiefly by these books, which played their part in each successive revival of worship, that the continuity of the true Anglican spirit, with its peculiar brand of reverence, sobriety, moral earnestness and sturdy realism, was assured.'

Part II

DEVELOPMENT OF THOUGHT

CHAPTER FIVE

THE HISTORIC PARTIES

Division under Tudors and Stuarts—High Church: Eclipse and Restoration—Oxford Movement—Anglo-Catholics—Broad Church: Rise and decline of Latitudinarians—The Evangelicals: Wesley, Whitefield and the Evangelical revival—The various parties overseas

EVERYONE WHO knows about Anglicanism knows about the parties into which it is divided. On the continent they are popularly supposed to represent different churches. A few years ago, before the present enlightenment had begun to spread, it was not uncommon for an Englishman in France to be asked, 'Do you belong to the High Church or to the Low Church?' with the implied assumption that they were two separate organizations.

Actually they are the glory of the Church. This is by no means the common view. Normally they are derided by critics and mourned by friends. As we have already reminded ourselves, some of the former have gone so far as to describe them as opposed religions and to allege the impossibility of combining them within one organization. However, it still remains true that each of them reflects a real aspect of Christian doctrine. The miracle is that they can stress their own aspect of the truth as strongly as they do without falling apart. It is surely a good, even a splendid, thing to have groups of people so unwilling to surrender any particle of the truth as they see it, and yet maintaining their unity in one communion and fellowship.

It is not suggested that this result is achieved without strain. In any organized body of people to whom belief appears specially important there must be continual tension. There are fashions in belief as in other things, and emphasis is always shifting. In a body where the differences are strongly marked the tension must be severe; to overcome it or disregard it requires an unusual amount of toleration. Anglicanism is probably the most tolerant of all Christian faiths, and yet not always has the tolerant attitude been particularly obvious. There have been times when representatives of one or other party were prepared to deny to the rest any right of inheritance in the Church. In the end, however, good sense, Christian charity or sober judgment has prevailed. It is the fact that since the century of the settlement there has been no split on party lines. Individuals of course have left the Church because of doctrinal disagreement, and one talks, without undue stretch of language, of the Methodists' as a low church schism and the Non-jurors' as a high church schism. But neither of the latter pair was, strictly speaking, on doctrinal grounds such as have provided the barriers between the present parties. The one was largely a matter of organization and the other of politics.

To the outsider the Anglican Communion must appear a curious amalgam. Even those of its own members who are not professed theologians or historians may find themselves confused over the constantly changing terminology used to denote the shifting changes of opinion. To the initiate it has all the attraction of a kaleidoscope whose colours are continually separating and merging again to form fresh shapes and combinations. On practical grounds this may sometimes cause an embarrassment for which the charm of variety may seem too high a payment. It would of course be intolerable if there were no common ground between the parties. But essentially there is a hard core of basic conviction derived from creed and catechism and bible which persists all through the changes. So long as that remains intact the Anglican feels that he should enjoy the fullest freedom of opinion and allow it to others. After all, is there not a text about 'the liberty wherewith Christ has made us free'?[1]

In any case a proper understanding of the parties can best be achieved by tracing out their main doctrinal emphasis and sketching their historical development. Happily the chief schools of thought have maintained some identity through the centuries, and in spite of certain inevitable changes it is not difficult to follow their fortunes.

We begin with the oldest—the High Church party.

High Church

It is tempting, and probably accurate, to see the beginning of high-churchmanship in Queen Elizabeth I herself, who brought its attitude of mind into the Settlement from her father Henry VIII. He, it will be remembered, as a theologian and defender of the faith, was determined to allow no change in the general ethos of the Church in spite of the substitution of the royal supremacy for the papacy. Elizabeth appears to have clung to this attitude in her own private chapel as far as possible during the changes involved by the reigns of Edward and Mary. When she herself came to the throne and was invited by Pius IV to send representatives to the Council of Trent, she declared that she was 'as good a Catholic as any' but insisted that the proper representatives of the Church in her dominion should be her own English bishops, who, having been canonically appointed, had as much right as any other bishops to be members of the council.[2] Her point was not allowed at

Rome, but the fact that she made it so strongly should be sufficient to show her own theological position. We have already seen how that position is further revealed in the detailed arrangements of her 1559 Prayer Book.

The Queen could not recover all the ground lost in 1552 because of the strength of the Puritan opposition. Many of her own clergy and laity felt themselves so definitely on the side of the Reformed as against the old-style Catholics that they were prepared to carry the ecclesiastical revolution much further than the known wishes of the Queen would allow. Nevertheless people like Matthew Parker saw the point clearly enough to recognize the need for a middle road between Geneva and Rome. Even while accepting a new emphasis in matters of faith, they were determined to keep what they believed to be the old historical constitution of the Church. It was to this position that Hooker gave an immense theological authority. He did not do it by taking a party line. On the contrary he effected a synthesis between the evangelical, the catholic and the rationalist strains. He did not even go so far as the Prayer Book in claiming apostolic authority for the threefold ministry. But he did claim authority for the Church. He exposed the futility of the puritan contention that everything has been already settled by the bible. He claimed that the bible itself is to be interpreted by reason, and that where the bible is silent the Church must speak. It was this that provided a foundation for the High Church party. 'The use of the people of God' was emphasized as a guide for the faithful Christian. That contention brought in the whole historic argument. The Church was a continuous organization and respect must be paid to its whole history.

It is easy to see that such an attitude could easily deteriorate into a mere antiquarianism. In due course that fate was to descend upon more than one generation of the party holding these views so devastatingly that the aphorism 'high and dry' became a common controversial cliché. But that desiccated condition never lasted long. Life always revived through the recollection of what the Church had been and was.

The Body of Christ could not become completely desiccated. Fresh vitality always poured in from the revival of faith if the stress on order threatened to choke the breath of the Spirit. In the beginning at least faith and order helped and supported each other in the struggle against Rome on the one side and the sectaries on the other. In its ideal form this type of Anglicanism could hardly be better described than in the words used of Dr Routh, one of its later representatives:*

*President of Magdalen College, Oxford, 1791–1854.

97

'In his own person he represented the particular type of Catholicism characteristic of High Churchmanship: a devotion to Catholic truth in all its splendour and fullness, a devotion rooted in massive patristic learning: a spirituality drawing its nourishment from the Prayer Book: a sense of the oneness of Church and Society, with the Church sanctifying every side of national life and giving to society a Godward purpose and direction: a loyalty to an England whose national character was influenced more by theology than commerce.'[3]

The divine of whom those words were written died in his hundredth year in the middle of the nineteenth century, having lived long enough to see these ideas re-born in the Oxford Movement. Newman dedicated to him his book on the *Via Media*: 'To M. J. Routh . . . who has been reserved to report to a forgetful generation what was the theology of their fathers.'[4]

But this is to anticipate. The work begun by Elizabeth and Parker was really completed by Bancroft, who was Bishop of London from 1597 to 1604 and was translated to Canterbury the year after the Queen's death. He had been the protagonist against the Puritans long before James called upon him to take a leading part in the Hampton Court Conference, in which the Puritan intention to transform the character of the national church was defeated. Bancroft effected a reform on his own lines. He obtained an acceptance of the Book of Common Prayer and the Thirty-nine Articles, a new set of canons and a new translation of the bible, a revision of the ecclesiastical courts and a reorganization of the visitatorial system. It was on such lines that original high-churchmanship completed the Settlement and brought to an end the reformation period in England.

Eclipse and Restoration
The movement thus inaugurated was developed and pushed to a fatal extreme by Laud and his school. No one could reasonably deny Laud's sincerity, ability and devotion. He had immense zeal but his zeal was not according to discretion. He generally had the law on his side and his opponents had little legal case against him. His mistake lay in failing to realize that law is not enough. Life is more than law and if the law does not continually adapt itself to growing needs, the spirit of the times will become too strong for it and break its bonds. Laud himself had a stiff, uncompromising spirit that sometimes made him morally wrong when he was legally right.

His business was to restore order and decency in the Church after the confusion and slackness of the pro-Puritan period. He took up a generation later where Bancroft had left off. He insisted upon the due observance of the canons, and brought under discipline not only the clergy but as many of the laity as he could, quite without respect to their rank or position. He saw that an attempt was made to keep the churches up to standard both in their fabric and in their worship. He defined the position of the Church of England among the religious bodies of Europe, supporting episcopacy in Scotland, effecting political alliance but not ecclesiastical intercommunion with the reformed churches of the continent, and entering into negotiation with the Greek Orthodox. This emphasis on order was combined with an effort to maintain what he believed to be the catholic standards of faith. He resented the Calvinism of the Puritans and did his best to keep to the front a teaching more consonant with the love and tenderness of God. He also—and this was to prove his own undoing and to provide endless difficulties for his Church in later days—cemented more closely than ever the union between Church and Crown. The absolutism of the Tudors, which had had a practical foundation in the good-will of the nation, became under the Stuarts an unpopular doctrine of Divine Right. It was an important element in the faith of High Churchmen. They paid dearly for it. If Cranmer died because in the end it failed him, Laud was beheaded because he clung so faithfully to it.

After the martyrdom of Laud and his King there came the period of the Commonwealth, and with it the eclipse of every kind of Anglicanism. The Prayer Book was banned; and Independency, the predominant religion of the army, strove unsuccessfully to find a substitute for it. The deprivation made Anglicans long for it the more. At the Restoration reaction against Puritanism was inevitable. It was High Churchmanship that came into its own with the monarchy. The ideals that Laud had preached were now in the ascendent. There ensued one of the greatest periods of Anglicanism. Members of the clergy like Beveridge, Bull, Cosin, Pearson, Jeremy Taylor, William Wake, and laymen like Thomas Browne, John Evelyn, Robert Nelson, Izaak Walton made the second half of the seventeenth century illustrious, earned for the Anglican clergy the title of *Stupor Mundi*, and won admiring encomiums from the Catholics of the Continent.

It was the Revolution that brought a check to this high-churchly progress. Many of the best of the high churchmen felt bound by their allegiance to James. They did not distinguish between a canonical and an absolute oath, and although their leaders had gone to prison rather than obey James's order to have the Declaration of Indulgence read in the churches, they would not offer him more than a passive resistance. Consequently eight bishops, including Sancroft, Archbishop of Canterbury, and about four hundred priests refused to take the oath of allegiance to William and Mary and were deprived. Thus began the Non-juring Schism which drained off the cream of high churchmanship from the national church.

Those who carried on the schism at least did good service in making liturgical experiments and keeping alive the sense of catholic continuity in doctrine and worship. Those who remained in communion with the establishment had little sympathy with Dutch William's Calvinism. Enough churchly sentiment remained to make possible something of a revival of high-churchmanship in the reign of Queen Anne. Indeed it received unexpected popular support. During the impeachment of its most conspicuous leader, the London mob crowded round the Queen's coach crying, 'We hope your Majesty is for High Church and Dr Sacheverell'.

This excitement, however, was no more than a flash in the pan. For the greater part of the eighteenth century the high church party ceased to be influential, and in the second half its influence almost disappeared. It had lost its close attachment to the crown. Indeed under the new régime it found its former loyalty something of an embarrassment. The Whigs and Latitudinarians now stood nearest the throne. It perforce fell back on its consciousness of the independent character of the Church, and it was still sufficiently attached to the traditional line in politics to earn for the Church the title 'the Tory party at prayer'. It looked with some disdain on the dissenting bodies and kept itself strictly aloof from them. It had been left high and dry in a new sense. But its greatest days were to come.

The Oxford Movement

The strongest reinforcement it ever received came to the High Church Party from the upheaval variously known as the Oxford Movement or the Catholic Revival. By the beginning of the nineteenth century the high church party had become chiefly centred in the men who ran the SPG and SPCK. Some of these stalwarts helped to form the 'Hackney Phalanx' (or the 'Clapton Sect'), which served to balance, though it never equalled in fame, the body of evangelical laymen known as the 'Clapham Sect'. It has been said that while the Church was preached at Clapton the Gospel was preached at Clapham, a caustic saying which has enough truth in it to make it bite. Two fruits of the High Churchmanship of the period were the National Society (founded for the promotion of elementary education in 1811) and the Additional Curates Society (founded to bring the ministrations of the clergy to the poor in 1837), both of which organizations are still doing excellent work.

The impetus that gave fresh life to the party and, as revolutions do, eventually carried it much further than the original participants would have been willing to go, was a violent reaction against the growing secularization of the state as a result of the Reform Bill of 1832 and against the state's increasing readiness to interfere in Church affairs. This institutional loyalty to the Church was linked with an inspiration derived from Scott's romantic medievalism, Wordsworth's nature mysticism, and Coleridge's mixture of philosophy, piety and poetry. Together with these influences went a renewed emphasis on Sacraments, now seen with new eyes and accepted in a more lively way. A combination of all these strains can be seen in Keble's *Christian Year* (1827) a book of poems we have already mentioned, which proved so popular as to run through ninety-five editions in its author's lifetime.

It was the same Keble who, according to Newman, launched the Oxford Movement in 1833 with his Assize sermon at St Mary's, Oxford. His subject was 'National Apostasy'. That is the phrase by which he described the State's amalgamation of a number of bishoprics in Ireland without consulting the Church. The way for the movement had been prepared by the frequent association in the Oriel College common room of the three most famous leaders, Keble, Pusey and Newman, to say nothing of lesser lights like Hurrell Froude and the later Dean Church. Nurtured in an academic circle the movement was primarily theological. It endeavoured to arouse the clergy to a full sense of what the Church was and what their own office in it implied. And then it set about helping the Church, clergy and laity together, to be the Church. Theology however was the means, not the end. The real aim of the movement was sheer holiness of life. That is probably what made it so intensely popular in the country parishes.

Originally there were no very obvious signs or trappings to distinguish individuals and churches belonging to the movement from any others. But soon, as people's minds were freed from the insularity within which they had been bound so long, they began to look back to the past and around to the Continent, for ways in which their catholicity could be better expressed. Careful investigation showed that it was only custom and not official regulation that had led to the abandonment of many of the historic adjuncts of worship. There seemed no reason in the nature of things why the Eucharist, for instance, should not be celebrated in Anglican churches with as much ceremony as in the churches on the Continent or, for the matter of that, in the Roman church next door. Indeed the Mass vestments, so far from being forbidden, were actually ordered by the Book of Common Prayer. So ran the argument, and though the original Tractarians* were as surprised at this turn as anyone, there were soon a number of churches up and down the country where all the colour and splendour of 'full catholic ceremonial' was to be found. Indeed it was soon asserted that the Anglicans, inheriting the Englishman's genius for orderly parade, were more careful about it than their Roman neighbours.

Naturally, such changes did not take place without much bitter opposition. We draw a veil over an aspect of nineteenth century history that reflects no credit on the churchmen of the period. Undoubtedly there was provocation. The clergy caught this infection much more rapidly than the laity, and often forced exasperating changes on quite unprepared congregations. But there was on the other side a measure of fanaticism, a good deal of rowdyism, and a whole weight of sheer ignorance. It was now that the expression Anglo-Catholic began to be used as a term of abuse. Originally it had been respectable enough. It was even applied by the Tractarians to their series of reprints from typical high church divines of the classic period. It was in its early use intended to denote a type of churchmanship that, while being fully catholic, was nevertheless neither Roman nor Orthodox. But now it came to be applied only to the advance-guard of the movement. The terms Puseyite, Tractarian, High Church were left behind or regarded with faint contempt. To be an Anglo-Catholic meant not only to wear vestments, to reserve the Blessed Sacrament, and to emphasize the corporate reality of the Church as the Body of Christ, but to teach openly the virtues of private confession, to sing Mass in place of Matins at the most popular hour for service on a Sunday morning, and to cultivate such extra-liturgical devotions as Benediction and Stations of the Cross.

Needless to say there presently developed an *avant-garde* who did not like the term Anglo-Catholic because it was not catholic enough for them. They dropped the first half of the phrase and wished to be known as 'Catholics' *tout court*. That might have been excellent if the Romans had not been already known in common speech by that title. With two sets of claimants to the name it is now never quite certain which of the two churches is under discussion. The situation is made the more paradoxical by the claim of a small section of Anglo-Catholics to the right 'to do everything that Rome does' without contravening their oath of canonical obedience to their own bishop. They are the Anglican

*So called from the Tracts in which the first propaganda of the Movement was conveyed.

ultramontanes who, in order to show their zeal for unity with Rome, become more papal than the Pope and leap to obey his slightest behest. Among them there are some zealous pastors, but their position is so paradoxical as to make them an 'astonishment and a hissing' on both sides of the border. Scorn, however, has never yet blunted the keen edge of fanaticism; what adds to the piquancy of the situation is that they are balanced, as we shall see presently, at the other end of the Anglican scale by an equally small but devoted body of puritan fundamentalists.

Broad Church

Today this title is hardly ever heard. But it stands for something of quite special importance in the make-up of Anglicanism. It implies an emphasis on the element of freedom in religion. There will always be people who dislike too much authoritarianism and who instinctively rebel against the feeling that they are 'cribb'd, cabined and confined' either physically, mentally or spiritually. A man must have space to breathe or he ceases to be a man at all. That there is plenty of room for such a temperament in Christianity becomes evident on a moment's reflection. To set men free was one of the purposes of the Incarnation. Christ came to give his life a ransom for many, to buy them back from slavery to sin and death. St Paul shows how the freedom with which Christ came to set us free includes release from the dominion of law. Religion is not to be legally interpreted. It offers no *quid pro quo* payments or rewards. It implies a readiness for infinite surrender and is sure of an infinite response.

Those who are of such a spirit are likely to experience some distaste for rules, definitions and authorities. They do not wish to be tied down. In the intellectual sphere they will be inclined to dispense, as far as possible, with fixed creeds and dogmatic formulas. They will not wish the expression of doctrines to be too narrowed down; they will wish to leave room for broad views. In the sphere of government they will recognize that some organization is necessary even for Christians, but they will wish to keep it as loose and ill-defined as is consistent with adequate management, and they will certainly not be willing to elevate any particular constitution into the position of a dogmatic necessity.

At the period of the Reformation it could be said that this spirit or point of view was most clearly expressed by Erasmus. Perhaps that is why he never became an effective reformer. He was too scholarly; he saw too many sides to a question; he had a foot in both camps. Today historians regard him as, of all theologians, the most typical of the Anglican spirit. This is not the temperament that leads great movements or founds great churches. It cannot see anything in terms of plain black or white; all shades of grey creep in to confuse the issue. In times of crisis, when issues must be clearly perceived, such a temperament stumbles and is lost. It is only when peace returns that the broadminded man comes into his own.

The Reformation at its height gave little opportunity for the display of this quality. Forces were arrayed too definitely against each other. It might be said of course that the Church of England was in itself an effort to display this spirit. And so indeed it was. That was implied in its very character as a national church and in its determination to keep within its fold as great a proportion as possible of the nation. It tried to unite followers of the new ways together with those who stood by the old, so long as they all alike accepted the royal supremacy. But just as both evangelicals and catholics developed parties to maintain their respective points of view, so also did the comprehensive and liberal 'broad churchmen'. In the temper of the times, however, it was not easy to stand out for any special breadth of view. The national church itself was broad enough; within it all was tolerance, without, the issues were sharply drawn and one naturally came down on one side of the fence or the other. In any case, the habit of sect-forming once begun was speedily accelerated. If one had a specially strong conviction one was more likely to form a society of one's own with a few like-minded friends to further it than to remain in the national church nursing a hope that the little leaven would ultimately leaven the whole lump. That at least became the tendency as soon as it was seen that the Puritan effort to subvert the whole polity of the Church of England would fail.

It was not until the latter half of the seventeenth century, when the religious settlement had been finally concluded at the Conference of 1661, and the Royal Society had been founded to cultivate the new ways in science, that the emergence of liberal views became so evident as to suggest the need for a specific party within the Church and to demand a name for it. Those who held that 'forms', whether of doctrine, government, or worship, were not really important were called 'men of latitude' or Latitudinarians. Whether the name ought to be attached to the attractive body of teachers known as the Cambridge Platonists may be disputed.

At any rate in their case the implied description is a fair enough estimate of their attitude to what one may regard as the externals of religion. But to be at all just to the Cambridge men one would have to add to this somewhat negative description an intense devotion, a philosophic mysticism, and a practical pastoral sense that were almost unique at the period. The group originated in that stronghold of Puritanism, Emmanuel College Cambridge, but reacted violently against both the rigourist dogma of the Puritans and the cynical ethics of Hobbes. They insisted on the importance of reason and upon the capacity of the soul for a mystical union with God.

Their leader, Benjamin Whichcote, Provost of King's, survives for us mostly in aphorisms, as he preached from very short notes. He emphasized a doctrine that was to become a favourite with William Law, namely, that what Christ did *for* us must become effective *in* us. Ralph Cudworth, Master of Christ's and Regius Professor of Hebrew, performed his best service in answering Hobbes' *Leviathan*. John Smith, Fellow of Queen's, was the great preacher of the group. Henry More, Fellow of Christ's, was the nature mystic who was widely studied in his subject and might with a little less caution have run the danger of becoming a theosophist. It has been said that he 'represents the quintessence of Cambridge Platonism. He lived so completely within it that he seemed unconscious of the disturbances without'. [5]

The chief point of their teaching was an emphasis on the spirit rather than on the letter; they would allow more liberty of worship than the typical Anglican and more liberty of doctrine than the Puritan; they held firmly to the fundamentals of the faith, while expressing some agnosticism with regard to details; they left the bible to speak for itself but regarded its authority as lying in its power to speak direct to the heart; they altered the balance in theology from a Latin transcendentalism to a Greek immanentism; they combined a love of external nature with an aspiration after an inner union with God. They thus prepared the way both for the mysticism of Thomas Browne and William Law and also for the full Latitudinarianism of the eighteenth century.

The Latitudinarians properly so called inherited the liberalism of the Cambridge Platonists without their mysticism. Intellectually no doubt they were moved by the progress of the new scientific age and temperamentally they were influenced by the progress of the Enlightenment on the continent. To these impulses was added the incentive of the royal Calvinism. With Reform on the throne there did not seem much future for traditional high-church Anglicanism. Consequently it was deemed wise to forsake the outer bastions of the faith and fall back on the main defensive positions. Even they were to be subject to some reconstruction. One ex-Presbyterian minister named Fowler, who later became bishop of Gloucester, wished to drop the Athanasian Creed. The precentor of his cathedral, Daniel Whitby, argued against the apostolic succession and later questioned the doctrine of Christ's deity. The point of attack from the more disputatious of the Latitudinarians was the doctrine of the Trinity. That challenge culminated in an extreme view known as Deism, which in its cruder form taught that God, having created the world, ceased from any further interference in its affairs. A surprising number of divines seemed to find an approximation to these views compatible with retention of their office in the Church.

Unfortunately Latitudinarianism in theology became allied with Whiggism in politics. The Hanoverians were glad to use the 'latitude men' for their own purposes, and to reward them with suitable preferment. Dr Samuel Clarke, who had doubts about the divinity of Christ, was appointed chaplain to George I; Benjamin Hoadly, who could see no particular use in any special form of church, ministry or sacraments, was made bishop successively of Bangor, Hereford, Salisbury and Winchester. The former was answered by the very voluminous Cambridge theologian Daniel Waterland, and Hoadly by the devout, brilliant, mystical Non-juror William Law. The response of the orthodox theologians to the challenge of deistic Latitudinarianism was most telling. It is, indeed, often estimated that the general decline in practical Anglicanism during the later eighteenth century was amply balanced by its magnificent defence of the chief doctrines of the Christian faith.

In the middle of the nineteenth century the title Latitudinarian went out of fashion. A new type of liberal had come into being even more intellectual but far less political than the prototype. For him was coined the name Broad Churchman. It is said to have been invented by Arthur Hugh Clough, who no doubt thought it might depict the type of mind described in his own verse:

> 'And almost everyone when age,
>   Disease, or sorrows strike him,
> Inclines to think there is a God,
>   Or something very like him.'

That at least is the kind of impression that many severely orthodox churchmen derived from the authors of *Essays and Reviews*. This book was published in 1860, the first great manifesto of the Broad Church school. It claimed 'to illustrate the advantage derivable to the cause of religious and moral truth, from a free handling, in a becoming spirit, of subjects peculiarly liable to suffer by the repetition of conventional language and from traditional methods of treatment'. Of the seven authors the most noteworthy were Frederick Temple, afterwards Archbishop of Canterbury, Mark Pattison, later Rector of Lincoln, and Benjamin Jowett, later Master of Balliol. The attempt to break through the conventional aura that surrounded the discussion of sacred subjects was epitomized in Jowett's suggestion that the bible should be read 'like any other book'. The demand created a tremendous *furore* at the time. Two of the authors were condemned by the Dean of Arches, but the Judicial Committee of the Privy Council reversed his decision. The episode marked a stage in the development of Anglican thought. It was afterwards never possible to go back to the old inhibited method of dealing with religious subjects. There were rearguard actions still to be fought, but free and unfettered discussion in the sphere of theology had come to stay.

The Privy Council had already in 1850 shown its determination to keep the doors of the Church as wide open as possible. In that year it decided in favour of G. C. Gorham, a clergyman who had nearly been denied ordination altogether on account of his doubtful views on baptismal regeneration. He later had the question raised again by the redoubtable Bishop Phillpotts of Exeter, who after examining him at great length refused to institute him to the new living to which he had been duly presented. The Judicial Committee did not presume to decide the doctrinal issue, but gave the case in Gorham's favour on the ground that his (minimizing) view of the effect of baptism did not actually contradict the formularies of the Church.

The Committee took an equally decided line against narrowing the limits of churchmanship by its judgment in the Colenso case of 1865. Colenso was the Bishop of Natal who had adopted what appeared to be an extreme form of the new critical method of studying the Bible. He gave free utterance to his conclusions and he was brought to book by his metropolitan, Archbishop Gray of Cape Town. On his refusal to retract he was deposed and excommunicated by the South African bishops with the Archbishop at their head. On appeal to the Judicial Committee of the Privy Council the Committee declared that 'the Crown had no power to constitute a bishopric in a colony which has its own independent legislature'. This, of course, made void any authority that the Crown had given the Archbishop of Cape Town over the Bishop of Natal. The Bishop was thus left in possession of the temporalities of his see. What had not been foreseen was that the judgment also had the effect of making the Church of the Province of South Africa a voluntary body independent of the English courts. In that case the Church in South Africa could exercise its spiritual authority and the excommunication of Colenso still stood. That, in fact, is how the matter rested. Some of Colenso's followers rallied round him and continued to use the emoluments now secured to them for the purpose of church work regardless of the inhibitions of the properly constituted authorities of the diocese. The result was a small and insignificant schism which, unfortunately, has not even yet been healed.* Two points were made clear by the controversy: the independence of the Anglican Communion overseas and the difficulty of extruding any minister on account of broad views.

A more representative Broad Churchman was Thomas Arnold (1785–1842), a Fellow of Oriel, who reacted violently against the Tractarianism of some of his colleagues and became famous as the headmaster of Rugby who revolutionized English public school education. He had a passionate devotion to the person of Christ but a thorough hatred of the catholic doctrine of the ministry and sacraments. He would have liked to see the boundaries of the national church expanded to include all denominations except the Jews. Clough, Dean Stanley and Thomas Hughes (author of *Tom Brown's Schooldays*) were all his devoted pupils.

An off-shoot from this type of thought is represented by Charles Kingsley (1819–75) and Frederick Denison Maurice (1805–72). Both disliked the Tractarians. Indeed Kingsley had a world-shaking controversy with Newman, which drove the latter into writing his *Apologia* and so produced one of literature's finest autobiographies. Both Maurice and Kingsley had a liberal outlook on life and learning; and both exerted great efforts to make social welfare recognized as an immediate concern of the Church, an effort that was to produce lasting results. Kingsley applied this teaching to bodily as well as social hygiene and became the chief exponent of 'Muscular Christianity'. He was also famous for his novels, writing them as a vehicle of his social teaching and displaying in almost equal proportions his love of nature, his distrust of Rome, and his passion for adventure and romance.

Maurice was the greater thinker. Kingsley always looked up to him as 'the beloved master'. He supplied the intellectual basis for the positions Kingsley held and popularized. He had come over to the Church from a unitarian background and embraced its ordered life and constitution with an eagerness quite incomprehensible to Arnold. His *Kingdom of Christ* is a monumental work supplying an essentially Catholic philosophical theology for the benefit of a Quaker who wishes

*A vigorous and objective account of these controversies can be found in A. O. J. Cockshut, *Anglican Attitudes*.

to understand *au fond* the ethos of institutional Christianity. In Maurice, Broad Churchmanship begins to merge into Liberal Catholicism and approximates to the new section of High Churchmen who were not afraid of the fresh fashions of biblical study. Owing to their allegiance to the creeds and sacraments these last were able to absorb the critical and historical method without losing their orthodoxy. The main stream of Broad Churchmen also cultivated the new methods of study, but sitting loose to the institutional safeguards so highly regarded by their catholic-minded colleagues, they ran the danger of falling into Modernism. But that is another story, which we must discuss in a later chapter.

The Evangelicals

Perhaps the proper antithesis to High Church and Broad Church should be Low Church. We prefer the term Evangelical because in these days it is regarded as more positive and respectable. It does also represent a well-known type of Christianity recognized throughout the world as contrasted with the type known as Catholic. As the title of an Anglican party it is a comparatively modern term. The original expression was Low Church, which was used by the end of the seventeenth century to denote those who repudiated the sacramental and sacerdotal ideas of the High Church. Such teachers eliminated ceremony and mystery as far as possible from worship and held an Erastian view of church government. They thus had obvious affinities with the Latitudinarians. The name Low Church was in fact regularly used for the Latitudinarians before the term Broad Church became popular. It then seems to have fallen into abeyance until party feeling began to run high in the middle of the nineteenth century when it was taken out, refurbished and applied to the Evangelicals, whose position and background we must now discuss. But it must be remembered that Low Church had a sinister connotation which did not apply to the designation Evangelical. As some churchmen were said to be 'high and dry' and others 'broad and hazy' so still others were said to be 'low and lazy'. The typical low churchman was said to settle down to the enjoyment of his emoluments without exerting himself unduly to earn them. The implication was that spiritual earnestness had drained out of both 'high' and 'low'. The substitution of 'catholic' and 'evangelical' implied that the breath of life had entered into them. Whatever their critics thought of them, both parties were now alive; and that is why they preferred to be known by names that had a positive content.

The justice of this point of view can be seen at once when we begin to trace the history of the Evangelicals. It is a mistake to begin their story in the eighteenth century with the Wesleyan revival, as if this particular apprehension of Christian truth was now seen for the first time in the Church of England. Actually there always has been an Evangelical or Low Church party in Anglicanism. Just as the High Church party can be said to have its origin in people like Elizabeth I, Parker and Laud, so can evangelicalism be said to have begun with Cranmer, Edward VI, and also with the puritan* exponents of continental protestantism, who found their way into the Church of England and nearly succeeded in disrupting it. The defeat of the puritans' attempt to refashion the Church after their own heart in the Elizabethan Settlement and again in 1604 and 1662 did, of course, mean the end of complete comprehension. It meant that those who despaired of finding satisfaction for their spiritual needs within the national church left it to form fresh societies for themselves.

There were, however, a not inconsiderable number of those who held roughly the same puritan outlook, but felt they could still remain, without hurt of conscience, in the established church. If, as they claimed, forms of ecclesiastical government were not important, then why not accept as harmless those already established? They could still maintain within that framework the general puritan ethos and manner of life. There would be no great difficulty in the doctrinal field. The articles were already written largely from their point of view, and the doctrine of the sacraments was fluid enough to allow them considerable freedom of thought and expression. Besides, the extreme dissentients did not agree precisely among themselves. There was no guarantee that even when they were freed from the shackles of the establishment they would stick together. A prophetic eye might easily have foreseen the fissiparous character of dissent and anticipated Swift's withering scorn of the ultimate narrowness:

> 'We are God's chosen few
> All others will be damned.
> There is no place in Heaven for you
> We can't have Heaven cramm'd.'

On the more positive side there was still the lingering feeling that ideally a nation should have only one religion. The puritans who remained within the Church, even after the Restoration, may well have

*The term puritan seems to have come into the English language from the Latin *purus*, *puritas* via the French *puritan*. It is first found about 1572 (the year of the St Bartholomew massacre in France). It was applied to those members of the English Church who did not think its reformation had gone far enough, but wished to see it still further purified from Romish and non-biblical elements.

been moved to maintain the unity of the Church on national even if not on purely ecclesiastical grounds.

Whatever the reason, many of them did remain, and they formed the continuing nucleus of what today we call the Evangelical Party. That their position was far from being intolerable can be seen from the fact that even a number of those churchmen who did think the form of government important, nevertheless held a position identical with theirs in matters of doctrine. Whitgift was an early example of this school. He was a strong disciplinarian and a determined opponent of all who wished to subvert the polity of the Church. Both as Bishop of Worcester and as Archbishop of Canterbury he served Elizabeth's establishment policy with consummate ability. Yet he was a Calvinist at heart, and was even responsible for the committee that in 1595 drew up a set of Nine Articles whose pronounced Calvinism makes the Thirty-Nine Articles seem very mild in comparison. Of course, the Queen would have none of them and they were never imposed upon or adopted by the Church. Another Bishop of Worcester who showed much the same combination of catholic order and puritan faith was George Morley (1660–2). He was one of the bishops who took a firm stand at the Savoy Conference, and after it even refused the saintly puritan Richard Baxter permission to resume his pastoral duties at Kidderminster. It must have gone sorely against the grain, for his doctrinal opinions were not far removed from those of Baxter.

Through all the kaleidoscopic changes of the following centuries it is possible to trace the continued importance of this point of view. The general dislike of Rome and the consequent avoidance of 'form and ceremony' brought the prevailing tone and temper of Church life very near to the puritan level. Even the high churchman was not as easily distinguishable from the general crowd as he became in the nineteenth century. This merely means that the rival tendencies had not yet hardened into organized parties. If a party is to be defined as 'a section of a larger society, united to carry out the objects of the whole body on principles and by methods peculiar to itself',[6] then the only thing that was lacking to turn these schools of thought into parties was the unity and discipline implied in specific organization. As an intermediate stage, the unifying force was supplied by politics. During the eighteenth century the high churchmen were identified with the Tories and the low churchmen with the Whigs. These political affiliations did no good to the spiritual work of either group. The high churchmen had to be stabbed broad awake by the suffering of the Non-juring schism. The low churchmen were inspired with new zeal by the Evangelical Revival.

This movement, inaugurated by the preaching of John Wesley (1703–91) and nourished by his brother Charles' hymns, actually began, as the name Methodist implies, as a high church movement with all the high churchman's love of method in religious faith and practice. It changed its character when it left the sheltered quadrangles of Oxford for the savannahs of Georgia and the valleys of Wales, and when John Wesley exchanged the influence of William Law for that of the Moravian elders. Wesley under the latter influence had an experience of conversion which he believed to be as definite and clear-cut as that of St Paul. He used all his great gifts as an orator to reproduce the experience in the lives of his auditors. They belonged to the new proletariat springing up in England as the result of the industrial revolution. Children were usable in the mines and mills. The population increased with extraordinary rapidity and its growth caught the Church unawares. There were inadequate means for the pastoral care of the new working class and too few buildings in which their spiritual needs could be met. It must be admitted too that the Church was too slow in awaking to the situation. Wesley, who had the temerity to take the world for his parish and was consequently refused entry into the parish churches, gathered the thousands of his listeners in the open air and found the new freedom conducive to the type of conversion he wished to encourage.

Wesley was not only a great preacher; he also had a genius for organization. Originally his societies worked within the framework of the national church. Eventually they broke away, first, because the establishment was not quick enough to find a place in its organization for the new army of lay preachers introduced by Wesley to supplement the efforts of the few ordained clergymen who shared his views and his work; and second because in his impatience at the delay on the part of the English authorities in providing a sufficient ministry for his people, he began ordaining presbyters on his own behalf. The fact that he also presumed to consecrate Thomas Coke as 'superintendent' for America was responsible for the beginning of the immensely strong Methodist Episcopal Church in that country. But it made an inevitable breach with the Church of England.

> 'Wesley his hands on Coke hath laid
> But who laid hands on him?'

Not all those affected by the preaching of Wesley left the Church. A considerable number remained but they did not form the bulk of the evangelical party or even dictate its characteristic theology. That honour falls to the followers of George Whitefield, a friend of Wesley's, who as a young graduate had actually taken over the leadership of the Oxford Methodists, when the Wesleys sailed for Georgia. He it was who actually started the open-air preaching and introduced Wesley to it. He seems to have been even more successful in moving multitudes than Wesley himself. Later a theological difference sprang up between the two men. Whitefield belongs to the puritan strain in Anglicanism and accepted the Calvinistic teaching of predestination and determinism. Wesley, on the contrary, was originally a high churchman, an Arminian and a strong 'freewiller'. In this respect Wesley was a good deal nearer the main stream of Anglican thought than Whitefield. But as Wesley's followers left the fold, it was the following of Whitefield that moulded the future evangelicalism of the Anglican Church.

It was inevitable that many of the low churchmen should be influenced by this display of evangelical zeal and its success in the conversion of many thousand souls. They reproduced its methods, as far as they could, within the stiff organization of the Church, but they were not willing for the most part to accept the evangelists' disregard of parochial boundaries. It was felt, reasonably enough, that while itinerancy might be good for evangelism, it was certainly bad for pastoral care.

It has been said that, whereas the two great evangelists took the world for their parish, the leading clergy of the evangelical party took the parish for their world. They combined the preaching of conversion with devoted pastoral care. They dwelt lovingly on the doctrine of the Atonement and instilled the Pauline doctrine of unmerited grace: 'Nothing in my hand I bring, simply to thy cross I cling.' They taught their people to read the Bible and to sing hymns. Their churches were large, cold and bare. This did not matter for the sectarians, whose building was, in point of fact, a small, tightly packed Chapel, but it told heavily against the old Gothic parochial buildings already denuded of their medieval glory. It was no easy task to warm up the atmosphere of a great barren church with the fire of heart-felt worship. The marvel is that, with so few of the normal advantages, it was so frequently done.

Such enthusiasm disturbed the lazy and the apathetic. It aroused opposition, which in some instances turned to persecution. Most of the bishops were against it, and it was by no means easy for members of the clergy who had shown themselves to be evangelically minded to obtain preferment. To meet this difficulty, just as their puritan ancestors had set up specially paid lectureships in the parish churches, so now the evangelicals began to buy up the advowsons of livings so that they might themselves have the right of presenting the incumbents. This, of course, led to reprisals on the part of the high-churchmen and became a notorious abuse, which had to be stopped by official action.* Before the end, however, the Simeon Trustees, the most famous of the evangelical trusts, had become the patrons of more than 150 benefices.

The Simeon Trustees were founded through the energy of Charles Simeon (1759–1836), one of the best known leaders of the evangelical party, who gave his life to a long ministry in the town and university of Cambridge. He was appointed to the incumbency of Trinity Church while still a deacon, fought down the determined opposition of the parishioners, and long before his death had become the acknowledged religious leader both of town and gown. He was concerned in most of the organizations that owed their origin to the evangelicals. The greatest of them was, and still is, the Church Missionary Society, founded in 1799 for 'missions to Africa and the East'. Later the CMS widened the scope of its missions until it absorbed most of the evangelical zeal. In fact, it did more than anything else to keep the party together.

But foreign missions were not the only activity expressing the genius of the evangelicals. To them, under the leadership of Lord Shaftesbury, was chiefly owed the suppression of the slave traffic. One of the more notorious slave dealers, John Newton, was converted and ordained, becoming a recognized leader of the Party as Rector of the city church of St Mary Woolnoth. Lord Shaftesbury is also given credit for the Factory Acts, which did something to mitigate the lot of the children and adults who were caught up in the remorseless machine created by the Industrial Revolution. Recent researches, however, have shown that the honour for this achievement cannot be assigned to one individual or one party. Some credit must go to central churchmen like George Bull, the 'ten hours' parson, who did not find evangelicals uniformly sympathetic when he was carrying on his campaign for the shortening of hours in pit and factory.

The political strength of the party lay in the fact that in the 'Clapham Sect', a body of wealthy and distinguished laymen, living as close neighbours around Clapham Common, they had a powerful spearhead of the movement ready to make a thrust in any required direction. They were especially interested in the education of the poor. In days when there was no governmental system of education they did valuable work in preparing the ground for the National Society and its great system of church schools all over the country. This they did through people like Robert Raikes and Hannah More, who established

*Benefices Act 1598 (Amendment). Measure of Church Assembly 1923.

the first Sunday Schools. In them the poor acquired the whole of their academic learning; elementary instruction was given in secular as well as religious subjects.

The manner of life inculcated by the evangelicals was austere. The theatre, dancing and cards were frowned upon. Sunday was chiefly noteworthy for the absence of both work and amusement. Even those who did not think it necessary to attend public worship would be expected to confine themselves to 'Sunday books' in private. The only relaxation allowed to the natural man was in the pleasures of the table. By setting such a standard the evangelicals made a marked impact upon the social life of their day. From the accession of Queen Victoria they began to enjoy the sympathy of the throne and they became more responsible than anyone for what we now consider the unnecessary pruderies and repressions of the Victorian age. Nowadays we are too inclined to view them through the peep-hole of 'The Barretts of Wimpole Street', but in spite of their oddities and lack of sophistication, they did impress a great ideal upon the country, and the impression has not yet entirely disappeared. With their emphasis on conversion they were individualists, having very little use for the Church as more than a conventional society. Consequently, the future was not with them. With the new upsurge of romanticism, catholicism, and collectivism in the nineteenth century they fell out of the lead, not without much bitter struggle and many rearguard actions against the Tractarians. By the twentieth century they had become an accepted part of the general pattern, one element in the Anglican tapestry, seeking, as we shall see, new forms of self-expression, but nevertheless standing out less conspicuously from the whole, and including in their ranks only a fraction of the clergy. But their missionary work is still *facile princeps*; it is a standing miracle that out of such resources they are able to do so much.

If our account of the parties has seemed to confine itself almost entirely to the English scene, our defence must be that we have been concerned to disclose their origins, and that they did actually spring up on English soil. But it would be a mistake of the utmost magnitude to conclude that they are confined to English soil. Wherever Anglicanism is planted, there the same differences begin to appear. Sometimes our overseas members have been heard to complain that we have carried our differences into their lands, and there is, of course, some truth in the complaint. But there is more to be said. So long as Anglicanism retains its historic character, so long will tensions arise within it. To hold the whole truth in perfect equipoise is granted to few individuals and not many groups. The alternatives are either to split up when the imbalance becomes too obvious, or to hold together in the belief or the hope that equilibrium will be sufficiently restored. The latter is the Anglican way.

The prevailing theological colour of national and provincial churches is often decided by historic or geographic circumstances. Thus the Scottish Church, largely because of its Jacobite and Non-juring sympathies, displays a 'catholic' colour. The Church of Ireland on the contrary, pressed between the millstones of Presbyterianism in the north and Roman Catholicism in the south, has evolved a unique combination of high church teaching with low church ceremonial. The United States, as befits a country that has drawn its population from all parts of the world, offers an almost infinite variety. The very name Protestant Episcopal reveals the combination of the two main strands. Its Prayer Book pays the debt of gratitude owed to the Episcopal Church of Scotland, which first gave it a bishop; its general organization is of the democratic type generally associated with protestantism; its teaching and practice reveal the strong individualism which is a marked feature of the American character. Canada, on the whole, retains the low churchmanship of the early missionaries but is fast developing an ethos of independent churchmanship in distinction from the United Church, which it has been strongly urged to join. But in all these cases there is no strictly 'monochrome' national church. In all of them varieties, sometimes of an extreme kind, exist.

Much the same thing must be said of Australia and New Zealand. The latter still retains some of the low churchmanship of the Victorian era in which the chief effort of colonization took place; but this has been subject to a good deal of development and the general churchmanship today approximates as closely to the type known as 'central' as is to be found in the whole Anglican communion. In Australia ecclesiastical colour varies from state to state and from diocese to diocese. While West Australia and Queensland are predominantly 'high', New South Wales contains one diocese, Sydney, where the churchmanship is more rigidly 'low' than anywhere else in the world. Africa and India in their various parts reflect the respective ecclesiastical colour of the missionary societies that first evangelized them. South Africa affords an almost solitary instance in which the generally 'high' tone of the province has led to a small low-church schism (in the unfortunate affair of Bishop Colenso).

Other dioceses in the vast continent of Africa tend individually to present a more than usually monochrome appearance. As they differ sharply from one another there have been some inter-diocesan clashes in the past. A notable instance occurred when Bishop Weston of Zanzibar charged his neighbours of Mombasa and Uganda 'with the grievous faults of propagating heresy and committing schism', because they had joined in a united communion service with non-conformists in the Presbyterian Church at Kikuyu. But those difficulties have been smoothed over and it has even been found possible for the 'lowest' and 'highest' dioceses to join together in the formation of a new province.

In India, the similar collocation of missions with differing theological complexions has not prevented the most interesting experiments in church unity of our time. The most famous of these ventures led four dioceses of South India with the consent of Lambeth to leave the Anglican Communion in order to form a new organization with several other denominations. The severance was deemed to be necessary because not all the ministers of the new Church of South India had received episcopal ordination. But this disability is in process of remedying itself and it is hoped that, after an interim period of thirty years, there will be no obstacle to the declaration of complete intercommunion between the Church of South India and all the Anglican Churches throughout the world.

Other schemes in North India and Ceylon have been framed on the basis of the experience thus gained. It is expected that they will achieve the same end without incurring the same disabilities.

It is obvious that if Anglicanism suffers some disadvantages through its inclusion of many different points of view and its comprehension of widely differing parties, it nevertheless enjoys great advantages and incurs great responsibilities. The opportunity of combining with people of so many types must make for a largeness of mind that is the opposite of sectarianism. Great controversies, of course, leave a certain innate tension behind them, and it is never quite possible to get back beyond them as if they had never been. But to many such largeness of mind will appear at least a close approximation to the temper of the New Testament.

This attitude has to be acquired by every faithful Anglican, not merely because theoretically it is fundamental to his church's creed, but also practically because he is bound to find himself rubbing shoulders with fellow Anglicans of strangely contrasting views. There is hardly such a thing as a completely 'monochrome' diocese in the whole Communion. And that, as we have seen, is true even where there is no establishment to hold a national church together. The differences are nearly as clearly marked in the United States as they are in England. It is true that the American clergy remain much more faithful to their

Prayer Book than the English, but that is probably because revision is easier and the clergy have a stronger voice in making it. The same comment would hold true of other provinces and national churches. But it does not obscure the fact that the differences are there, and that they are native to Anglicanism.

This singularity lays upon the Anglican Communion a great responsibility in respect of the growing movement for the reunion of the *disjecta membra* of the Body of Christ. Here is a communion that straddles the greatest of the fences dividing the two main sections of Christianity from each other. It has a foot in each of the opposing camps, Catholic and Evangelical. It can hold out hands to both sides. Inasmuch as it combines both elements in its own communion, it need have no shame or bashfulness in helping others to do likewise. Even if they had accomplished no more than this, the parties would have done a good work.

CHAPTER SIX
MODERN LIBERALISM

*The 'Summer' period—Development of theological thought in first decade of twentieth century—
Lack of religious consciousness—Textual and literary criticism of Bible—Modernism: Theory
of evolution and doctrine of progressive revelation—Study of comparative religion—Liberalism—
Kenotic Theory—Mysticism*

IT WILL not be possible satisfactorily to understand the idea of
Anglicanism unless we know something of what Anglicans are thinking
today. Thought in these days changes very rapidly but perhaps we
could allow ourselves leisure to look back over the first half of the present
century. That should help us to trace the formation of current trends
and to estimate their place in the whole set of Anglican life. We have
already seen the effect before that of the successive High Church,
Broad Church and Evangelical movements.

The Summer Period
When the twentieth century opened, the Anglican Communion was a
sort of amalgam of all three. Behind was the background of the Victorian age with its combined ignorance and competence, its insularity
and its world-wide power. It had produced the greatest period of
missionary expansion the Church had yet known. At the same time even
its bishops had a merely adolescent knowledge of liturgical and canonical matters.

Its two great venerations were for the Reformation and the Bible.
The former was beginning to suffer a little under the well-remembered
attacks of Tractarians like Hurrell Froude, but the Catholic Emancipation of 1829 and the subsequent restoration of the Roman hierarchy in
England had given rise to fresh fears. Consequently, church life was
becoming more concentrated if less widely diffused. Daily services were
now the rule rather than the exception. They were attended, of course,
merely by a small élite of leisured people but they at least formed a
nucleus for the great congregations that gathered on Sundays. There
was a growing interest in the sacraments although in the eyes of many
sacramental practice still left much to be desired. The effective faith of
the country was in its assured future. Most people believed in the
inevitability of progress and felt that, whatever may have been the
temporary set-back due to such episodes as the Boer War, all would
come right in the end. It was still the period of Sunday clothes and of the
church parade, of conventionality and respectability. The observance of

religion was the recognized way to ensure one's place in the established order of social life, and so to place oneself in the main stream of progress.

The first decade of the twentieth century has been described by Ensor[1] as a period of sunrise succeeding to sunset, and others have spoken of it as the 'summer period'. The upward tendency of Anglicanism was best illustrated in the great Pan-Anglican Congress of 1908. And no one can properly understand the emotions that congress roused in the breasts of the English Churchman without reading Scott Holland's essay on it in his *Bundle of Memories*,[2] perhaps the finest piece of ecclesiastical journalism ever penned. For many an Englishman it meant the first full realization that he was not a member of a small, isolated national church but of a world-wide communion that extended even beyond the confines of his 'far-flung empire'. The consciousness of what some of the attendant overseas bishops had done and suffered for the cause of the common religion cast a halo of romance and adventure over the whole conception of the world-wide Church and consequently over the humblest congregation and parish priest. It brought to the rank and file a vision of Anglicanism that had hitherto been shared only among the scholars and administrators.

Nevertheless, when the tumult and the shouting died it was evident to the discerning that all was not well. Far too large a proportion of the population was not effectively touched. It is true that the vast majority of them were baptized and married in church, but Moorman[3] calculates that no more than 20 per cent attended church regularly. Even those who filled the churches had for the most part only a diffused idea of religion. They took little account of the authority of the Church. A man's religion was his own concern, and one church was about as good as another. The sacraments were not much more than picturesque symbols. Religion in short was very thinly spread and theology was almost entirely lacking.

So at least it seemed to the leaders of a more churchly turn of mind, those who had imbibed and carried a stage further the teaching of the Tractarians. The feeling led them to chide their congregations for their respectability and smug conventionality. If only they would come to church for the right motives! So Bishop Gore exclaimed in a characteristic utterance: 'What this country needs is not more Christians but better Christians, not more church people but better church people.' It is hardly surprising that many took him at his word, and when the First World War broke up the social habits of a lifetime they stayed away from church and never recovered the habit of church attendance.

It is evidence of the perennial difficulty of an established church: how to concentrate on aiming at perfection and at the same time to bring all and sundry within sound of the gospel. In this first decade of the century, when, in order to get their favourite seats at the Sunday services, the faithful had to arrive early and wait in crowded porches, the proportionate number of regular communicants was not large. They were without much conception of 'corporate holiness' and they were afraid of excess in any direction. Choral matins was still the height of worship for the professional and wealthy classes, choral evensong for the lower middle class and domestics. A fair number from both classes who had sufficient leisure would attend both services.

Rise of Criticism

It is interesting that this development should have taken place and that Anglicanism should have entered upon its summer period just at the time when the critical method of biblical study was claiming its early successes in the world of scholarship. It was, of course, not much known as yet, but was nevertheless greatly feared, among the ranks of the regular church-goer.

The results of the lower or textual criticism were already universally accepted. After all, the efforts of the linguistic scholars were simply to provide the best and most accurate text; and everyone recognized that such a text must be the necessary foundation for all subsequent work. In its efforts to assist in the establishment of such a text English scholar-ship had earned tremendous prestige as the result of the brilliant work of the famous Cambridge trio—Westcott, Lightfoot and Hort. However illogical such a distinction may seem, the ready acceptance accorded to the lower or textual criticism was certainly not paralleled by any complacent acceptance of the higher or literary criticism, that is, the criticism that dealt with the date and composition of the individual books of the Bible. For one thing that particular branch of scholarship was not deemed to be English but German; its main theory bore the name Graf-Wellhausen; and the English scholars such as Pusey who had made early acquaintance with it had turned against it. Further it seemed to apply to the development of religion, even the revealed religion of Israel, the theory of evolution which, whatever progress it had made among scientists, was still regarded as essentially anti-religious by the rank and file. As a consequence, adoption of the new method would mean a reversal of many traditionally received ideas —the date of creation, the order of law and prophets, many of the miracles, and in general the idea of the infallibility of scripture.

Perhaps it was its last great effort to meet the challenge of such ideas that helped to give Anglicanism its unity and strength during this decade. Or perhaps it would be more true to say that there was a double effort, to assimilate what was valuable in the new teaching and at the same time to make very sure that it did no harm to true religion. Enlightened circles were beginning to feel that the solution of the difficulty lay in the doctrine of progressive revelation. The inevitable progress that Victorians read in the signs of the times and the evolution that they learnt from the scientists were both united under this doctrine in God's ordering of religious development. If one could only disentangle the strands of the Old Testament one would find that they revealed a gradual religious education of Israel, parallel to the evolution of ideas which Herbert Spenser maintained was revealed in the general history of the human race.

However that may be, anyone going up to Oxford in the year 1904, as the present author did, must have realized that he was stepping into a new world. Outside, everyone he knew at all intimately, even his teachers, were still sticking to the old ideas, but here the new thought and the new methods already reigned supreme. Driver and Sanday were the two great teachers in biblical subjects. It was the year of the publication of Hastings' *Dictionary of the Bible*. Its sober volumes marked an epoch in the history of biblical criticism and had already superseded the more adventurous and fanciful *Encyclopedia Biblica* of the year before.

Behind this lay a careful consideration of the contribution made to the new ideas by the comparative study of religions. Robertson Smith's *Religion of the Semites* had appeared in 1890 and had done him no good with his own Presbyterian denomination in Scotland, but in the English universities it was regarded almost as a sort of bible in itself. Frazer's *Golden Bough* had opened up the ground, in spite of its too facile collocation of rites and customs bearing a superficial resemblance. His application of his comparative methods to the religion of the Hebrews was not to appear till 1919, when he published his *Folk-lore in the Old Testament*. These wider studies brought a little life to the somewhat dry-as-dust methods of Hastings' *Dictionary*. Nevertheless it must be confessed that the method pursued in the theological school at that time was almost entirely critical and historical. It was only the excitement of engaging in a new and adventurous course of study that kept interest alive. It was not easy at first blush to see its connection with religion.

This is not, of course, to say that elsewhere the practical effect of these studies was not being eagerly canvassed. In Germany Harnack from the depths of his immense learning had produced a small popular book in 1901, *What is Christianity?* which endeavoured to sum up the new research as it affected, not the Old Testament only, but the essential elements of Christianity. Under his interpretation the effect was to reduce Christian faith to belief in the fatherhood of God and the brotherhood of man, while Jesus himself appeared in the guise of a Liberal Protestant reformer. This was the kind of thing that might appeal to a good many British politicians but it drew a sharp *riposte* in the following year from the French savant Loisy in *L'Evangile et L'Eglise*. He pointed out that this was not Christianity as the world had known it for nearly two thousand years and denied that the new studies made it necessary to dispense with the Incarnation, the sacraments and the Church.

Oxford, being still the most definitely Anglican centre of the country, was assisted to maintain its orthodoxy by its attachment to the Church and by that Church's emphasis on the creeds and sacraments. The lead given by its theological faculty was to accept the new learning but to be cautious about drawing doctrinal conclusions from it. If its scholars were not, like the Germans, in the vanguard of progress, framing new theories and starting new movements, there was a magisterial quality about their work which helped to provide a rallying point for many who might otherwise have been lost in the uncharted seas of speculation. Most of them had been pastors before they became teachers, lecturers or professors. If their writings were definitely academic, their priestly functions were not far from their mind, even when they had pen in hand. By contrast one young historian, Thompson of Magdalen, was unable to maintain this judicial poise. In his *Miracles*, published in 1911, he seemed to couple the gospel miracles with those of the middle ages as equally unworthy of credit. His work brought him under the discipline of his bishop but it produced no echo among the theologians, although the veteran Sanday leapt to his defence. The younger members of the faculty combined in writing a symposium that was intended to sum up the position in theology as far as the current advance in critical studies had carried it. Their book, published in 1912, was called *Foundations*. Ronald Knox, who had succeeded G. K. Chesterton as an ecclesiastical satirist in defence of traditional positions, found in it *Some Loose Stones*, but on the whole it served well its purpose of combining credal Christianity with biblical criticism.

Modernism
Nevertheless, it is undeniable that there was a good deal of unrest

123

engendered by the new methods of study. People who had been accustomed to base their faith on an infallible book were finding it hard to adjust themselves. Either they must take the trouble to find out what the new teaching was all about, or they must remain theologically in the old ways while progressing forwards in every other department of thought. The second alternative would produce a serious dichotomy in their minds. A third possibility was to give up bothering altogether. The last is the course that too many people seemed likely to adopt. There arose a consequent anxiety on the part of many theologians to adapt their teaching to the needs of 'the modern man'. Indeed his name was continually on their lips and it seemed as if everything was to revolve round the modern man. That he had as much right to feel secure in his faith as anyone else went without question. What was questionable was whether anyone has ever a right to absolute security, and whether modern man would feel any more secure if the claims of history and theology were reduced to the fewest and simplest. Anyhow the attempt was made, and the guise under which it was made was known as Modernism.

There were, in fact, two types of modernism and they nearly cancelled each other out. The first was a Roman Catholic teaching resting on an essentially philosophical foundation. It had little influence in England or America but spread mostly in France and Italy. Two of its best known leaders were Loisy, the Frenchman, and Tyrrell, the Irishman. It relied effectively on the teaching of Ritschl that no fact is without value and it assumed that the value is more important than the fact. In the long run, if you produced the values, the facts did not really matter. Applied to the gospel and its transmission, this meant that the new science of biblical criticism could be accepted, even in its most extreme phases, without doing any damage to the Christian faith. It did not matter if the whole historical foundation of Christianity were corroded away; the structure of Church, creed and sacraments would still stand. Its foundation was not history but faith. Those who believed and practised the religion of the Church would find themselves in the ark of salvation: they would inevitably reach their destination and they need not worry about the truth of events that allegedly happened long ago. Now this might have been a comforting evangel for an academic philosopher who had no time for history or for a practical man of business who had no time for academic pursuits and was glad to commit his eternal welfare to the system of the Church. But it was a complete reversal of the age-old boast that Christianity, unlike other faiths, is a historical religion. In the event it received, as we shall see, short shrift from the Roman Catholic hierarchy.

The other modernism, which gained much more currency in Anglican circles, was of an almost contradictory character. It placed its whole weight on history. It used much the same critical method as did the Catholic modernism but it believed profoundly that by the methods of scientific criticism it would be possible to peel away all accretions until the final substance of irrefutable historical fact was left. The adherents to this theory did not realize, of course, that such historical fact when found could only relate to space and time and could, therefore, prove nothing about the spiritual or eternal sphere. They were sure that the facts were there to be reached and that when found they would contain the real gospel. The result, however, of their careful investigation of the facts was that there remained so little of the ancient creed with unquestionable historical support that Christianity became almost unrecognizable. The Virgin Birth, the Resurrection, the Ascension, the Descent of the Spirit, the apostolic ministry, the 'effectiveness' of sacraments, all disappeared under this kind of solvent and it was questionable whether the residuum was recognizable as Christianity at all.

A somewhat modified form of this teaching was embodied in the *New Theology* of an Anglican turned congregationalist minister, R. J. Campbell, which was published in 1907 and seemed likely to start a new movement. It laid tremendous stress on the human side of Jesus's story. It claimed that his humanity was perfect and that no one could really tell what were the limits to the capacities of perfect human nature. It was thus strongly immanentist and strove to ignore the essential difference between human and divine. It sought to make the miracles more credible by ascribing them to the perfect human element in the person of the Christ. These ideas were attractively presented in the style of the popular lecturer, but their shallowness did not appeal to theologians. Although they found a response for a time among the general public they met a stout opponent in Bishop Gore. Under his guidance the author himself came to see their hollowness, retracted them, and became a Canon and Chancellor of Chichester Cathedral.

The way in which the Christian world met the threat of Modernism to what was believed to be its essential faith was both interesting and varied. The Roman Church took the line of most complete resistance and set about exterminating the heretical views by the speediest possible methods. In 1907 Pope Pius X issued the decree *Lamentabili*, followed by the encyclical *Pascendi gregis*, which analysed the Roman type of Modernism and banned it in every part. As there remained some suspicion that this drastic action had succeeded in driving the discredited teaching underground, leaving a good many crypto-modernists among the working clergy, these measures were followed three years later by the imposition of an anti-modernist oath. This meant that a few of the leaders such as Loisy and Tyrrell were excommunicated. Others like Duchesne were silenced, while some distinguished laymen like Baron von Hügel were left untouched but with the consciousness that a sword of Damocles was suspended over their heads. On the whole the measures seem to have been successful, although inevitably they have involved from time to time the secession of some learned scholar who has found the intellectual discipline of his church too strait for him.

The Anglicans dealt with their particular type of Modernism in a very different way. To begin with, a society, the Modern Churchman's Union, was formed to further its ends. Its magazine, *The Modern Churchman*, was ably edited by Dr Major, an expatriate Australian who had all his countrymen's courage and directness of speech. It was in vain that the members differed from one another and contended that they were arguing not for any set of conclusions but only for a certain method of approach. Dr Major had no such hesitations and made clear to what a small compass in his view Christian dogma should be reduced. The result was that at the annual conference of the union held at Girton in 1921 and in Dr Major's preface to the number of *The Modern Churchman* reporting the conference, the aims of the more extreme section of the members were laid bare. Public opinion was revolted by the revelation. The movement lost what popularity it had and dwindled, like the Liberal Party in politics, to a position of comparative insignificance.

There was another reason why there seemed no point in maintaining any longer a modernist party. The scientific method of historical and literary criticism, which had been the main plank in its platform, had been by this time very generally appropriated. The clergy from the universities had all been trained in that method and by the use of it they were now prepared to defend the traditional creed. Hewlett Johnson, then Dean of Manchester, later to become known as the communist Dean of Canterbury, did yeoman service in editing a magazine called *The Interpreter*, which popularized the methods and results of critical study, and so immunized the public against the fever of modernism. Even the more intelligent laymen were beginning to know something about the new methods and to be less afraid of them.

Liberalism
This new attitude, which effectively defeated modernism, is best

described as Liberalism. The word was a term of bad omen because it had been used by Newman and the Tractarians to stigmatize all that they most disliked. To them, however, it had implied a distrust of all definiteness in religious teaching combined with a determination to make the ecclesiastical subservient to the secular administration. In its new context, however, the term meant simply freedom to use scientific method in the study of the Bible and the Church. It did not seek, like modernism, to appeal to 'modern cultivated man' by softening away the claims of dogma; it did not dissolve institutional religion into a mere philosophy; it believed that the historical facts behind the creed could stand up to historical enquiry. In the first quarter of the twentieth century this 'conservative liberalism' succeeded in establishing itself in nearly every corner of Anglicanism.

Not quite every corner. It is interesting to observe the success and failure of this new spirit in religious thought. It did in point of fact split the evangelicals. For them, with their stress on protestantism as the religion of a book, the attack on the infallibility of scripture was much more serious than for the catholics with their emphasis on the Church. There was a section of them who refused even to consider it. The bible was the Bible, the Word of God; it did not admit of questioning; it must be simply accepted. They turned their back on the new learning and became known as 'conservative evangelicals'.

There was even an extreme wing of them, known as Fundamentalists, who went back to the old views of verbal inspiration. They combined their biblical literalism with a puritanical attitude to life which was in many respects reminiscent of the old Puritans who tried to change the Church of England from within during the period of Elizabeth I and her immediate successors. They were pre-eminently conspicuous for their zeal and devotion. They gathered school-children into bodies of Crusaders, undergraduates into 'Varsity fellowships, ordinands into specialized colleges. They formed a small but solid enclave within Anglicanism but were in ethos less like Anglicans than were the Methodists or even some of the other separated bodies.

Thus weakened by the defection of their conservative and fundamentalist elements the bulk of the evangelicals began to show their acceptance of the new methods. They too must have a society to encourage the acceptance of their views. They began rather precariously in 1906, and it was not until 1923 that they effected a strong combination in the AEGM (Anglican Evangelical Group Movement). Even so the society after a few years of useful service dropped into insignificance, not because of failure but because of success. The views for which it stood were too widely accepted to need a special organization for their promotion. Members of the party who accepted the academic discipline began to be known generally as Liberal Evangelicals. That was taken to mean that they not only shared the modern view of the Bible but also were interested in developing general culture and stood only a little left of centre in churchmanship.

Paradoxical as it may seem, the people who were least disturbed by the new methods were the Anglo-Catholics. They had translated the somewhat academic piety of the Tractarians into the glory and colour of catholic worship in the slums. There they had lived by the Church, creed and sacraments. The bible had never been so much of a fetish to them as to the evangelicals. In any case they were quite used to the idea that the Church produced the bible and even if the bible were questioned they could always fall back on the authority of the Church. Specifically, moreover, in 1899 Gore and Scott Holland with others, whose catholic standing could not be doubted, had given in *Lux Mundi* an instrument by which, through the doctrine of the all-pervading Logos, the conclusions of science and the theory of evolution could be harmonized with traditional teaching. It is true that there were a few like G. K. Chesterton and Ronald Knox who made fun of the Anglican compromise, but their self-chosen *métier* was to make fun and they were not taken very seriously. Also there were a few who were more traditionalist than the Pope; but they were obviously treading a tight-rope, and the only interest they roused was to see which way they would fall. The vast majority of Anglo-Catholics could be divided into two sections: the academically minded, who accepted the new methods to a man; and the pastorally minded, who did not mind either way; they were quite prepared to accept the training they had received, but their main interests lay elsewhere; in the parishes they had more important things to teach than the doubtful authorship of J, E, D, and P.

Thus Liberalism in the early part of the twentieth century became almost universal among the Anglican clergy, except the extreme wings of catholics and evangelicals. The clergy, however, were cautious about recommending it to their laity. The first sharp reactions had damped the enthusiasm of those who would have liked to proclaim it as a new gospel, while the excesses of the modernists had frightened many who did not wish to be tarred with the same brush. The result was a widening gap between the pulpit and the pew. Biblical references were often made by the preacher in one language and understood by the congregation in another. It was only by slow degrees and by diligent work in the schools and bible classes that the gulf could be bridged. Inevitably some of the intelligentsia were lost in the meantime; but the position was retrieved. Today it would have to be said that what was true of Oxford and Cambridge in the first decade of the century is now true of almost the whole body of intelligent Anglicans, clerical and lay: their approach to the Bible and theology is at least superficially liberal.

Kenotic Theory

One of the most interesting questions that faced the new liberalism was perhaps the most important of all, that of the Person of Christ. The traditional doctrine was that in the Incarnate there was a conjunction of two complete natures, perfect Godhood and perfect manhood, with two wills but with only one personal element which was supplied by the eternal Logos. The Council of Chalcedon in 451 had once for all stated in the clearest possible terms that each of the two natures was complete and perfect and that they were united ontologically without separation but at the same time without intermingling or confusion. The Tome of Pope Leo, which was accepted and endorsed by the Council, had gone further and explained that although in virtue of the union the two natures could share their particular qualities they did in fact act distinctively, so that it was as man that Christ felt pain and suffered hunger, as God that he performed his miracles and rose from the dead.

It was this suggestion of an alternating balance that seemed unreal to the Anglican theologians of the early part of the twentieth century. As we have seen, the modernists cut the Gordian knot by eliminating the miracles altogether. There were others, however, like Charles Gore, Bishop successively of Birmingham and Oxford, who wished to retain the miracles while keeping a firm hold on the humanity of Christ. They relied on the famous passage in Philippians[4] where St Paul speaks of Christ 'emptying himself' of his divine power and glory while he lived as man among men. The Greek word for emptying is Kenosis and the theory they evolved to explain the Incarnation was known as the Kenotic Theory. This meant that in reading the story of Christ we must never bring in his divinity to explain any of his earthly actions. He was the prince who came disguised as a beggar and must always act true to his disguise, only in this case there was a real laying aside of his royal state. This was why in certain instances Christ could quite truthfully profess ignorance and incapacity. If we ask why then was he ever able to perform miracles at all, the answer is that some of the miracles attributed to him can be explained on scientific grounds, some have probably been exaggerated in transmission, some may have been due to the direct intervention of God, while some may have been due to the otherwise unknown capacity of perfect manhood. Only extreme Modernists regarded them as figments of a pious imagination.

Gore, as we know, had already played a great part in *Lux Mundi* and had succeeded in uniting the two streams of liberalism and catholicism. But even his great prestige could not induce general acceptance of the Kenotic Theory. It was difficult to see what could be the precise value in an Incarnation that held the divine element of the union in complete suspense. Nor did the theory fully account for the obviously super-human elements of the gospel story.

William Sanday, the Lady Margaret Professor at Oxford, who had been one of the main supports of the moderate liberal section of theologians, tried to help by introducing the new science of psychology. Great play was being made at the time with the discovery of the subconscious, and Sanday tried to use it as a key to unlock the mystery of Christology. The subliminal self, he suggested, was the ideal location for the eternal Logos in the Christ. It was there that in the case of genius the source of inspiration was to be found. No doubt there, below the threshold of consciousness, the ancient prophets had first heard the word of the Lord. Was not that the fitting abode for the Word in the Incarnate? The suggestion, however, was laughed out of court. The professor was using an instrument from another science before it had been properly forged. The subliminal consciousness was not only the home of genius; it was also the lair of the tiger and the lion. Indeed most of our psychological terrors are battened down under the threshold: that is therefore no very obvious abode for the eternal Word. Nevertheless the enquiry was worth making. If we are to entertain the suggestion of two centres of consciousness in Christ, we may still have to take something like it into consideration. Sanday, however, found himself drifting further away from the moderate position. Chivalrous to a fault, he defended Thompson in his controversy over miracles. He was himself involved in controversy with Gore, Thomas Strong (the Dean of Christ Church) and N. P. Williams (who was to succeed him in his professorship). Ultimately at the Church Congress of 1912 he effectively declared in favour of the modernist position.

A more acceptable proposal for a solution came from Frank Weston, Bishop of Zanzibar. His book, *The One Christ*, was short but it was clear and concise, and was recognized as a remarkable production to come from an Anglo-Catholic missionary working on the fringe of civilization. Weston's view was that we must continually recognize the unity of Christ's person. We must not think at some times of the Man at work and at others of the Logos. And inasmuch as the personal element is supplied by the Logos it is always—even when Christ appears at his weakest and most human—the Logos who is at work. The Kenosis appears in that he can only work through human nature with all the limitations and disabilities to which humanity is subject. This 'God as man' theory seemed at least to fit more satisfactorily than any other the prologue of the Fourth Gospel. Weston's book had a great vogue and is still to be reckoned with in any discussion of the subject.

Mysticism

A further influence, producing a considerable effect upon Anglican thought in the early twentieth century, was that of Mysticism. Again it was perhaps characteristically Anglican that in manifesting a special interest in this type of thought English churchmen should modify it and adapt it to their own needs. There was of course an initial prejudice to be overcome, Anglicans were not in the least attracted by stories of stigmata, ecstasies, levitations, and so on. They did like to hear about St Francis preaching to the birds. Indeed they became interested enough in the rest of his life to dedicate to him one or two new churches. But in general they reduced their idea of mysticism to that of a specially intense spirituality, about which they were willing to learn so as to deepen their own religion.

The original impetus, we may suppose, came to the scholars from the American William James's *Varieties of Religious Experience* (1892). This helped them to understand about 'once-born' and 'twice-born' people and to reconcile the traditional Anglican consciousness of steady growth with the evangelical emphasis on conversion. The scholarly world was further illuminated by Dr Illingworth's magnificent trilogy, *Personality, Human and Divine* (1894), *Divine Immanence* (1898) and *Divine Transcendence* (1911). But what opened the eyes of the general public to the nature of this form of religion was the publication of Inge's Bampton Lectures on *Christian Mysticism* (1899). Here in clear and literary English was conveyed the impression of an incarnational religion that could use the presence of the Eternal Word in Jesus of Nazareth as a key with which to unlock the mystery of the universe and of human personality. If Inge was more of a detached observer than of a practitioner, if he did go out of his way to raise a supercilious eyebrow over realistic views of the sacraments, nevertheless he enabled Anglicans to see the Logos reflected not only in the works of Christ but in the beauties of nature, in the liturgy of the Church, in the aspirations of the soul that was 'in Christ'. If he himself put more emphasis on the psychological side of religion than the ontological, he did not conceal the fact that the New Testament holds out the prospect that we may be made partakers of the divine nature and that through the sacraments there may be set up an essential relationship between Christ and the Christian soul.

Further, by its emphasis on the threefold way of Purgation, Illumination and Union, mysticism offered an ordered scheme of spiritual development. By its dissection of these main stages into a number of smaller steps it gave the learner an opportunity of analysing his own spiritual state. And by its emphasis on such exercises as meditation and contemplation it taught him how to foster his expected growth. In short, although comparatively few were prepared to accept all the details of the Mystic Way as a rigid and necessary scale of religious progress, the revived teaching opened up new vistas of opportunity and threw a halo of romance and adventure around the everyday practice of religion. This timely teaching brought a new warmth into current Anglicanism, and was a much needed counterpart to the academic speculations of liberalism.

The movement was not confined to Anglicanism. It found massive support and a whole world of new learning in a work by the Roman Catholic modernist layman, Baron von Hügel. His *Mystical Element of Religion*, published in two volumes in 1908, was really an enormous commentary on the life of St Catherine of Genoa. The saint herself was buried under a vast mountain of erudition and of crabbed German English that took a good deal of sifting out into intelligible sentences. But the book as a whole was pure gold. The division of religion into intellectual, institutional and mystical elements has become classic, but what was even more important was the ponderous defence by one of the most learned men of his day of catholic practice and liberal thought united in the heartfelt perception of the indwelling Christ. With the publication of *Mysticism* by the Baron's Anglican pupil Miss Evelyn Underhill in 1911 the floodgates were opened to a spate of literature on the subject. Miss Underhill was almost unique among modern writers in that she had come, not to God through a belief in Christ, but to Christ through a belief in God. That fact gave to her writing a certain austerity that prevented it from descending into anything like mawkish sentimentality. When mysticism found its way again into Anglican piety, it did not manifest itself in any awkward extravagancies. It was really a strong re-affirmation of the saying of William Law that in the sphere of religion what is done *for* me is of no value unless it is done *in* me.

If then we find the calm confidence of the Anglicanism of the first decade of the twentieth century already somewhat undermined by the spread of liberalism with its restless, questioning spirit, we have to remember the compensation offered by the spread of interest in mysticism. Nothing perhaps could ever restore the complacent superiority of Victorian days, but its place might easily be taken under divine guidance by a more truly religious spirit relying upon the knowledge of Christ's presence in the soul. How far that happened we may be able to trace in the sequel.

CHAPTER SEVEN

HEY-DAY OF ANGLO-CATHOLICISM

Effects of the First World War—Parliament's rejection of proposed new Prayer Book 1928—Establishment of National Assembly—Progress of liberalism—New scientific studies of Old and New Testament—Revival of Anglo-Catholicism and its results

IN PURSUING the story of the development of Anglicanism as a way of thought[1] we can either try to follow the advance along the whole front—which would be a very difficult and complicated proceeding—or we can do what the archaeologists do and sink an investigating shaft at carefully spaced points. The latter seems the easier, as well as the more interesting, measure to adopt in the present instance. We have already made a beginning by examining the first decade of the present century, when the Victorian age was disappearing into the past and taking with it the belief in the fixity of conventions and the inevitability of progress. We might find another suitable point of investigation at the end of the first quarter of the century, from about 1925 to 1934, when the world was suffering from the reaction after the First Great War and had not yet prepared itself for the second.

Effects of the First World War

Perhaps the most widely felt result of the First World War was the effective break up of convention. The age of the church parade, Sunday clothes and courtesy calls was gone. The war had absorbed the energies of the whole nation. It had turned habits inside out, broken down long-established taboos, and introduced a much more hand-to-mouth existence. With the break in social habits had come a change in moral and religious conventions. The church-going habit had perforce been broken and was not easily restored. Men and women who had found a life of conventional morality easy enough in the fixed circumstances of home life, had found it infinitely more difficult when they had been herded together in a completely new environment where the old restraints were no longer effective. They did not settle back easily after the war into the old grooves. There was a consequent revolution against the Christian ethical tradition with an emergence of what was called the New Morality. Combined with the current secular humanism the determination to be one's own master in the moral realm was reminiscent of the neo-classicism of the renaissance period.

In the theological sphere the war meant a temporary end to German prestige. The massive learning and imaginative brilliance of German scholarship could not be long submerged, but there was a useful breathing space in which British and American studies could set themselves on their own feet. Also the war had settled some awkward questions. The Kikuyu troubles, in which the bishop of one African diocese had threatened a schism because another had broken rubrics governing admission to Holy Communion, had somehow become lost to sight, just as in the sphere of secular government the question of women's suffrage had ceased to cause agitation. In much the same way the debate on miracles seemed for the moment to be less important when the new wonders of atomic science began to occupy the forefront of attention.

In two particular respects the Church received severe blows. The first was the failure of the National Mission of Repentance and Hope in 1916. It had been a gallant effort to keep spiritual issues to the front at a time of great pre-occupation. But it was probably ill-timed at a moment when the pressure on the nation's energies was mounting to its utmost tension and there was, as yet, no certainty of ultimate victory. However, one ought not to say of any spiritual effort that it has been a failure, for one can never tell what hidden effect it has had. But we are bound to attempt a historical judgment, and the general verdict is that, on statistical grounds at least, the effort cannot be accounted a success.

The other blow fell in 1927 and 1928 when a revised Book of Common Prayer, which had been in preparation for twenty years and had passed through all the necessary ecclesiastical procedure, was actually disallowed by the House of Commons. Its defeat was due to pressure brought to bear upon members of parliament by small but vehement groups of extremists from both the catholic and evangelical sections of church members. The evangelicals raised the cry of 'No Popery', and although Davidson, the Archbishop of Canterbury, affirmed that no new doctrine had been introduced into the new Prayer Book which could not be found in the old, it was difficult, if not impossible, to show that there was no change of emphasis. The catholics, who were fewer in numbers and probably had less influence, objected to the proposed revision largely on expert liturgiological grounds which had little significance for the multitude. For the moment it looked as if the Church, thus rebuffed, might demand its own disestablishment. But in the end the bishops eased the situation by announcing that they would not take action against any priest who, while departing from the authorized liturgy, confined his departure within the limits set by the pattern of the new book they had approved. On the whole, in spite of the anger caused by Parliament's action at the time, there has been some satisfaction that the 1928 book did not come into use. Ever since that controversy liturgical knowledge has been growing apace. Instead of being regarded as an utterly arid and static branch of study, it has now become one of the most progressive and exciting departments of theology. It is expected that when the new proposals for the reform of the liturgy become authoritative they will differ widely from those of 1928.

The anger caused by the débâcle of that year was all the greater at the time because it was confidently believed that a *modus vivendi* had been reached between Church and State, in accordance with which the Church would be left effectively free to fulfil her own spiritual functions in her own way. This arrangement had been contrived as the result of the Life and Liberty Movement which had begun in 1917, before the war actually ended. In it the leading figure had been William Temple, who later became Archbishop first of York, then of Canterbury. His aim, in which he was seconded if not led by the reigning archbishop Randall Davidson, was to find a democratic government for the Church based on adult membership. The old convocations were left untouched, but a National Assembly, consisting of three houses of Bishops, Clergy and Laity, was set up to act as a central legislative body for the whole Church of England, with subordinate councils at diocesan, rural deanery and parochial levels. This involved a considerable measure of centralization and the organization of a kind of ecclesiastical Whitehall at Church House. Once the National Assembly was in being, ecclesiastical measures passed by it were examined by a committee of both houses of Parliament. If that committee saw no objection to them they were expected to be accepted formally by Parliament. If, however, the committee were doubtful and could not persuade the Assembly to withdraw or amend them, they would have to go through the normally long and tedious Parliamentary procedure for ordinary bills. It had been assumed that Parliament would be interested only in measures that affected the rights and property of the citizens. The shock was, therefore, all the greater when it set itself to adjudicate upon recondite questions of faith and worship.

However, that is one of the penalties, not merely of the establishment, but of encouraging the laity to take an interest in theological questions. In spite of this set-back, the National Assembly has successfully passed a mountainous heap of measures and the administration of the Church's affairs has been subjected to a root-and-branch reformation. The changes effected have brought a vastly increased efficiency into the conduct of ecclesiastical business. But what is far more important than the mere rectification of faults in the machine is that a whole organization has now been provided by which the Church could, if necessary, manage her own affairs independently of the State. If disestablishment were forced upon her, or if she felt it her duty to demand it for herself, she would, at least, know that on the day of her separation she would be able to keep her own house in order. Probably such a thing could never have been said before in the whole history of *Ecclesia Anglicana*.

Progress of Liberalism

We saw in the last chapter how the defeat of Modernism left behind a spirit of scientific enquiry which was accepted by the main body of theological teachers whatever their party colour. The ease with which this spirit spread was largely due to the fact that the biblical scholars had combined to establish what were sometimes called 'the assured results of criticism'. This success had made the whole process respectable. Ordination candidates were drilled in those results and in the 'progressive revelation' of which they were supposed to be evidence.

Between the wars, however, some doubts were thrown by independent researchers on some of these assured results. In the Old Testament Professor Welch questioned the accepted date and meaning of Deuteronomy. Did it really belong to 621 BC and did it really insist on one and one only central shrine for all Judaism? Since 621 was the sole fixed chronological datum in the reconstructed history of the Old Testament literature, this was a serious doubt indeed. In the issue few people agreed with Dr Welch but his defection was symptomatic of the uneasy glances that were being thrown at J, E, D, and P.

An even more illuminating question was being raised with regard to the Psalms. In the pre-war days it had been assumed by the young student that most, if not all, the Psalms were to be ascribed to the Maccabean period. It had often been the recreation of the theological undergraduate to find from internal evidence the most credible date within that period to which he could pin any particular psalm. But now we were learning to treat the psalms as elements of liturgy, often with an epic or dramatic flavour. As such they must have been subject to all the influences that still shape and reshape our hymns today. Consequently, we must expect many of them to be much older than our scepticism had led us to judge. One can still remember the titter that went round the Examination Schools at Oxford when the redoubtable Dr Gressman announced in his broken English, 'Der are *no* Maccabean psalms'.

What was even more staggering was the revelation of the civilization of ancient Sumeria as the result of Woolley's excavations at Ur of the Chaldees. Hitherto we had known of nothing to compare with the early pyramid period of Egypt, but here was a culture that produced artistic products like the famous gold figurine of the 'Ram caught in a Thicket', and they were dated about 4,000 BC. They were so staggering that an Old Testament professor, returning to Oxford from the exhibition in the British Museum, said 'I think we must have got our dates all wrong'. But further discoveries served to confirm the dates, and we became conscious of a highly advanced Mesopotamian culture already thoroughly established many centuries before the Hebrews left the neighbourhood to start their separate existence. It began to be realized that some of the elements of Old Testament culture, which had been thought due to post-exilic Babylonian influence, were really part of the common inheritance of the Semitic peoples occupying Mesopotamia and the Fertile Crescent. As study of these cultural types developed, it began to appear likely that there might have been a common background or framework to the related Semitic religions even in the historic period. In 1933 Professor Hooke published his *Myth and Ritual*, which sought to show that there was a common pattern in which King and God were closely associated together with the forces of nature, so that the King, representing the Saviour-God, died and rose again with winter and spring in order to ensure the continuance of the fertility of the soil and the national life. This process was reproduced in the New Year cult to effect a kind of sympathetic magic. Traces of this cult, could be found in the Old Testament, particularly in the so-called Coronation Psalms, and could be evidence that it once occupied a leading place in Hebrew religion.

Professor Hooke found himself supported by a growing body of Scandinavian scholars. Anglicans were more concerned to show that the vagueness of this outline in the Old Testament was evidence of the marked difference between the Hebrew religion and that of its neighbours. Even if they had the same background the picture presented by the religion of Israel itself was entirely unique. Just as the prophets had used outstanding incidents in the secular history of their people to show God in action, and so to produce a *heilsgeschichte*, a history of salvation, so the priests had moulded the common elements of worship into a cultus that aptly expressed the nature of the one, holy God of Israel.

In the meantime something equally exciting had been happening in the sphere of New Testament studies. An Anglican scholar, Canon Streeter, had carried the documentary analysis of the synoptic gospels as far as it would go, and his book, *The Four Gospels*, published in 1924, received the unusual honour of translation into German, and still remains a standard work. Anglo-Catholic scholars accepted these results and in the same year revealed the definite conjunction of the two streams of liberalism and catholicism in a symposium entitled *Essays Catholic and Critical*. The next step was to get behind the documents composing the gospels to the oral sources from which they were compiled; but that was a German triumph and does not belong to our present story.

What is important for our immediate purpose is to record that new conceptions had arisen with regard to the character of Jesus. We left the story at the point where the main feature was Harnack's description of Jesus as a kind of liberal protestant reformer, proclaiming the Fatherhood of God and the brotherhood of man. That picture was shattered by the great philosopher-theologian-musician-medical missionary Albert Schweitzer. He pointed out that this description of Jesus left out of reckoning all his references to the approaching end of the world. He prepared a new picture of Jesus as a sincere, fanatical, mistaken apocalyptist who believed that the new Messianic age would be immediately ushered in by his own self-sacrificial death, and who taught that in view of this imminent end everyone should begin to practise at once a completely other-worldly code of ethics. Schweitzer's book was translated into English under the title *The Quest of the Historical Jesus* as early as 1910 and was referred to in the Church Congress at Cambridge of that year. But it only slowly made itself felt. One remembers the Cambridge scholar, Professor Burkitt, saying years after that he thought he was the only follower of Schweitzer in the country. Catholic Anglicans welcomed it because it conclusively defeated the view of Jesus preached by protestant modernism; but they left it to a non-Anglican, Professor Dodd, to challenge Schweitzer's 'imminent' eschatology with his own 'realized' eschatology, teaching that Jesus had proclaimed the beginning of the Kingdom of God in his own lifetime. And Schweitzer's views did help them also in calling a halt to the monistic attitude which merged the sacred with the secular, the Kingdom with the World. It assisted them to emphasize the distinction between the two ages, between the life that now is and the life to come, between the world and the Church, even to understand the relation between Jesus and Christ.

It was in regard to this last element in the continual debate that Anglican scholarship was able to render a new service. A part of the modernist case had been that it was possible to separate completely the historic Jesus from the dogmatic Christ. If one disentangled the earliest elements in the gospels, one could find there, it was alleged, the simple moral teacher who was a carpenter's son and who gave himself up to death in the belief that his witness for truth could help his people. All the supernatural elements, turning this simple Galilean peasant into the cosmic Christ, were really later figments foisted upon the original history. This interpretation was effectively exploded by two Cambridge scholars Hoskyns and Davey in their book, *The Riddle of the New Testament*, published in 1931. They showed that, with the best will in the world, it was quite impossible to find this alleged primitive picture of Jesus. The gospels were written, like the epistles, by men who already believed that Jesus was the Son of God and were anxious to persuade others to accept that belief. Even if one went behind the documents and teazled out the earliest strands of oral teaching, the same condition would be found. There simply was no part of the New Testament in which the writers were not convinced that Jesus was the Messiah and trying to teach other men so. We must take it then that the New Testament is not dry-as-dust chronicle. From cover to cover it is interpretation. The conclusion is inevitable that this is the only picture of Jesus that we have. It is a portrait of the Christ. We cannot dissect it into varying features of several dates. We must accept it or reject it as a whole.

It is evident that with the work of Hoskyns and Davey we have entered a post-critical period of Bible study. The results of literary analysis are not abandoned; they are greedily accepted. But they have not fulfilled expectations; they have not brought us to a purely objective view of Jesus. The writers of the New Testament were believing Christians. Their writings were probably intended to be read in church to other believing Christians. They were not, after all, meant to be read quite 'like any other book', or even as an anthology to be analysed and dissected. They had a positive message to convey and that message was of primary religious importance; it was nothing less than the plan of God's salvation.

Anglo-Catholicism

The results of the critical period in biblical studies were well summed up for members of the Anglican Communion in a volume called *Doctrine in the Church of England*. It was the work of a commission set up by the two archbishops in days when there was much perplexity about the extent to which an apparently destructive criticism was likely to go.

Many faithful Anglicans were also asking themselves whether men who held the extreme modernist views had any right to retain office in the Church. The archbishops had foreseen that a careful study of the subject was likely to take a long time and they wisely took care that members of their commission should be young enough to have a good prospect of seeing the work brought to a conclusion in their own lifetime. In the event, the commission took sixteen years to complete its work. It was appointed in 1922 and published its report in 1938. Inevitably it met with a mixed reception; it went too far for some and not far enough for others. It was typically Anglican in that it did not endeavour to rest its findings in profound philosophical principles, about which no one would ever agree. It was content to point out what was the general consensus among scholars on the subjects discussed—which ranged, in point of fact, over the whole creed—and revealed how wide a range of opinion on controversial matters was consonant with Anglican loyalty. The volume did a vast amount of good in providing a *vade mecum* for the clergy and in assuring the laity that there was an Anglican mind on these matters. Unfortunately, the outbreak of war in the year following its publication diverted attention; and by the time the war was over it had been forgotten by the majority. It is probable, however, that those of the older generation who have retained their copies and have had reason to refer to them in recent years have been surprised to find how good and useful a book it is.

About the course of post-war biblical study we shall have to say something in the next chapter. In the meantime it is necessary to notice that the effect of the work between the wars had been to throw increasing emphasis on the idea of the Church. It is indeed extraordinary how widely the revival of churchly ideas had spread. The beginning, no doubt, was to be found away back in the Oxford Movement. But at first the Tractarian insistence on the Church had aroused little but antagonism among the rank and file of the laity. There was an ingrained prejudice against the idea: people brought up to regard the Reformation as the golden age of spiritual religion were not likely to have much use for the church. Jesus and his teaching were simple; the Church and its claims were complicated. The Church was blamed for having obscured the original clarity of the gospel. The consequence was that while congregations were willing enough to hear about Jesus, they were impatient of any teaching about his Church. Up to the time of the First World War, the preacher in a normal parish church felt constrained to apologize if he dwelt on the subject of the Church.

Now, however, in the period between the wars, there was a great change. The critical examination of the Bible, the loss of the theory of its infallibility, drove people back upon the Church. Here was authority and here was security. Further, the development of biblical scholarship was teaching people to think of the bible as a church book. This view had not gone so far as it was to go later, but already the old aphorism 'the Church to teach and the Bible to prove' was taking on a new depth of meaning. Even the Old Testament studies, with their emphasis on myth and ritual and their view of the psalms as part of the cultus, were encouraging the new and exciting study of the Church's worship and liturgy. Paradoxically, the very shock administered by Parliament's rejection of the Prayer Book of 1927–8 made church people realize themselves as parts of a separate entity as against the State and made them look anxiously to see what the Church would do to assert its independent rights.

All this acted as a kind of background to the mounting influence of the heirs of the Oxford Movement. That movement had long ago passed out of the university common rooms to affect the parishes up and down the land. When its academic principles were translated into terms of practical worship they were found to include such details of ecclesiastical furniture as lights, and vestments, and incense and all the ceremonial splendour that hitherto had been associated in most people's minds with Rome. This was the way, said the parish priests, in which the Catholic Church had been accustomed to worship for centuries and as the Anglican was the Catholic Church in this land it was only right and proper that her people too should worship in that way. In any case, Elizabeth I in the relevant rubric of the Book of Common Prayer had actually ordered the use of the ancient vestments and they were merely acting under lawful authority in obeying her.

The easiest way to find out how things should be done was to look at the Roman Catholic churches in the neighbourhood. But an effort to show that this did not involve the following of any Roman authority was made by some who wished to restore the ancient Use of Sarum. It was thought that this would be recognized as something distinguishably English and therefore non-Papal. The hope was vain. It was perceived that the Salisbury use was less practical than that of modern Rome and it was laughed out of court as a 'British Museum Religion'. Consequently, in the movement for liturgical reform it was the pattern of Rome that was found handiest and was most widely followed. Normally only such elements of ritual and ceremonial were adopted as could be held to fit reasonably into the Prayer Book pattern, but a facility for borrowing from one's neighbour is notoriously easy to accelerate. It was not long before a small section of the clergy were claiming the right to incorporate the whole papal system into their parishes. They seemed a little puzzled and hurt that the Pope did not accept their obedience on those terms. They were, apparently, still more puzzled that the Anglican authorities should be disturbed and resentful at their attitude.

This was the hey-day of Anglo-Catholicism. As we have seen, the Tractarians themselves had used the name, and had employed it, just as the term Anglican had originally been employed, to imply a catholicism that was English as distinct from Roman. In that sense it was still used by the majority. Some, however, felt they could do without it and would have preferred to be known simply as Catholics. Others, both among moderate supporters and downright opponents, used it as a reproach, almost a term of abuse, to designate an extreme wing of Anglican ultramontanists. Consequently, there were many whose lives and work had been vitally affected by the movement but who were, nevertheless, unwilling to associate themselves with the name.*

Actually by this time the vast majority of the clergy were indebted in varying degrees to the movement. There was now very little violent opposition or persecution. Even the suspicion, under which members of the movement laboured, was beginning to evaporate as more and more priests who had been trained in its teaching found themselves elevated to the episcopate. True, the dioceses to which they were appointed were, for the most part, overseas in the mission field, but they were able to make their influence felt in wider circles when they came home to share in some of the more spectacular manifestations in which the movement now indulged.

It must be said that throughout this period the movement was brilliantly led. A 'Fiery Cross' campaign maintained the vigour of the parishes. But what was of outstanding value was the series of congresses held in the Albert Hall in London at intervals from 1920 to 1933, the latter being the centenary of the birth of the revival in Keble's Assize Sermon at St Mary's, Oxford. Some of these congresses included open air events such as a reception in Hyde Park and a High Mass at Stamford Bridge. But the main feature was always the gathering in the Albert Hall where crowds of earnest (and often perspiring) catholics listened to papers from some of the most learned theologians in the country, papers which they could never have understood but which they seemed to find pervaded by a numinous atmosphere at once reassuring and stimulating. In any case great enthusiasm was engendered

---

*It is interesting that the best history of the movement, by the Lutheran Archbishop Brilioth, is entitled *The Anglican Revival* (1925).

and maintained. It was assisted by some noteworthy personalities. Perhaps the greatest of them was Frank Weston, the theologian bishop from Zanzibar, whose fine presence, magnificent voice and obvious devotion constituted a symbol of the physical and spiritual qualities for which the movement stood.

It must never be forgotten that below all the frills and fripperies, and beyond all the discipline and dogmatism there was a very real, warm and heartfelt spirituality. What provided the vitality of the movement was the consciousness that here, in the lowliest church and the meanest altar, there was a double line that led on the one side to heaven and on the other to the heart of the believer. All the colour and romance brought by the movement into drab lives, whether lived in slum, suburb, or palace, was the natural expression and cradle of such a belief. The altar was the generator of a vivifying power that ran direct to the domestic hearth, the factory loom, the office desk. It set a halo about every element of private and public life. It gave a touch of glamour to the most commonplace existence.

Results of the revival of Anglo-Catholicism

The extent of the influence exercised by the Catholic Revival is impossible to estimate. It is probable that its uncritical admirers have claimed in some respects more for it than is its due. We have already suggested that some of its emphasis on daily services had already been anticipated in the springs of the Evangelical Movement; though there the impetus had been lost and the catholics had to begin all over again. Further, there had been a general movement of church reform initiated by Bishop Samuel Wilberforce of Oxford which had won for its followers the name of 'good churchmen'. That movement had been hardly distinct enough to earn for itself the honour of capital letters, but it had led to a raising of standards in priestly life, in liturgical competence, and in business administration. It helped to provide an extensive fringe of anglo-catholic clergy, men who would not have given themselves the name and who would never have striven after the decorations, but whose essential teaching and practice were catholic, whose private devotions were derived from catholic sources, and who were prepared to incorporate into their services as many catholic practices as their people were prepared to accept. When due allowance is made for such qualifications it is possible to say that there is scarcely a church in the whole length and breadth of the Anglican Communion today that has not been to some extent affected by the Catholic Revival. Even those most opposed to it have suffered some of that influence. It would not be far from the truth to say that the average evangelical church services are conducted today much as Newman would have liked to see them conducted during the period of his ministry in the Church of England.

More specifically it is worth noticing the tremendous change that has come over both the parish churches and the cathedrals, especially in England. The vast majority of them are open and in use every day. Their fabrics are well tended. Even the terrible devastation of the two world wars, which was mostly restored from public funds, gave an opportunity for the raising of large sums and putting the buildings in a better state of repair than they had enjoyed for many centuries. Interiorly they have been 'beautified' almost beyond recognition. Indeed the renewal of a sentimental taste for Gothic resulted in the destruction of much good work that had gone out of fashion. The United States showed greater wisdom in maintaining their colonial style churches intact to be a continual joy to those English visitors whose taste had attained a wider range of appreciation. In any case, it is true to say that Anglican churches throughout the world are well kept and give evidence of loving care combined with a gradually deepening knowledge.

The cathedrals were less quick to seize their opportunities than the parish churches. For one thing, just as the Oxford Movement got under way, they lost a large part of their endowments in the efforts to redistribute some part of the Church's income and make better provision for the pastoral care of the vastly increased population. There was also a genuine conflict of opinion whether they were meant to provide the best possible service for a small élite (as their closed-in choirs appeared to indicate) or whether they were intended to act as evangelizing centres for the multitude (as their great naves might seem to suggest). The fact that neither answer was historically correct was not to the point; the question was what was to be done with them now. Actually both uses became more fully exploited; the choir was the natural home of the week-day services while the nave was almost always used for Sunday services and for services of great civic or national importance. It was the genius of Dean Bennett of Chester that employed the cathedral for a further use—the spiritualization of the tourist traffic. Instead of being treated as intruders, the tourists were welcomed, they found the chapels and the treasures in good order and regularly used; they were faced by notices providing them with a running commentary on everything they saw; and they were made to feel that they were in the house of God whose children they were. The rejuvenation of the cathedrals spread rapidly from Chester throughout the country.

The improvement in the fabric and furnishing of the churches was paralleled by an improvement in the conduct of the services. As we have already suggested, the cathedrals, all the way from Tudor times, had preserved a great tradition of church music. The peculiarly Anglican element about it had been the opportunity given to composers to produce worthy musical settings for the daily office with its canticles and anthem. The tradition thus developed was subject to the incidence of changing fashion, and not all the music it produced could be called good by any standards, but the tradition was maintained and it encouraged a purity of tone for boys' voices that has never been surpassed. Such music had suffered one of its bad periods in the early nineteenth century, but the new vitality infused by the anglo-catholics encouraged musicians to take fresh heart of grace.

Hymn-singing was largely an inheritance from the evangelicals, especially of the Wesleyan variety, but now the practice became so universal as to demand special hymn-books that were, in effect, anthologies of religious verses and tunes from many quarters. Both *Hymns Ancient and Modern* and the *English Hymnal* were fruits of the movement. Even Oratorio was not neglected. Although it may seem absurd to set Stainer's *Crucifixion* side by side with Handel's *Messiah* they both met the same need, and while the cathedral choirs were performing the latter in their spacious building, the former was providing a means of devotion and comfort in hundreds of humble churches up and down the country.

But the great change of a liturgical character brought about by the movement was the substitution in many churches of the Sung Eucharist in place of Matins at the most popular hour of Sunday morning worship. To get the Eucharist so recognized and attended was to display the sacramental character of Christianity as nothing else could. To very many it brought a revelation of what worship could mean. It was a step that had become necessary if Anglicans were to display, under the new conditions of biblical and liturgical learning, their recognition of their historic heritage as part of the Catholic Church. But it must be confessed that the gain was won at great cost. Few things are more disturbing to a congregation than drastic changes in the service to which they have been accustomed for generations. And few changes could be more drastic than the substitution of the Sung Eucharist for the choir office. It may be questioned whether it was always introduced with the sympathy and consideration for other people's feelings that might have made it acceptable. It was, in fact, the bitterness arising from the rapidity with which such changes were made that helped to give the

The Medieval Heritage of the
Anglican Church

1
The native British church, established in the third
century, was gradually driven westwards by the Anglo-
Saxon invasions and developed a strong monastic
tradition. Remains of beehive-shaped monk's cells such
as this one in Dingle, Co Kerry (*c.* 700) can be found in
many places in Cornwall, Wales and Ireland

2
The Chapel of St Peter on the Wall at Bradwell juxta Mare (*c.* 654) was founded by St Cedd, Bishop of the East Saxons

3
The elaborate illumination and writhing animals seen on this opening page of St Mathew's Gospel from the Lindisfarne Gospels are typical of eighth century Celtic and Saxon art

4
The tenth century Saxon Church of St Lawrence at Bradford on Avon is a
particularly fine example of pre-Norman architecture

5
The Church of St Andrew, Greensted, Essex, is a rare example of an early wooden church. The nave was probably built in 1013

6
The massive pillars of the nave of Durham Cathedral are
characteristic of the best Norman architecture

7
The choir of Salisbury Cathedral is famous for its pure
and elegant thirteenth century Gothic style

The English Reformation

8
Erasmus (1466–1536), who was one of the greatest
scholars of the Reformation period, visited England
several times and was a friend of John Colet and Thomas
More. His refusal to associate himself with extremist
views in the Reformation disputes shows the same
tolerant and broad-minded attitude now characteristic
of the Anglican church

9

Henry VIII's desire to annul his marriage with Catherine of Aragon prompted his renunciation of papal supremacy in 1531, when he took the title of Supreme Head of the Church of England

10

The title-page of the Coverdale Bible, the 'Great Bible' of 1535, from which are derived the psalms as they appear in the Book of Common Prayer

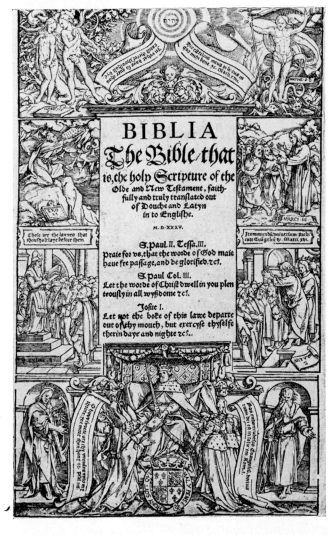

11

Thomas Cranmer, Archbishop of Canterbury from 1533 until his execution in 1556, was the architect of the Book of Common Prayer

12

The table of contents of the first English Prayer Book produced by Cranmer in 1549

13
Paul's Cross was from Anglo-Saxon times the centre for
official proclamations. During the Reformation period
many controversial sermons were preached here in the
shadow of Old St Paul's. It is seen here on a panel from a
1616 triptych

THE
HOLY
BIBLE,
Conteyning the Old Testament,
AND THE NEW:

Newly Translated out of the Originall
tongues: & with the former Translations
diligently compared and reuised, by his
Maiesties speciall Comandement.

Appointed to be read in Churches.

Imprinted at London by Robert
Barker, Printer to the Kings
most Excellent Maiestie.

ANNO DOM. 1611.

14
The title-page of the Authorized version of the Bible
published in 1611

15
Richard Hooker (1554–1600) was the author of the famous *Treatise on the Laws of Ecclesiastical Polity*, 1594, the Church's reply to puritanism, which asserted that the authority and teaching of the Church must be respected side by side with Biblical revelation

16

John Donne (*left*), Dean of St Paul's from 1621 to his death in 1631, was one of the greatest Anglican poets and preachers. His memorial effigy in St Paul's depicts him in his shroud at his own request

17

William Laud (*above*), Archbishop of Canterbury from 1633 to 1645, was a fierce opponent of Calvinism and upheld the Anglican doctrine of the 'real presence' at the Eucharist. He was beheaded in 1645 for 'attempting to overthrow the Protestant religion'

18
The engraved title-page of the 1662 Prayer Book. The Act of Uniformity in the same year made its use compulsory in all churches

19
The seven bishops of St Asaph, Ely, Chichester, Canterbury, Bath and Wells, Peterborough and Bristol committed to the Tower in 1688 for refusing to endorse James II's Declaration of Indulgence which gave freedom of worship to non-Anglicans, Roman Catholic and Puritan alike, but was suspected of being a cover for the establishment of Roman Catholicism

The Great Period of
Anglican Church Building

20
St Paul's Cathedral, Wren's masterpiece, was completed in
1710 and is the greatest example of English baroque architecture

21
St Bride's, Fleet Street, has one of Wren's most beautiful spires

22
The Church of St John, Smith Square, built in 1728 and designed by Thomas Archer, is an example of elaborate English baroque. It was badly damaged during the Second World War

23
The interior of St Stephen, Walbrook, often considered the finest of the Wren churches, has an elaborate dome supported on eight arches

24
Galleried interiors and pulpits dominating the congregation reflect the emphasis placed on the sermon during the
eighteenth century. In some cases, as in the Parish Church
of St Mary, Whitby, these features were added to a
basically mediaeval structure

25
An engraving by William Hogarth showing an eighteenth
century congregation at worship: 'The Industrious
'Prentice Performing the Duty of a Christian'

The Evangelical Revival and
the Anti-Slavery Movement

26
John Wesley (*left*), founder of Methodism, whose practical rejection of the doctrine of the apostolic succession led to the breakaway from the Church of England

27
George Whitefield (*below left*), one of the greatest preachers of the Evangelical Movement

28
Much of the awakened social conscience resulting from the evangelical revival was directed into the movement for the emancipation of the slaves. William Wilberforce (*below*), the leader of this movement, was a devout churchman and a founder of the Church Missionary Society and the Bible Society

29
(*Right*) A contemporary engraving commemorating the freeing of the slaves in 1832

30
(*Below*) Thomas Clarkson, one of the founders of the Anti-Slavery Society, addressing an Anti-Slavery Convention in 1840

The Nineteenth Century

31
John Keble (1792–1866), whose famous sermon on National Apostasy in July 1833 marked the beginning of the Oxford Movement

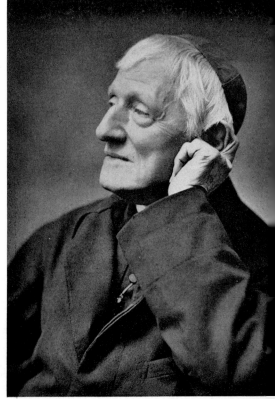

32
John Henry Newman (1801–90), one of the leaders of the Oxford Movement, was converted to Roman Catholicism in 1845

33
Keble College Chapel (*above*) is one
of the best examples of the work of
William Butterfield, the famous
Victorian architect and himself a
follower of the Oxford Movement

34
(*Left*) Samuel Wilberforce
(1805–73), son of the anti-slavery
leader and Bishop of Oxford and
Winchester, contributed much towards the general raising of the
standards of parish and diocesan
work which was one of the direct
results of the Oxford Movement

35
Charles Gore (1853–1932), who
founded the Community of the
Resurrection in 1892, was closely
associated with the revolution in
the church's attitude to social
reform

36
Frederick Denison Maurice
(1805–72) was, with Charles Kingsley, the driving force behind the
Christian Socialist Movement which
challenged ecclesiastical indifference to economic evils

The Missionary Work of the Church

37
(*Left*) Thomas Bray (1656–1730) founded the Society for Promoting Christian Knowledge in 1698 and the Society for the Propagation of the Gospel in 1701

38
(*Below*) A letter of thanks to the Society for the Propagation of the Gospel signed pictorially by Red Indian Chiefs

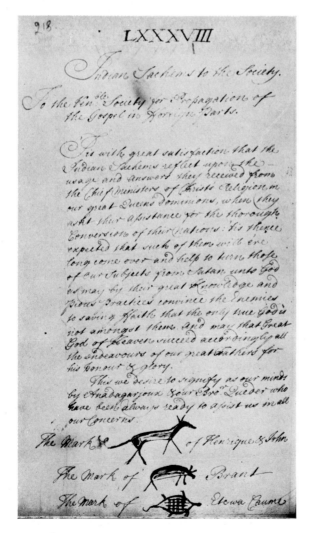

39
Samuel Adjar Crowther, who was
the first African bishop, was consecrated Bishop of the Niger in 1864.
He was rescued as a boy from an
illegal slave ship and converted to
christianity

40
A river baptism in Mashonaland,
Southern Rhodesia

41
A crowded congregation gather for
the consecration of the new church
at Odibo, Damaraland, South
West Africa

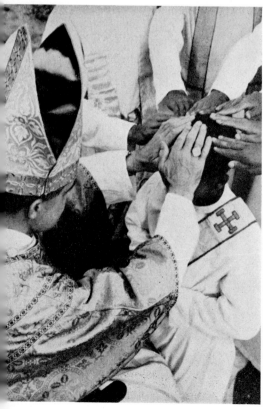

42
Bishop Nigel Cornwall ordains a
new priest in Borneo

43

(*Above*) Schoolgirls from Dogura, New Guinea, dressed in grass skirts on their way to prayers in the Cathedral, built by the Papuans for their own use only fifty years after the first appearance of missionaries in their land

44

Putiki Maori Church, New Zealand (*below*) is famous for the elaborate Maori carvings with which it is decorated

The Episcopal Church of the United States of America

45
The oldest episcopal church in America is Bruton Parish Church in Virginia, which was built between 1710 and 1715

46
St James's, Goore Creek, South Carolina, has a typical American colonial church interior. The royal arms can be seen high up on the East wall

47
Samuel Seabury, the first American bishop, was consecrated in 1784 by a group of Scottish bishops who were able to act independently of the political disability which affected the English bishops during and after the American War of Independence

48
Work on the Cathedral of St Peter and St Paul in Washington was begun in 1907 and is still going on. This view of the sanctuary illustrates the elaborate gothic style in which the United States national cathedral is being built

The Life of the Church Today

49
William Temple, Archbishop of Canterbury from 1942 to 1944, was particularly respected for the work he did towards promoting international understanding on the basis of Christian principles

50
One of the most encouraging features of the Anglican Church since the Second World War has been the lead it has given in the Ecumenical Movement. Here Dr Fisher, Dr Ramsey and other Anglican bishops are seen with Bishops of the Eastern Orthodox Church at the 1958 Lambeth Conference

51
The John Piper mosaic of Christ on the road to Emmaus over the altar of the Church of St Paul, Harlow New Town, is one of many examples of what the Anglican Church has done to encourage the arts in recent years

52
Since the Second World War many new churches have been built following new trends in design and building technique. St Oswald's, Tile Hill, Coventry, is one of five new churches in expanding districts of the city

Anglo-Catholics a bad name and indeed turned their title into a term of abuse. Not nearly so much trouble was aroused by such extra-liturgical services as Benediction and Exposition of the Blessed Sacrament. They were more reprehensible in the eyes of authority, but they were generally conducted as additions to, rather than as substitutes for, the congregation's normal worship, so that they aroused less opposition.

What met with far more widespread approval was the practice of frequent communion, which was now much encouraged. The Prayer Book regulation stated a minimum requirement of three times a year, of which Easter was to be one. Even that was better than the Roman minimum requirement which was understood to be once only, at Easter. Actually it had been the practice for some time in most Anglican parishes to instruct confirmation candidates that they should make a voluntary rule for themselves of monthly communion. There was a danger that this monthly idea might become completely stereotyped, as if there were some ancient tradition behind it. Indeed, the first Sunday in the month did appear to the unsophisticated to be some special kind of 'Communion Sunday'. Now, however, the Roman rule of attendance at Mass every Sunday was translated into the Anglican formula 'the Lord's service on the Lord's day', and communicants were encouraged to make their communion as frequently as they could make adequate preparation. As a result in many cathedrals, parish churches, and college chapels there were small numbers of communicants every day, while on Sundays the number of regular communicants went up enormously.

A further element of church life in which the Anglo-Catholic movement showed an outstanding effect was the revival of monastic communities. This development was of tremendous and increasing importance, but as we shall presently be devoting a chapter to it, we shall not stay to dwell on it now. There is, however, one other feature which is apt to be overlooked and which must, therefore, be specially emphasized. It is the interest now evinced in sociology. The Church is sometimes blamed for not having done more to assist in the elimination of poverty and of the evils that so often follow in its train. This accusation is not altogether fair. Poverty could be eliminated only by political action and it is not the Church's business to conduct political action. It is the Church's business to point to evils that need to be remedied. She may perform a useful function in seeing that proper study is made of the best ways of removing the evils. It is certainly her business to succour to the best of her ability all who suffer from them. But the parliamentary programmes she must leave to the parliamentary

members she has inspired and perhaps taught. Granted that preliminary caution, it will be remembered to the Church's credit that there
had been a regular tradition of interest in these matters from Kingsley,
Maurice and Westcott to Gore, Barnett, Scott Holland and Carter.
The Christian Social Union was formed to unite enthusiasts in the cause.
A good deal was done in the way of putting down and investigating
slums. Here and there people like Basil Jellicoe were able to raise
money for pulling down bad old houses and building up new flats.
Eventually an organization of Anglo-Catholic leaders was developed
to hold summer schools of sociology and to carry on the work of study
and propaganda that had been so brilliantly inaugurated by Scott
Holland in his magazine *Commonwealth*. The basic teaching was thoroughly incarnational. The eternal Logos, who was the eternal reason of God
active in creation, was the same who had taken upon himself human
nature in Jesus of Nazareth, who used the Church as his body and
conveyed his presence and power in its sacraments. If the sacramental
view were justified then it ought to apply to the social and economic
interests of the nation as much as to the specifically religious. In its
hey-day Anglo-Catholicism must, and did, appeal to every side of life.

CHAPTER EIGHT

RISE OF ECUMENISM

Post-war situation: Church's attitude to divorce—Effect of the Welfare State—Discriminate baptism—Church schools—Clergy housing and stipends—Effects of radio and television—Biblical theology and the Church—Rise of ecumenism: Lambeth Conference 1920—Discussions with Roman Catholics, Eastern Orthodox, Old Catholics and National Church of Sweden—Formation of World Council of Churches—Inauguration of Church of South India—First and Second Ecumenical Conferences

IN OUR effort to examine the modern situation of the idea of Anglicanism we have made two probes, the first at the beginning of the twentieth century and the second at the end of the first quarter. At the first period we found liberalism triumphant, at the second catholicism. We might now sink a third shaft at the end of the second quarter, that is about the middle of the century.

Post-war situation

The first thing we have to notice is the effect of the Second World War. If the first had shaken the habits and tested the morals of the people, the second had done so in a heightened degree. It was not that the suffering involved in the second was more intense than that of the first. In some respects, indeed, the second was a gentleman's war compared with the first; there was less foot-slogging and less trench warfare. But it was more expertly carried on and its effects went deeper. The whole nation was involved in a completeness of effort that was not achieved even in the first global war. Also the actual destruction involved was greater. In particular, churches, with their wide expanse of roof and their convenient space between roof and ceiling in which incendiaries could get a firm hold before being discovered, proved particularly vulnerable.

This meant that the habit of church-going, which had never recovered from the effect of the first war, received an additional blow. The results of evacuation, of lack of fuel, of the ruinous state of many churches demanded a certain heroism on the part of those who continued faithfully to observe the duty of public worship. The nucleus that did so were the salt of the earth. They were joined by those who were like-minded when the exigencies of the war were over. Together they acted as a rallying point for some at least of those who, on returning to civil life, found it difficult to return to the old habits of regular worship. Although the defection of many was most marked, and alarming statistics began to be published about the retreat from religion, the steadfastness of the minority had its reward. As soon as the first un-settlement of the return to peace-time conditions was over, there began a slow but gradual return to the habit of chiurch-going. It is true that there has not resulted anything like the pract cal association of respect-ability with a necessary church-going habit which was characteristic of the Victorian period. Today there are too many rival attractions to make that possible. Nevertheless it can be argued that the present freedom evidences a sincerity and a determination that are of special importance in building up the morale of a nation.

One very bad effect of the dispersal of families in the course of the war had been the spread of unfaithfulness to marriage vows. Such an untoward result of the prolonged parting of husband and wife might not have been unexpected, but there was a paradoxical element in the consequent situation after the war was over. Under the teaching of the 'New Morality' sexual licence was regarded as natural and pardonable, and 'sin', which was taken as the theologians' old-fashioned name for it, had become a music-hall joke. Yet adultery was still almost univer-sally regarded as an offence that could not be forgiven, and, where it was discovered, must be taken as an inevitable reason for breaking up a home and a marriage. To meet the growing demand the law of divorce was made easier, with the result that the number of divorces in England rose enormously.

In spite of this attitude on the part of the state practically the whole of the clergy of the Church of England refused to celebrate the marriage of divorcees, and its great women's organization, the Mothers' Union, refused to admit any divorcees at all to membership. At the same time the Church continued to offer its pastoral care to those who had contracted such marriages, and especially sought to do all it could for the children of the resultant 'broken homes'. Parallel difficulties were experienced in other provinces of the Anglican Communion, particu-larly in the United States. The defection from the Christian standard of marriage would certainly have gone even farther than it did had it not been for the stand made by the Church.

Another post-war influence that seemed likely to detract from the importance of the Church in England was the emergence of the Welfare State. The idea that the state was responsible for the welfare of each individual citizen from the cradle to the grave was new, if not in political theory, at least in political practice. It is true that many of the functions the state now undertook to discharge had formerly been the concern of the Church. It was not much more than a century since the state had first begun to interest itself in education, while some of the benefits that had once been the fruits of charity were now offered on a basis of mutual co-operation between state and citizen for the first time. All this was at least partly the result of Christian teaching, and Christians as a whole rejoiced heartily at the culmination of so many centuries of effort. But it meant that the need for the Church would not in future loom so large in many people's minds. The former recipients of charity would look elsewhere for the satisfaction of their needs. On the other hand the clergy would be set more free for the spiritual work of their office. It would need some time before it became generally realized that there was still work of a welfare kind for the voluntary societies to do. However close-meshed the net of the Welfare State, there would always be some needy cases that would escape it, and in many others there would be need for a personal and unofficial sympathy that could not be provided by a government organization. In all this welfare work the ministers of the National Church would still be expected to play their part.

It was perhaps due to the essential honesty of the clergy that just at this time, when numbers and importance seemed to have diminished, some of them should have raised the question whether they were not receiving new members into the Church on too easy terms. This question applied not to adult converts, but to children brought to be baptized. Ought these children to be received indiscriminately, as might appear to be suggested by Jesus's saying 'Suffer the little children to come unto me and forbid them not', or ought some enquiry to be first made whether they had an even chance of being brought up 'to live a godly and a Christian life'? Some of the clergy felt so strongly on the matter that they began to exercise discipline on their own authority and refused to accept children for baptism unless they had the requisite number of god-parents, unless the god-parents were of the approved pattern, and even unless the parents attended church regularly and the older children of the family were regular at Sunday School. It was natural that where these measures were introduced suddenly there should be difficulties with parishioners, and equally natural that the bishops and central authority generally should soon begin to take official notice of them. But one cannot very well understand the genius of Anglicanism without recognizing the individual and independent zeal of such members of the clergy, or the fact that they had brought to light a pastoral issue of real difficulty, or their apparently reckless disregard of the immediate harm they might do, or their unwillingness to wait for and to shield behind a decision of Convocation. Yet it must be remembered that in the still more difficult question of divorce, the parochial clergy, almost to a man, had voluntarily accepted the bishops' lead and refused to use the protection allowed them by the state for the marriage of divorcees.

The reason for the apparent discrepancy may be that in both cases the clergy were moving towards a more rigourist interpretation of Christian life and manners. Their riposte to the growing secularism of the world was not to follow into a half-world of naturalism and religion, but to emphasize the more strongly the distinctive character of Christian teaching and conduct. The Lambeth Fathers, as we have seen, in their Conference of 1948, asserted their Christian humanism, but the clergy in their constant struggle against the corrosive influences of the world were more inclined to emphasize the particularist character of the Church. Always in any National Church there must be a continual tension between universalist and exclusivist tendencies. That kind of tension makes itself felt in every part of the Anglican Communion but nowhere more crucially than in England. It is compelled to adjust a theoretic humanism to what must often seem a rigourist application. In any case, there can be no doubt that after the Second World War the line between the Church and the world was more clearly drawn than it had been before. If we had fewer church people, they were better church people. The number of attendances at church was smaller, but the number of communions made was greater. The ranks of believers had been consolidated, but there was a larger body who looked over the wall and knew little or nothing about us. In the age of relativity and atomic science, in the age of nuclear fission and nuclear fusion, in the age that had seen the horror of Hiroshima and was afraid, we had at least a solid body of earnest Christians better equipped than they had ever been before to meet the challenge of doubt and despair.

The Church of England also had the advantage of some quite material assets. Thus the Education Acts passed by the Government in 1944 and 1945 not only ensured that every child in the country should have the opportunity of learning something about religion and taking part in public worship, unless its parents or guardians actually withdrew it, but also gave the churches favourable financial terms for the rebuilding and maintenance of their schools. The financial assistance was even increased a few years later. The unevenness of Anglican reaction was striking. Some dioceses took full advantage of the offer and retained practically all their schools while others felt even the residual burden left them by the state too heavy to bear and allowed the control of most of their schools to pass into secular hands. A more happily concerted effort was made to retain and even extend the Church's part in the training of teachers. Some of the bishops, who from the superior height of their public school training could see little value in the church elementary school, could nevertheless see the importance of training the teachers in Christian principles and rudimentary theology. It was a pity that more sermons were not preached from the text, 'This ought ye to have done and not to have left the other undone.'

One of the reasons why some of the bishops did not feel able to raise the necessary money for their schools was that they were already over-burdened with efforts to re-house their clergy and to provide them with adequate stipends. The rising cost of living and the difficulty of securing domestic help had made the lot of the clergy trying to maintain their roomy vicarages on fixed stipends particularly hard. But here the Church of England was splendidly served by the business-like management of its central funds. In the year 1948 the old Ecclesiastical Commissioners for England were amalgamated with Queen Anne's Bounty to form the Church Commissioners. The new body took advantage of the opportunity to invest a suitable proportion of their assets in equities instead of land and gilt-edged securities and so succeeded in doubling their income. The benefit of this increase was passed on for the most part to the clergy. The improvement in the handling of endowments was met by a considerable increase in the generosity of voluntary gifts. But this did not happen without special effort. When the value of money is declining it is almost inevitable that relief should come much more slowly to the officers of voluntary societies than to those of governmental and industrial concerns. It is an aphorism that in such circumstances 'charities are the first to suffer'. The danger was not avoided in this instance. But at least help came before it was too late, and in making the clergy better able to do their work it was an added assistance to the spiritual task of the Church.

A further material aid to evangelization was afforded by the tremendous advance in the efficiency of radio and television. Here at least the Church was not slow to use its opportunity. In the fifteenth century the ecclesiastical authorities had been among the first to see in the printing press an aid to their own particular propaganda, and the Bible had been among the earliest of printed books. So now religion had still so widespread an interest among the bulk of the population that it was worth while for those who controlled the new means of publicity to devote a good deal of time to it in their programmes. Indeed, it was thought at one time that this use of the air might turn out to be the most effective instrument of evangelization. Although a 'radio mission' undertaken in Scotland disappointed such expectations, it is undeniable that the wide diversity of presentation, from academic discussion to solemn worship, has succeeded in reaching many who hitherto were either ignorant of, or indifferent to, institutional religion. These programmes have also brought religious consolation to many who, for one reason or another, have been unable or unwilling to attend church. They have proved an untold blessing to the sick and bed-ridden. At the same time the gradual increase in church attendance, which became evident during the period, suggests that they have not, on the whole, combined with other attractions to keep possible church-goers at home. A further and not unimportant effect of these programmes is that they have served to make Anglicanism much better known and understood throughout the world. The coronation of Elizabeth II brought to the continent an entirely new understanding of the ethos of the Church of England. This new understanding, as we shall see, had an interesting bearing on the relations between the churches.

Biblical Theology and the Church

In the last chapter we saw how the rise of Anglo-Catholicism had put a new emphasis on the doctrine of the Church. Interest in this element of theology began to take on a special force outside the ranks of the recognized followers of the catholic revival. It was assisted by a new fashion in the study of the scriptures known as Biblical Theology. The title may have seemed a little wounding to those who had always thought they derived their theology from the Bible, but it stood for something that was almost universally welcomed, a combination of practised techniques and new insights.

Biblical theology carried forward the reaction we have already noted against the almost purely literary studies of the previous generation. It did not surrender the conclusions reached, but went beyond them to appropriate more fully the positive ethical and spiritual content of the Bible. It was less anxious to explore the field of comparative religion than to interpret scripture by scripture. It insisted on regarding the Bible as a unity, containing one message from cover to cover. It recognized the significance of its historical chronicle and the means used by criticism to elucidate it, but it saw that the religious importance of this history was in its exhibition of the action of God. It concentrated its own interest almost entirely upon that aspect of it, upon its *heilsgeschichte*, or history of salvation. This treatment laid tremendous stress upon the differentia of the Bible. It implied that there was a marked difference between what could be known from the Bible and what could be learned elsewhere. Revelation was revelation, and it was to be found in the Word. The fact that this term Word or Logos was ambiguous and could be used just as validly of the eternal Son of God as of the scripture tended to throw a numinous atmosphere about the latter and to put what used to be known as natural theology completely in the shade.

Anglicans, after their fashion, were inclined to water down this teaching and not to let it carry them far from their characteristic humanism. Nevertheless, they found it made an interesting combination with their own special emphasis on the Church. After all the Bible *was* a church book. Hoskyns and Davey had shown that the gospels were imbued with a common, if unconscious, effort at interpretation. That interpretation expressed the mind of the early generation of church folk among whom the narrative had developed and assumed its current form. Professor Kilpatrick and Archbishop Carrington were soon trying to show that St Matthew and St Mark respectively were actually arranged as lessons to be read in church. S. C. Easton in America had performed the same service for the Fourth Gospel in lectures to his pupils as long ago as the end of the First World War. If the influence of the Church was probably at work in the composition of the documents, it was clearly there for all to see in the definition of the Canon. Everyone knew that the Palestinian Jews had settled the canon of what we know as the Old Testament at the Synod of Jamnia in AD 90 and that the Alexandrian Jews had included in their canon of the Septuagint also the books we know as the Apocrypha. Whichever was the right canon it was without doubt of churchly arrangement. Similarly in regard to the New Testament. It was the Church that decided which books should be included and which excluded. The struggle was prolonged and it was not until St Athanasius in the fourth century that we find a list of books precisely the same as our own. And when that list was finally authorized, it was the Council in Trullo (692) that acted on behalf of the whole Church in removing all doubt and prescribing exactly what books were to be accepted as sacred Scriptures.

Whatever, therefore, happened on the Continent, in the Anglican Communion the Bible and the Church went together, and Biblical Theology did not lose sight of the Church. This can be seen by way of illustration in the work of William Temple, Archbishop of Canterbury. Beginning life on the liberal side, and with suspected leanings towards Modernism that made some think him a doubtful candidate for ordination, he became more and more interested in the Church and sacraments. In his preface to the *Report on Doctrine in the Church of England* (1938) he contrasts the position of Anglicanism with those of Rome, of Wittenberg and of Geneva, and, finally rejecting them all, decides that the closest parallel to the Anglican Communion is to be found among the Eastern Orthodox. His successor at York, Dr Garbett, did not profess to be a theologian but towards the end of his life he wrote a fine trilogy of books which sought to elucidate the special character of the Church as he had known it. Garbett's successor at York, Dr Ramsey, had already in 1945 published what he described as an essay in biblical theology, *The Resurrection of Christ*, in which the place of the Church is fully emphasized.

The special interest in the Church thus started by the Oxford Movement and developed among the biblical theologians spread beyond the borders of Anglicanism and found a timely echo among the Free Churches. The Methodist Dr Flew gave evidence of that interest in his widely read *Jesus and his Church*. The Barthian emphasis on revelation as against natural theology had its counterpart in the recognition on all hands that if it was to do its work properly 'the Church must be the Church'. The end had come of the period when the main object of theologians and pastors alike had seemed to be to commend the Church to the world by showing how little difference there was between them. It became now a fundamental point of theology, held in common by Anglican and non-conformist alike, that Jesus had intended to found a visible church and that that church was intended to be one and indivisible. This decision, once recognized, marked the beginning of a new epoch.

The Rise of Ecumenism

It is, of course, clear that once the Christian world had made up its mind on this point and had realized that it could not be content with the idea of an invisible, a spiritual or gathered church, it must begin to make the most strenuous efforts possible to reunite the *disjecta membra* of the ecclesiastical organization as it currently existed. There were other less fundamental, but more immediately practical, reasons why such efforts should be set on foot without delay. The general decline in morality and the retreat from religion since the First World War indicated that it was high time for Christendom to close its ranks. Further, in the mission field the resurgence of political nationalism had been accompanied by a revival among such religions as Buddhism and Mohammedanism, to say nothing of some varieties of Hinduism. This revival was giving a good deal of anxiety to Christian workers overseas, especially as it was in some cases even beginning to copy Christian methods by sending missionaries to the West. The extremely disunited condition of Christian missions was a cause for scandal and a source of weakness too obvious to be any longer tolerated. In view of the increasing challenge of other faiths it was very necessary for Christians to show the utmost possible unity.

But these practical reasons were not so powerful as the simple recognition that unity was the will of the Church's Founder. It will never be wholly explicable why in some particular generation the wind of the Spirit will breathe on some special passage of Scripture and make it live afresh in the hearts of the hearers and move them to new and unprecedented vigour. In the previous century some such breath had brought new life to the apprehension of the command, 'Go into all the world and make disciples of all the nations', with the consequence that the nineteenth had become the greatest of all the missionary centuries in the long history of the Christian Church. In the present century the same lively attention was given to the prayer, 'That they all may be one', with the consequence that the movement towards re-union became much the most important feature of contemporary religious history.

In view of her own peculiar history it was almost inevitable that the Anglican Communion should take a leading part in this movement. Her old isolation had now disappeared. Her commitments in many parts of the world had brought her in contact with most nations, and although she was very far from being generally understood, there was a growing knowledge that she claimed to bridge the gulf between the pre- and post-Reformation worlds. She had, indeed, in her own membership some who laid greatest store by their historic connections and others who boasted most of their modern character. As a body, therefore, she could hold out a hand to either side and offer her services as a 'bridge church'. Although the suggestion offered a chance of easy ribaldry to cynics, who affirmed that the bridge was unsafe at both ends, interest steadily grew. It was, at least, intriguing to find a church that had already done what many were trying to do and had united both catholic and evangelical in one fellowship. There was little evidence of the same experiment elsewhere. The nearest parallel was in the national Church of Sweden, but that was definitely a Lutheran church and was, therefore, more completely committed to the theology of the Reformation than was the Anglican.

The actual history of the movement towards Christian reunion can be passed over the more rapidly since it has acquired a considerable literature of its own. But as far as Anglicans are concerned it should be noted how large a part of the incentive came from overseas. The provinces in the United States and Canada, which had taken the initiative in the summoning of the first Lambeth Conference, were equally forward in the initiation of the reunion movement. It was due to their pressure that the famous Quadrilateral was drawn up, the four points to be claimed as a basis of union—the Bible, the Creeds, the two Gospel Sacraments, and the Historic Episcopate. These were eventually (1888) interpreted as follows:

'A The Holy Scriptures of the Old and New Testaments, as "containing all things necessary to salvation", and as being the rule and ultimate standard of faith.

B The Apostles' Creed, as the Baptismal Symbol; and the Nicene Creed, as the sufficient statement of the Christian Faith.

C The two Sacraments ordained by Christ Himself—Baptism and the Supper of the Lord—administered with unfailing use of Christ's Words of Institution, and of the elements ordained by Him.

D The Historic Episcopate, locally adapted in the methods of its administration to the varying needs of the nations and peoples called of God into the Unity of His Church.'

On this basis the first steps had been taken in the period between the wars. The Lambeth Conference of 1920 had issued 'An Appeal to All Christian People' affirming that the Anglican bishops would be ready to exchange the laying on of hands in recognition of appointment to the ministry with the leaders of any church that was prepared to accept such terms of union. This was a dramatic gesture which challenged the attention of the whole Christian world, and made reunion a practical issue. It had the great merit of calling attention to the one overriding consideration of the whole discussion, namely the provision of a ministry commonly acceptable to the participating churches.

The catholic section of the Anglicans were quickly off the mark. In the following year, under the leadership of Lord Halifax and Bishop Gore, they began conversations with Archbishop Mercier of Malines about the steps that would be necessary before there could be any inter-communion between the Roman and Anglican Churches. These conversations never became official, although both the Pope and the Archbishop of Canterbury were cognisant of them. They lingered on for five years but were finally broken off in 1926 by the orders of the Papacy, when it realized that there was no prospect of submission on the part of any considerable section of Anglicans.

In the meantime discussions had been going on with the Eastern Orthodox. In 1922 the Ecumenical Patriarch recognized that the

Anglican orders were valid in the same sense that the Roman orders were valid. This recognition was also accorded by several other of the Orthodox Churches. It was hoped that a future Ecumenical Council would complete the establishment of full inter-communion between Orthodox and Anglican Churches, but the exigencies of world-history have made the summoning of such a Council impossible and there seems no early prospect of it being held.

A greater measure of success attended discussions with the Old Catholics, a body consisting of the old Jansenist church of Holland combined with the followers of Dr Döllinger (who had left the Roman communion after the publication of the Infallibility decree in 1870). With them the Polish National Church (now mostly in exile in USA) is closely associated. With these Old Catholics complete inter-communion was effected. The bishops of both sides share in each other's consecrations and the faithful are freely admitted to the sacraments in each other's churches. Not quite such close accord has been reached with the National Church of Sweden, but at least we recognize the validity of each other's orders, the bishops of either church have shared in the consecrations of the other, and the faithful of either are admitted, as a matter of hospitality, to the altars of the other.

While it was making these efforts on its own behalf Anglicanism was caught up into the main stream of the wider Ecumenical Movement. This movement was given an executive organization when the World Council of Churches was formed in 1938. The work it inaugurated was held up by the outbreak of the Second World War, although its members were able to maintain some sort of contact with each other even across the closely guarded frontiers. When the war was over and the Council was able to proceed with plans for a great ecumenical gathering, it had the encouragement of one great and unprecedented development. There had been many instances of union between churches that had the same general ethos and background. Many of the points of doctrine or organization that caused differences and actual splits in the post-Reformation period had since diminished in importance and had been judged too trivial to keep brothers apart. Consequently, many Methodist bodies had effected union with one another as had also many Presbyterian. But it had seemed unlikely that it would be found easy to bring about union between churches from opposite sides of the great Reformation divide. Yet something very like that had just happened in the mission field. In 1947 a Church of South India had been inaugurated in which were included Anglican dioceses together with missions of Methodist and Congregationalist parentage. It is true that, in order to effect that union, the Anglican dioceses had had, temporarily at least, to go out as a body from the Anglican communion, but it was confidently expected that after an interim period, during which the South Indian ministry would become wholly episcopal, inter-communion between the Church of South India and the Anglican churches would be fully effected.

It was, therefore, with a good deal of encouraging experience behind them that the various denominations joined together in the first great Ecumenical Conference at Amsterdam in 1948. Practically all the great churches were represented with the exception of the Roman Catholics. The Anglicans entered the Conference with full numbers but not such hopes as some, who expected that the result of so great a gathering would be the immediate breaking down of all denominational barriers. In any case, their own influence was not likely to be very obvious. They had no speaker who commanded general attention as did the continental theologian Karl Barth or the Czech communist Professor Hromodka. Nor could they offer anything like the financial support of the Americans. Nevertheless, they did add weight to the determination to carry on. They also helped to define the nature of the movement as something more than Pan-Protestant, and of the World Council as in no sense a super-Church. The object of the Council would be not to initiate schemes of re-union but to offer a forum for the discussion of inter-church affairs, to frame an organization for the presentation of Christian views on international affairs, and to offer material help in every kind of international difficulty or disaster that might befall.

This careful limitation in the scope of the movement, as represented by the World Council, was not universally understood, particularly in America. Those for whom Christianity was mainly a sentiment and for whom confessional allegiance had no strong meaning became impatient at the delay in effecting practical results. Greater hopes than ever centred in the second great assembly held at Evanston, a suburb of Chicago, in 1954. As far as numbers are concerned this must be reckoned as one of the greatest assemblies in Christian history. Indeed, the numbers were so great that the sense of intimacy was largely lost. It was recognized from the outset that proper debate would be impossible, and consequently a report was drawn up in advance, which the members were instructed to reject or accept but not to amend. The result was that the assembly did none of these things. It neither accepted, nor rejected nor amended; it contented itself with passing on the report to the constituent churches and commending it for careful study.

It was in the committees that on this occasion the best work was done, and it was there that the fundamental division between catholic and protestant interpretations of the common faith became most clearly recognized as the greatest barrier to unity. In this connection a good deal of attention was given to Anglicanism. Its representatives were not alone in insisting that for a proper understanding and practice of the Christian religion due place must be given to the catholic element. In this respect they were supported by some Swedish delegates and a powerful contingent of Eastern Orthodox, to say nothing of the Syrians and Old Catholics. Such a presentation of the case was new in the experience of many members. It was all the more important in that at least it helped forward the intellectual process that must be carried a long way before there is enough mutual understanding to offer ground of hope for the uniting of churches of the ancient with those of the modern tradition.

There was again a good deal of disappointment in America at the meagre results flowing from so gigantic an effort. Some leaders of the movement detected a tendency to despair of anything like organic reunion and a consequent willingness to rest content *faute de mieux* with a mere federation or an agreement to co-operate. Such pessimism was unjustified. Anglicans at least would never regard their ambitions or their duty as fulfilled by so slender a measure of union. It is true that Anglicans as a whole have been slow to rouse themselves to respond to this call. It is true also that even now it is effectively heard by a mere minority among the leaders and that the rank and file of church members have still to be made to obey it. Nevertheless the whole Anglican communion, speaking and acting through its bishops, has taken an official, even a leading, part in the movement and every diocese has its nucleus of faithful enthusiasts who are fully committed to the cause. Their goal, the only goal ever envisaged, is complete organic re-union. It is for this that they are in the movement. For this they have already made considerable sacrifices and are prepared to make more. They are not the least bit likely to be satisfied with anything less. Other people may be attracted by the idea of a great business merger, and others again by a practical scheme to co-ordinate and canalize Christian effort throughout the world. But the one thing in which the Anglican is interested is the knitting together of the Body of Christ. In so far as ecumenism is a means to that end, he is prepared to accept it as the outstanding and most necessary movement of the age.

Part III

ACTIVITIES

CHAPTER NINE

INSTITUTIONS AND SOCIETIES

Origins and objects—SPCK and SPG—Eclectic Society and the Clapham Sect—Church Missionary Society—British and Foreign Bible Society—Colonial (now Commonwealth) and Continental Church Society—The National Society—Church Schools and state aid after 1945—Woodard Schools—Mothers' Union—Church of England Men's Society—Girls' Friendly Society—Church Lads' Brigade, Church Girls' Brigade—Church Army—Industrial Christian Fellowship

No one can expect to understand the nature of Anglicanism who does not give full recognition to its propensity for forming societies. If the habit owes something to the medieval custom of founding a multitude of guilds and voluntary bodies within the small compass of the feudal state, it developed on distinct lines in the post-Reformation period when the establishment had been made secure, and the troubles of the Commonwealth were over.

The earliest of these societies were precisely religious and moral in scope and purpose. Their creation was due to reaction against the low moral standard of the Restoration court and society. We first hear of the Religious Societies, strictly so called, in 1678, when Horneck at the Savoy Chapel and Beveridge at St Peter's Cornhill gathered their earnest young men together in bands modelled on the atheistical clubs that were all too common in the London of that generation. The members met together regularly, put themselves under clerical direction, listened to lectures in preparation for their monthly communion, and above all provided a regular congregation for the daily services in many churches of London and Westminster. They incurred some opposition because they were alleged to lean to the Jacobite side in politics, but the bishops protected them. In Anne's reign they became a natural resort for the high churchmen. During the popularity of that party there were as many as forty of them in the metropolis and they spread through most of the provinces. Samuel Wesley had a flourishing society in his parish of Epworth, so that his son John was no stranger to this form of religious organization when he began the formation of his Methodist Societies. This latter development drew off the most enthusiastic members of the older societies, which seem to have died out about the middle of the eighteenth century.

In the meantime, however, they had been largely responsible for the growth of a considerable offshoot in the shape of the Reforming

Societies or the Societies for the Reformation of Manners. These were not so exclusively Anglican as the Religious Societies, and instead of existing in order to deepen the religious life of the members they were intended to act as a voluntary 'Watch Committee' or 'Council for Moral Welfare'. There were indeed laws and bye-laws whose purpose was to keep the streets and the stage clean, but they were seldom put into execution because few people were willing to give information that would involve a charge before the magistrate. In 1691 several lawyers and others began to band together those who were willing to lay such charges and to press for action to be taken upon them. The members of such groups never kept the third of the penalty that was paid to informers but ploughed it back into the funds of the societies. The movement had the powerful support of Queen Mary, Archbishop Tenison and a number of the bishops. In order to cover a wider range in the search for information they invited the co-operation of the dissenting ministers. This means that they acquired a low church and Whig flavour, which was not at all to the taste of the Religious Societies, whence hitherto they had drawn many of their best members. Nevertheless, before their decline set in the Societies for the Reformation of Manners had spread throughout the country and beyond to Ireland, Scotland and even to America. They were objected to on the ground that they were too inquisitorial and that they attacked only the poorer class of vicious person while those in high society were left to practise vice with impunity. A more cogent reason for their end was that the state was at length roused out of its apathy and saw that the law did its duty. Their cause had thus triumphed. But the fact that between the date of their inception and 1738 they had been responsible for over a hundred thousand prosecutions shows that they had not achieved their victory without considerable effort.

It is against such a background that we have to set the foundation of two of the best known of Anglican societies, both of which still flourish, SPCK and SPG. Their creation was largely due to the energy of a country clergyman, Thomas Bray, who in his parish of Sheldon near Birmingham had shown remarkable skill in the training of children. It was a period when the leaders of the Church were encouraging the clergy to pay special attention to this part of their duties. Bray published several courses of *Catechetical Lectures*, which were widely sold and brought him to the notice of Bishop Compton of London. Compton was responsible for the overseas work of the Church and was at the time specially concerned about the conditions in America and more particularly in Maryland. The Bishop enlisted Bray's interest in the colonial work, and so harnessed the energies of this remarkable man to a task that was to have an effect on the life of the Church both in England and beyond the seas even to the present day. But a country clergyman required powerful backing for such schemes as Bray soon developed. He found it among the societies of which we have been speaking. His most recent biographer says, 'Probably he found his allies among the young men of good standing who constituted the Religious Societies; they could add what he lacked, a social status to approach those eminent in Church and State.'[1]

His great idea was to encourage the clergy to read. For this purpose they needed books and he prepared to supply them by providing local libraries wherever they would be most accessible. This scheme he applied not only to English parishes but to the American colonies. He was bold enough to think that much could be done to civilize the young bloods in English country houses, and to tame their 'ferity', if their type of layman could be induced to join the scheme. The 'Associates of Dr Bray' still continue this work of providing clerical libraries some 250 years and more after its initiation. Although the greatly increased cost of publication has made the task more difficult there are still many of the clergy who have to thank 'Bray's Library' for the chance, not only of continuing their professional reading from the borrowed books, but also of buying some of them cheaply at the end of their year of currency in the library, and so of building up a modest library in their own home.

It was out of the need to make this valuable work financially secure that there arose the most typically Anglican of all societies, the Society for the Promotion of Christian Knowledge (SPCK). When it was seen that Bray could not be expected to find for himself the large sums demanded by the success of his work, four of his friends met together at Lincoln's Inn on 8th March 1699 and formed themselves into a voluntary society. The Venerable Society, as it later came to be called, was not satisfied with providing books for the colonies but began to send missionaries also. One thing led to another: the society soon found itself involved in the educational field. It became responsible for the provision of charity schools, and then began to seek an educational system for the poor of the whole country. Ultimately it became a handmaid to the bishops for almost everything that was needed by the Church at large, so that practically nothing could be done without the knowledge and support of SPCK. In recent years it has become obvious that so wide an expansion of interests could not fit an age of specialization. Today there has been much concentration of effort. There has been a renewed emphasis on the primary purpose of the promotion of knowledge, and the society is now the greatest of the religious publishing and book-selling organizations in the country. Nor has SPCK ever forgotten its overseas obligations. A great deal of its publishing has been for the 'younger' churches in the Commonwealth, and of course has dealt with books in many languages. It was thought at one time that English might become the *lingua franca* of these territories, but rising nationalism has put fresh vitality into racial tongues and the Society's work in this direction may not be eased as much as once was hoped.

SPCK is no longer responsible for finding the missionaries. That task was very early handed over to its daughter society SPG (Society for the Propagation of the Gospel). That society was founded within two years of SPCK, in 1701 to be precise. Bray's connection with Maryland and the fact that he had been made commissary for the Bishop of London for the American colonies made him specially conscious of the need overseas. He himself was responsible for the sending of a couple of hundred missionaries, but he could not continue the work single-handed. The close connection of the Church with the State made for endless delays and at first prevented the one adequate solution, the appointment of overseas bishops. The alternative was the formation of a society for America and the West Indies with the prime purpose of caring for the colonists. Hence the origin of SPG. In the meantime SPCK would still remain responsible for other overseas work. However, the specifically missionary task, apart from the publication of vernacular literature, soon became the sole responsibility of SPG. To its principal care for British emigrants it soon added the evangelization of non-Christian races. At the present time SPG has financial obligations towards more than sixty dioceses and maintains nearly a thousand European missionaries. But perhaps the greatest work it ever accomplished was the maintenance of Anglicanism in the American colonies for eighty years, an Anglicanism strong enough to withstand the shock of the Revolution and to provide firm foundations for the church of the future.

Both these great societies were incorporated by royal charter and were just about as official as they could be. Although in the paradoxical Anglican way they started in purely voluntary fashion and with a continuous stream of unofficial but devoted laymen assisting in their affairs, they have the Archbishop of Canterbury at their head with the diocesan bishops forming a large part of their governing bodies. This close association with authority tends to make them on occasion a trifle stuffy and stodgy. One would have thought that it would have made them thoroughly representative of the Church. But after a century of trial the evangelicals decided otherwise. The Methodist revival, which was sweeping the country, laid as much stress on the conversion of the heathen overseas as of the Christian at home. It was realized that the two established societies were not covering anything like all the ground. They had made the regions within the British Empire their special field, but increasing knowledge of the slave trade was opening the eyes of ardent evangelicals to the needs of heathens in a wider area. Through the initiative of the Eclectic Society, a body of clergymen, and its lay friends in the Clapham Sect, the 'Society for Missions to Africa and the East' was founded in 1799. The first missionaries were not Anglican but German Lutherans, who received part of their training in Berlin and part in assisting at a school started in Clapham for negro boys from Sierra Leone.[2] Wars with France made the East unavailable for missionary enterprise, and it was to Sierra Leone that these first missionaries were sent. But this happy consummation was not reached until 1804; so long had the preliminary negotiations taken.

The work of the new organization had begun with the active assistance of William Wilberforce, and it was he who had negotiated the first steps with the Archbishop and bishops. Official recognition was not sought but mere assurance of friendly interest. So little of that easy commodity appeared to be forthcoming that some of the friends doubted whether it was worth while going on. However, the rest were sufficiently encouraged by the somewhat lukewarm welcome accorded their schemes as to persevere. But the initial coolness on the part of authority tended from the first to mark the society, even after it changed its name in 1812 to that of 'Church Missionary Society for Africa and the East', with a certain partisan character and to make it adopt an attitude of aloofness towards the bishops.* It is true that by 1840 it had twelve bishops among its vice-patrons, but in the actual mission field it showed a tendency to control its own men and money without reference to diocesan policy which was naturally galling to the diocesan bishops. Difficulties were almost inevitable when it was the bishop who granted the licences while it was the society that paid the stipends of the missionaries. Such difficulties were bound to come to a head when you had an exceptionally capable bishop like George Selwyn and a self-opinionated committee[3] like that of Henry Venn both regarding themselves as responsible for the work in the same area. It is indeed a testimony to the Christian character of all concerned

*The fullest account is in Eugene Stock's three-volume *History of the Church Missionary Society*, 1899.

that the tensions and conflicts were never allowed to assume disruptive proportions.

In any case these troubles proved to be not much more than the growing pains of adolescence. As the Church became less afraid of evangelicalism and the evangelicals took church organization more completely into their system the society grew until it became what has been described as the largest voluntary missionary society in the world. However that may be, it has at the moment nearly a thousand missionaries in the field and its annual contributions to the work amount to £652,000.

Since we have discussed the CMS it seems almost inevitable that we should go on to mention two other organizations of strongly evangelical flavour, whose origin dates from much the same period, the British and Foreign Bible Society and the Colonial and Continental Church Society.* The former, familiarly known as the Bible Society, is not actually an Anglican society, as it includes a large non-conformist element in its governing body, but it was predominantly Anglican at the start and is fairly representative of at least one section of Anglicanism. The combination is less irksome than it is in some fields because the sole object of the Society is to print and publish copies and translations of the 'Authorized Version, without note or comment'. Its productions can therefore be used without fear or hesitation by most if not all of the myriad Christian organizations.

The British and Foreign Bible Society started in 1804 and arose originally out of the need for providing Bibles in Welsh. There was a story of a little Welsh girl 'who had walked over the mountains every week to read and learn the Sunday's text, since she had no Bible of her own; and who, when she had saved up pence enough to buy a Bible and had walked thirty miles to get one, found that not a copy was to be had'. It is a harrowing story, but the blame should not have been laid at the door of SPCK. It was, of course, the duty of the Privileged Presses to keep the Welsh Bible in print since they had the monopoly, but SPCK, which was largely Welsh in origin, had always had a soft spot for Wales and had done what it could. It had distributed five large editions of ten to twenty thousand each between 1716 and 1799.[4] That was a not altogether discreditable effort for a voluntary society with many other irons in the fire.

However, a happier note was struck when it was asked, 'if Bibles were to be printed for Wales, why not for the British Empire and the World?'

*The old 'Col and Con' has now changed its name to that of 'Commonwealth and Continental Church Society'.

On that broad foundation the Bible Society was erected into the biggest Bible-distributing organization ever known. It has been the handmaid of nearly all the great missionary organizations, and has translated the Scriptures into almost every known tongue.

In contrast to the Bible Society the Commonwealth and Continental Church Society is thoroughly Anglican and is even more strongly evangelical in the party sense of that word. It owed its inception to a Devon man, Samuel Codner, who made a fortune in Newfoundland and was shipwrecked on his way home. He vowed that if he survived he would devote his wealth to the extension of Christ's kingdom. This combination of the medieval and the evangelical spirit resulted in the foundation of the Newfoundland School Society in 1823. It widened its scope to general evangelization of the colonies and was so refounded in 1838, acquiring its middle name in 1861. The continental element in its title covers the provision of chaplains for English communities in many of the larger towns and health resorts of Europe. In the days when British residents on the continent were numerous this was an important work. Their comparative wealth enabled them to build many churches, and even where there arose no Anglican churches it was often possible to arrange for services during the holiday seasons in hotels or in the churches of other denominations. The work still continues although the British have been to some extent replaced by Americans, and there are other agencies besides the Commonwealth and Continental Church Society which provide resident or temporary chaplains.

We get back to the atmosphere of the older societies when we turn to the field of education. It seems odd that up to a century ago all the education of English youth was in private hands. The state had not even begun to wake up to its own privileges and responsibilities in the matter till 1816, when a Select Committee of the House of Commons was appointed to enquire into the education of 'the lower classes of the metropolis'. Even so it was seventeen years before the first grant of public money was voted for the erection of school buildings. Before that there had been a long history of voluntary effort. In the medieval period education in all its branches had been in the hands of the Church, and the cathedrals had played a conspicuous part in the provision of schools. During the Tudor period many grammar schools were founded by private individuals, among whom ruling monarchs were proud to be counted. Such schools were deliberately intended for the education of a governing class. It was not until the eighteenth century that much attention was given to the poor. The population was increasing rapidly, and the young were growing up in crass ignorance.

In 1781 Robert Raikes of Gloucester founded the first Sunday School, in which the children of both sexes were given the basic elements of education not only in religion but in secular subjects. Raikes' efforts were ably seconded by Hannah More and a long list of noble-hearted volunteers. An opportunity of fuller education was given to the children of the poor in the Charity Schools, one of the most typical of eighteenth century institutions. In them boys were taught reading, writing, arithmetic and the church catechism, while the girls generally replaced arithmetic with sewing or some other domestic accomplishment. The children wore a special dress and assembled annually in some cathedral or great church for a special service and sermon, when their singing seldom failed to draw tears to the eyes of the more generous and sentimental portion of the vast congregation. In the foundation and maintenance of such schools SPCK played a distinguished part.

One of the main difficulties in the way of popular education was, then as always, the provision of teachers. Two men, Andrew Bell, a military chaplain to India, and Joseph Lancaster, the Quaker son of a Chelsea pensioner, independently arrived at the same way of solving the difficulty. They set the older boys as monitors to teach and exercise discipline over the younger. Their method was generally approved and accepted, but not unnaturally there was a difference over their respective attitudes to the teaching of religion, Bell being staunchly Anglican while Lancaster encouraged a liberalism bordering on indifference. The supporters of the latter were first in the field with the foundation of a series of 'British' schools from 1808. Successful as they were, they were easily eclipsed by the National Society (1811) for the Education of the Poor in the Principles of the Established Church. Here again the stalwarts of SPCK did yeoman service. Joshua Watson acted as treasurer until he resigned rather than accept a grant from public funds. Luckily his colleagues were not of quite so stern a breed and they left the door open for the state to begin to take its proper place in the education of the poor. Even so it was not until the Forster Act of 1870 that government undertook to ensure, by the compulsory establishment of school boards, that there should be a sufficient supply of public elementary schools for every district in the Kingdom. Until that date the National Society had been responsible for the greater part of elementary education. Henceforth the 'dual system' was established in which an increasing portion of the burden was taken over by the state. 'National' schools still exist, and many of them have been rebuilt and re-equipped under the education acts of the twentieth century. It is noteworthy that, owing to the social changes of the present generation, many of the clergy have received in them the earliest stages of their own education.

As a result of a century and a half of work in the educational field, with all its ups and downs, there are still nearly 8,000 schools in England and Wales provided by the Anglican Church. Many believe that a great opportunity was lost at the time of the 1944–5 Acts. The Church might then, in view of the generous aid offered by the state, have advanced its position. In fact, however, the Church was suffering from the post-war anxiety about finance. The bishops were hard pressed to find a living wage and a suitable dwelling house for their clergy. Church buildings were not being restored without some expense to the ecclesiastical organization. From the money raised for education a considerable slice had to be devoted to the training colleges for teachers, which in the opinion of a proportion of the hierarchy were even more important than the schools. The effect of these factors was to make many of the local authorities adopt the easy alternative of becoming 'controlled', that is, to fall under the managerial control of the state, which was ready in the case of such schools to defray all costs while the Church retained the buildings. The financially stiffer alternative was to accept 'aided' status. This meant that the Church retained managerial control while the state assisted with heavy grants, which were actually increased by an amendment act in 1959. It is obvious that, of the two, 'aided' status is much more advantageous to the Church, but the effect of poverty was such that only 3,434 schools remained in that category (serving 429,636 pupils), while 4,411 (serving 475,535 pupils) became controlled.

It may seem surprising that secular pressure did not secure the abolition of the dual system, that is, partnership between Church and State. But the fact is that quite a proportion of the experts were and are in favour of maintaining some variety in the national system. Also there is a much happier relationship between the Church and non-conformity than there had been in the old days of the conflict between National and British schools. Further the difficulty of maintaining differing standards of religious teaching was met by the practice of arranging an agreed syllabus among the various denominations to be used by all, while a diocesan syllabus could be used in aided and Sunday schools to give specifically Anglican teaching.

It is interesting to note that keen as many of the English clergy are on their schools, their enthusiasm is surpassed by that of their colleagues overseas. Perhaps it is the daily contact with rival faiths that makes the latter especially glad of the opportunity to teach the young. Certainly they show themselves eager to do so, although the overseas churches have not the same hereditary association with elementary education as is the case in Britain. They have shown a laudable desire to co-operate with the state, and, where allowed, have provided in the ordinary curriculum the specific religious teaching which the state regards as outside its own competence. In Queensland, for instance, Anglicans make full use of the primary schools provided by the State. Denominational teachers are allowed a 'right of entry' and the Anglican clergy are well known for their practical application of the privilege. This, indeed, is shown in ordinary clerical parlance. The normal incumbent, if asked what is the size of his parish, will reply, 'Oh I have three churches and seven schools'—or whatever the correct number may be. He links the schools with his churches as the scene of his activities, although they are not his schools at all, but state schools in which he has merely the right to act as a visiting teacher in his own subject. Generally speaking his visits are fully appreciated by the school staff. The effect on the clergy is excellent, since they realize that in such circumstances it is an essential part of their training to learn the art of the teacher.

But to return to conditions in Britain. While this development of elementary education was going on, many of the old grammar schools had risen in the scale of importance to become great 'public' schools—the most typical element in English education, the training ground of the ruling class, in which character rather than learning was deliberately inculcated. Most of them are of Anglican foundation but sit rather loose to the official connection. They aimed to turn out Christian gentlemen, with the emphasis on the latter word. In 1848 Nathaniel Woodard, a hard-working parish priest, published his *Plea for the Middle Classes*, and founded a society to extend the privileges of the best form of educa-tion to them, especially to their poorer sections. The result has been the creation of a network of 'Woodard Schools' all over the country, where Anglican life and teaching can be seen at its best. More 'churchy' than most of the older schools they nevertheless reproduce the typical public school ethos and training. Indeed they are reckoned as public schools of a high standard and the best of them are among the leading schools of the country. The pity is that they find it no easier than do other schools to ensure the fulfilment of their founder's ambition to establish unity in education 'among the several classes of society'.

We come now to a group of societies which for want of a better name we can only call domestic. They are worthy of that name because they cater for the various sections of a home or family—the mother, the father, the girls, the boys. Thus there is the Mothers' Union, the Church of England Men's Society, the Girls' Friendly Society, the Church Lads' Brigade, the Church Girls' Brigade. They all belong to the nineteenth century flowering of Anglicanism. They had a difficult passage during the Second World War and, in the social upheaval that followed, it seemed doubtful whether they would survive. They seemed almost part of the capitalist society which was now rapidly disappearing. There were some devout Anglicans who thought it might be as well to let them disappear for another reason: they were only too successful in isolating the various sections of the family. Was not the right idea to get the family to worship together as a whole? Ought not father, mother and children to sit in the same pew together? Then why encourage this sectionalism? However, it was realized that each section of the family has its own particular interests, which it prefers to follow with people of its own age. This was no reason why the whole family should not present itself as a self-contained unit for worship on Sunday. So after a short period of struggle and readjustment the societies settled down to a new term of usefulness, if not with quite the same numbers, at least with quite as much enthusiasm as before the war.

Of these societies the Mothers' Union is by far the biggest and most important. It owed its inception to Mary Sumner, whose husband was son of the Bishop of Winchester (Charles Richard Sumner) and nephew of the Archbishop of Canterbury (John Bird Sumner). She had begun by gathering together the women of her husband's parish of Alresford,* and bound together thirty or forty of them in a Mothers' Union in 1876. To-day it has over sixteen hundred branches and more than half a million members. It was incorporated by Royal Charter in 1926. Its objects are:

1 to uphold the sanctity of marriage;
2 to awaken in all mothers a sense of their great responsibility in the training of their boys and girls;
3 to organize in every place a band of mothers who will unite in prayer, and seek by their own example to lead their families in purity and holiness of life.

How far they succeed in these objects is beyond the capacity of human judgment to tell. But they have certainly made a powerful impression on the present generation in regard to the first. It is quite possible that the modern relaxation of the marriage tie would have gone even further, if it had not been for the steadfast opposition to divorce

---

*It is said that the first time they arrived at the Vicarage Mrs Sumner was so terrified at having to address them that she ran upstairs to fetch her husband to do it for her.

put up by the Mothers' Union. Their programme has provided a rally-ing point for all those elements of society that have the stability of marriage most at heart.

In England the close limits that confine the objects of the Mothers' Union to moral and spiritual issues have been a marked advantage. Whether the limitation has been so great a boon overseas may be questioned. It is true that there are branches of the Mothers' Union in all parts of the Commonwealth and that even native converts are enlisted in the movement. But especially in Canada, as also to some extent in Australia and New Zealand, the Union is less strong than in England, while in the USA it scarcely exists. The reason is that in these areas a strong women's organization, generally known as the Women's Auxiliary, already exists in practically every parish. It is true that the main object is that of raising funds for necessary purposes. Parochial finance largely hinges on their efforts and they are quite indispensable. But there is not room for two great women's organizations in a single parish. Now that new methods of financing the parishes are being developed it is possible that a fresh and more specifically spiritual turn may be given to the work of such societies for women.[5] This would bring them much nearer to the spirit and function of the Mothers' Union.

The parallel society for men is the Church of England Men's Society. It is not, as its name might seem to suggest, confined to Englishmen.* Not only has it branches in other parts of the British Isles but it is strong in its affiliated societies of Australia, New Zealand and South Africa. In Canada, and to some small extent in USA, the same needs are met by the similar but unrelated Society of St Andrew.

The CEMS arose through the amalgamation of some small men's organizations in 1899 under the glamorous leadership of bishops like Cosmo Lang and Arthur Foley Winnington-Ingram. It spread during the remaining years of the century like a prairie fire. The easy and rapid growth may have been partly due to the fact that the rules of member-ship were not at all exacting. It was stricter than the Mothers' Union in confining itself to communicants, but it did not narrow down its aim to a particular social purpose like that of upholding the sanctity of marriage. Its rule of life was simply expressed: 'In the power of the Holy Spirit, to pray to God every day, to be a faithful communicant, and by active Witness, Fellowship and Service to help forward the Kingdom of Christ.' In effect, however, the emphasis has always been on the importance of work for the Church.

*A movement is on foot to facilitate expansion overseas by leaving out the reference to the Church of England in the title and calling the organization simply 'The Men's Society'.

The rapidity with which the movement spread was nearly its undoing. The membership became marked for quantity rather than quality, and numbers were regarded by those who had not seized the true inwardness of the movement as an end in themselves. It became easy to regard the local branch of CEMS as a mutual entertainment society. Two world wars were a severe test of its sincerity. Members who had been drawn away by the necessities of national service had to ask themselves whether it was worth rejoining, and such members of the clergy as had been compelled during the darkest days to fulfil their task without it, inevitably asked themselves whether it was worth the labour of restarting. For a short time the fate of the Society hung in the balance, but soon both clergy and laity began to realize how valuable such an organization could be in assisting the Church to take advantage of the situation as the country settled down to the new post-war conditions. The lesson of past mistakes was securely learned; continually growing emphasis was placed on the need for the assistance of the laity both on the material and on the spiritual sides of the Church's work. With the renewed emphasis on work and witness the Society began to re-establish itself in numbers and to enhance its prestige. At the moment of writing it has 1,816 branches and 33,000 members in England and Wales alone.

The Girls' Friendly Society antedated the Mothers' Union by one year. It was in 1875 that Mrs Townsend, disturbed by the dangers attending the lives of girls who left home to work in strange cities, gathered together a few people who were already working individually; and induced them to co-ordinate their efforts and form a nation-wide society. Success was immediate: branches were formed to band the girls together. Suitable provision was made to occupy their hours of relaxation, and hostels were acquired in which they could find homes away from home. It was a period when a large proportion of girls entered domestic service, and it was among them that the Society found its main field of operation. It was thus a typically Victorian piece of welfare-work. With the war years and the consequent changes that came over social conditions, the servant class disappeared and the Society ran into difficulties. These were successfully surmounted: the new class of business girl found the old facilities useful and today in England and Wales alone the GFS has 26,000 members and 1,096 branches.

In the meantime, however, the Society had achieved a great and unexpected expansion abroad. This development was most marked and instructive in Australia. There the social conditions of Victorian England scarcely prevailed, and there was no large class of domestic servants. But girls of a different type showed themselves glad to be brought together to pursue their common interests on a religious basis. The daughters of the local bank manager, doctor, schoolmaster, and parson joined happily with the daughters of the share-farmer and small tradesmen to form an organization of surprising health and vigour, in which team games began to do as much for the training of character as they had already done for the boys of the English public schools.

As a consequence the Society has developed in most countries of the Commonwealth as well as in USA; it has also reached out to many of the missionary dioceses. The flexibility manifested in Australia has shown itself in other countries also, each adapting the general purpose of the Society ('to provide opportunities for growth in knowledge of the Christian way of life') to its own immediate needs and circumstances. This example has even, as we have just suggested, influenced the development of the Society in England and Wales. It has been helped to rid itself of the old Victorian atmosphere of class distinctions and to help girls of almost every type. Relying upon an access of outside aid from the Ministry of Education and from such bodies as the King George Jubilee Trust it has been able to launch out into new works interesting itself in 'protected emigration', the acquisition of new hostels, the organization of holidays at home and abroad, and the provision of an extensive programme of useful and recreational subjects.

Another society that caters for young people is the Church Lads' Brigade with its feminine counterpart the Church Girls' Brigade. The latter is a small body best known in Manchester and the north, but the former is a nation-wide organization with its centre in London.

The CLB was first founded in 1891 at St Andrew's, Fulham, by a committee of which the popular A. F. Winnington-Ingram, later Bishop of London, was a conspicuous member. It incorporated the Gordon Boys' Brigade, whose crest it adopted to become its own badge. Its object was stated as 'to extend the Kingdom of Christ among lads and to make them faithful members of the Church of England or of other churches in communion with it'. To that end it employs a variety of means such as 'drill, physical recreation, games, sports, skills, crafts, and cultural work'. Its members wear a semi-military uniform, and their drum and fife bands are familiar features of many localities. Since the conclusion of the last great war the military atmosphere has been toned down considerably, but the Brigade has every reason to be proud of the contribution made by its past and present members in both world wars. This is shown by its long list of war honours which includes no fewer than twenty-two VCs.

Inevitably there is some friendly rivalry between the CLB and CGB on the one side as against Scouts and Guides on the other. The uniform of the Church societies both for girls and boys and the somewhat stricter discipline have advantages and disadvantages from the point of view of the young, but if the clergy decide for the Brigade as against other organizations it is probably because it is an entirely Anglican organization and they feel happier with something that belongs wholly to the Church.

One of the greatest concerns of Anglicans as of most religious bodies is for the huge mass of industrial workers who appear to be scarcely touched by the appeal of Christianity. In many countries the Church finds itself shut off from the interests and affections of the proletariat. But as usual England shows unique features. Here no open and avowed cleavage between Church and people exists. There is a great deal of ignorance and apathy, but no downright opposition. The average Englishman likes to think that he is on the side of the angels. If you asked him whether he was a religious man he would probably say No, but he would regard it as the greatest insult if you told him he was no Christian. Also from his earliest years, unless he has been brought up in some other denomination, he has been taught to think of himself as belonging to the Church of England. In all probability he was baptized in that faith, and it was some approximation to Anglican worship in which he was trained at school. In later life he may find he has missed Confirmation and consequently he does not become a communicant, but in common with at least half his companions he will expect to be married in the parish church and he will expect to be visited by the parochial clergy both in sickness and in health and to be buried by them when he dies. The C. of E. may be the church he normally stays away from, but nevertheless he always writes himself down C. of E. on formal documents and enjoys a real sense of belonging.

This situation seems ludicrous to many to whom a church means a solid congregation of 'gathered' and convinced Christians, and it is often used as a means of poking fun at the establishment. In reality of course it gives the Anglican clergy the most glorious opportunity of evangelism that exists anywhere in the world. If these people were not C. of E., they would almost certainly drift away to form an anti-religious opposition. From that might soon arise the stark antagonism between Church and people that characterizes so many countries. But in claiming to be C. of E. they lay themselves wide open to such influence as the Church is able to bring to bear upon them.

The problem is, as always, how to exercise that influence. The main effort is made by the clergy in their normal parochial ministrations. Such ministrations have become more difficult in recent years owing to the decreasing number of clergy in proportion to the population. But if house-to-house visiting becomes harder, visits to hospitals and industrial concerns become on the whole easier. Indeed many large stores appoint one or more local clergy as chaplains; government offices have lunch-hour services; and many large concerns have their own religious society or guild. An interesting fact is that the incentive for these enterprises generally comes from below. It is the employees who ask the executives for permission to set such activities on foot. Normally they assume an inter-denominational character but it is naturally the clergy of the national church who are expected to be most active in these undertakings.

Such advances, valuable as they are, still leave almost intact the barrier that is sometimes felt to exist between clergy and laity. An experiment or two has therefore been made in following the French example of 'worker-priests'. Ordained men have been allowed to take work as artisans, in the hope that they may be able to become intimate with their workmates and influence them in the direction of Christianity. It is contended that this is the method of the incarnation exhibited in Jesus himself and imitated by his early followers such as the fisherman Peter and the tent-maker Paul. It is hardly likely that the experiment will attain such notoriety in this country as in France, where the barrier between the Church and the masses is much more obvious. In any case it has not assumed such proportions as to warrant full discussion in this book. One should note however in passing that, if pursued, this method may meet an experiment being made from the opposite direction, that is to say, of ordaining men who already occupy full-time posts in other professions. Such 'part-time' priests would have to overcome the difficulty of serving under two masters, but they would certainly help to fill the depleted ranks of the clergy and they might assist in the cultivation of mutual sympathy of clergy and laity, and so further the cause of evangelization.

In any case we have to recognize that some of the best work undertaken for the evangelization of the masses is being done by two *ad hoc* societies: the Church Army and the Industrial Christian Fellowship, both of which are essentially lay organizations.

The Church Army was founded in 1882 by Prebendary Wilson Carlile, being incorporated ten years later. It frankly copied the methods of the Salvation Army both in its use of bands of musicians to assist its open-air preaching and in its development of a host of social organizations for the relief of poverty and suffering. But it never allowed the band to become essential to its development, and in fact that side of its activities has practically died out, although the silver cornet that Wilson Carlile used to play is still preserved with great reverence in his old church of St Mary-at-Hill. Spiritually the CA has always had behind it the ordered life of the Church with creeds, ministry and sacraments. Its lay officers, known as 'captains' and 'sisters', work under the ecclesiastical jurisdiction of the bishops and clergy, although in all internal matters they are subject to the authority and discipline of their own society.

In recent years the CA has grown into an immense organization covering a network of activities both at home and overseas. It provides officers, both men and women, as parochial workers; it conducts missions in town and country, and maintains vans for the work of itinerant evangelization; it specializes in moral welfare work and keeps homes for mothers and babies in distress; it has whole-time workers constantly on duty in many of the prisons as well as others who pay periodical visits; it has its trained workers among the Scouts and Guides, in youth and social centres and among the defence forces; it has developed a quite considerable press and publications department, acting not only as printers but as film and strip producers; it maintains hostels for working women and men, holiday homes and homes for elderly people; it provides help for disabled men and also for prisoners' families, and even finds room for assistance to distressed gentlewomen and professional men as well as rest homes for impoverished clergy. In fact the Church Army does everything possible to fill the gaps in public assistance for which the Welfare State has not yet succeeded in making provision. At the back of all its efforts there is a strongly evangelistic purpose. Its officers 'strive for conversion, consecration, and loyal churchmanship in those among whom they work' and so endeavour to introduce their protégés to the best available of both evangelical and material worlds.

By the side of this variety the Industrial Christian Fellowship seems surprisingly single-minded and almost academic. It was formed in 1918 by the amalgamation of the Christian Social Union and the Navvy Mission. Its object is to study industrial relations in the light of the Christian ethic and to help the putting into effect of Christian principles in everyday life. Like the Church Army, the ICF trains lay missionaries, but in this case they are not put into uniform as are the officers of the CA. They are expected to make contact with artisans and members of the trade unions, and to try by such personal contact to bridge the gulf between the Church and the proletariat. Their purpose is mostly accomplished in talks during the dinner hour and by the distribution of pamphlet literature which is specially written for such readers. They also do a valuable task in reverse by bringing the results of their experience into the Church's domestic societies, such as CEMS, and so preventing the Church from sinking too deeply into a rut of its own.

To avoid becoming tedious that is as far as we shall go in the story of Anglican societies. It should be realized, however, that we have merely touched the fringe and have not necessarily mentioned the most important. Two others for instance leap at once to the mind, the Children's Society and the Mission to Seamen, each of which continues to do work of tremendous value both to Church and nation. It is hoped, however, that enough has been said to show that the canalizing of enthusiasm in the work of special societies is a marked feature of the Anglican way of life.

CHAPTER TEN

RELIGIOUS COMMUNITIES

Revival of monasticism in nineteenth century—Importance and extent of Anglican monastic movement—Women's communities—Men's communities—Friars—Communities overseas

ONE OF the most striking features of the development of the Anglican Communion during the last hundred years has been the growth of communities of men and women living under vows. This revival of monasticism was due to the inception of the Oxford Movement in 1833. But there were not wanting earlier efforts in post-Reformation Anglicanism at a coenobitic life, nor were there wanting signs in the contemporary situation that some such development would again arise.

P. F. Anson, an interesting example of a Roman Catholic writing sympathetically and with knowledge a standard book on an aspect of Anglicanism, sees the latter signs in the popular recitation of the daily office.[1] From the early days of monasticism the main duty of monks and nuns had been the *opus dei*, the chanting of the seven canonical 'hours' of daily prayer. Cranmer's Book of Common Prayer had condensed these hours into two and brought them within the scope of the average lay congregation. We have already pointed out the popularity of these daily offices in the first half of the eighteenth century. After a lapse the popularity revived among the followers of the Oxford Movement in the second half of the nineteenth century. What more natural then than that the concentrated attention given to this form of piety should direct the interest of those who practised it to the institution from which it sprang?

This may be guess-work. But there is no doubt about the earlier efforts to establish monasticism in the heart of Anglicanism. The first of them was the family community set up by Nicholas Ferrar at Little Gidding near Huntingdon in 1625. The life, charity, and industry that characterized this institution earned the unstinted admiration of people like Charles I, whose Queen had taunted Anglicans with the small aid they gave to devotion, and like Izaak Walton, who immortalized it by his literary genius.

Unfortunately it inspired an equal hatred among the Puritans, who described it as an 'Arminian Nunnery', and whose soldiers sacked it during the Civil War in 1646. It was in any case too much of a family affair to attract many postulants and the effort finally petered out, leaving behind no other offspring than a fragrant memory. A number of distinguished people expressed at one time or another the intention or the hope to found some similar community. John Evelyn wished to combine piety with the new science that produced the Royal Society in some institution of a similar kind. Edward Chamberlayne in 1670 wished to found a Protestant Monastery which should care for the education of young ladies. Anson thinks that these and similar designs were inspired by the example of the old English communities, some of which had, since the Dissolution, set up their houses on the continent, and also by the example of the French communities which were admitted as refugees to this country after the taking of the Bastille.

William Sancroft, when Dean of St Paul's, became the spiritual director of twelve ladies who wished to retire from the world, but unfortunately their leader found an easier way to satisfy her needs by conforming to the Roman Church—a fate that was to prove all too common in the early efforts to establish the Religious Life in Anglicanism. Mrs Godolphin lived the life of a religious, as far as possible, against the unsympathetic background of the Restoration court. Bishop Burnet narrowly stopped Princess Anne from contributing largely to a proposed Protestant Nunnery. Bishop Ken, after he left Wells, ministered to what he described as 'a kind of nunnery' consisting of 'two good virgins', the Misses Mary and Anne Kemys. Better known is the fact that William Law, the Non-juror, acted as director at King's Cliffe, Northamptonshire, to a widow, Mrs Hutcheson, and Miss Hester Gibbon, sister of Gibbon the historian.

Overseas early in the eighteenth century Governor Codrington left £30,000 for the express purpose of founding a religious community under vows. Its main business should be to maintain three hundred negroes on his estates in Barbados, which were to be kept whole, and to practise both medicine and divinity. The terms of the bequest could not, at the time, be carried out in their entirety, although a grammar school was founded and later a famous training college. It is only today that a religious community for men has been started there under the auspices of the Community of the Resurrection, and thus the original intention of the testator at long last is being fulfilled.

In England the foundation of religious houses followed swiftly, after all this preparation, on the emergence of the Oxford Movement.

Newman gathered a few young men together at Littlemore and trained them in an extremely austere manner of life. The group was generally described as 'the monastery', but Newman himself denied that it had any right to the title. In any case, most of its members who had not preceded him actually followed him to Rome after his secession in

1845. A similar fate overtook a group of young men gathered together by Frederick Faber at Elton in Rutland. Its nucleus was a Society of St Joseph instituted for visiting the sick. Faber and seven of his Brothers were admitted into the Roman communion in the same fatal year 1845.

The first great and lasting step, however, had already been taken in 1841 when Marian Rebecca Hughes was dedicated to a religious life under vows by Dr Pusey at St Mary's, Oxford. It was not until eight years later that she became the foundress of the Society of the Holy and Undivided Trinity with its home in Oxford. By that time four other Anglican sisterhoods had been established.

Before going further with the history of the Religious Life in Anglicanism, this may be a good opportunity for considering the extent and importance of the monastic movement. The point may easily be missed, because, by its very nature, monasticism escapes publicity. Certainly today the outsider is generally unaware of the magnitude of this new phenomenon in English life, and even more ignorant of its growth in other parts of the Anglican Communion. Even Anglicans themselves are only dimly aware of what is happening. If they are not in sympathy with Tractarian teaching, they probably still regard the monk and the nun with considerable distrust. Indeed, there is much ingrained prejudice and inherited tradition still to be overcome in this respect. Nevertheless, the spiritual influence of this great development is quite literally incalculable. Statistical sources of a possible estimate are not easily attainable. But it is evident that the property owned by so many communities and the charitable uses to which it is put must make of them an important factor in the national life.

Not even the number of existing communities is easily calculated. The official *Guide to the Religious Communities* issued by the Advisory Council gives the number as 115 but the book already mentioned by Peter Anson makes it 121. The discrepancy is at least partly due to the omission in the former case of institutions such as the Australian Bush Brotherhoods, recruited from priests who make only temporary promises. In any case, it should be realized that the numbers, impressive as they are, refer only to communities, that is whole societies, and not to individual houses, cells or branches, of which any community may possess a considerable number. It is impossible to give any census of the total number of members of these communities, but it is probably safe to say that few, if any of them, are as small as were the 'smaller monasteries' at the first stage of the dissolution during the Henrician Reformation. The popular statement that there are twice as many Anglican nuns today as there were nuns in England at the beginning of the Reformation is probably not far short of the truth.

Another point that is not generally realized is the heartbreaking struggle that this success represents. It is not the opposition from outside the movement that has been so hard to withstand. That after all was to be expected and could be lived down; the gainsayers were gradually silenced by the obvious benefits conferred on society by the 'religious'. It was rather the lack of staying power manifested by the early communities themselves, and their tendency to pass over to the Roman obedience, that created the main difficulty. In addition to the 121 that still persist, Anson lists 65 that have perished through sheer inanition and also 11 that have yielded to Rome. That means that just over sixty per cent have survived. Finally, still using Anson's enumeration, it should be noticed that of the communities that remain 92 are of women and 29 of men.

An interesting question that always arises in regard to monasticism is how it is to be integrated into the normal organization of the Church. In its fourth-century beginnings it was very much a lay movement, and had little to do officially with the hierarchy. In the Greek east the local bishop gradually made his authority felt in any monastery within his own area. The General Councils endorsed that arrangement. In the Latin west, on the other hand, the monasteries managed to free themselves from local episcopal control. After the Cluniac reform in the tenth century, monasteries began to owe obedience to the mother house from which they were founded. This arrangement overlapped diocesan and even national boundaries. The local bishop had perforce to yield his authority to the Pope, who alone could exercise the right of appeal over an international organization. Such orders as the Friars and the later Jesuits stemmed directly from the Papacy and owed direct obedience to it.

In Anglicanism the monastic movement developed against the wishes of the bishops and even against their general opposition. Consequently, for a long time the communities had little relation with the episcopate. But as more sympathetic clergy began to be appointed to the bench, an effort was made to put an end to this anomaly. What is sometimes described as 'a typical Anglican compromise' was reached. An advisory council was appointed, consisting of six members from the communities, six experts nominated by the bishops, together with a diocesan bishop as chairman, placed there by the Archbishops of Canterbury and York. An advisory council, of course, has no authority, but at its meetings suggestions can be made, tension eased, problems thrashed out, and possibilities of dispute circumvented. It must be said that this experiment in the new style of government by consent has so far worked out very well. There is today very little conflict between the religious and the bishops. Most diocesans are only too happy to recognize the good work done by the communities either by continuous intercession in the case of the enclosed, or in the fields of home and foreign missions, of education and charity, in the case of the active societies. Such bishops are glad to show their approval by offering their assistance in any way possible. Some of them are prepared to act as visitors, and some even as wardens of individual communities. If any conflict does arise, it is most likely to be over liturgical practices, the bishops wishing to stand as close as possible to the standard set for the national church, while the societies may wish to exercise the liturgical independence that has generally been accorded to the religious throughout the ages.

But to return to the course of our history. The first religious community to be founded in the Anglican Communion after the Reformation and to achieve a settled existence was the Sisterhood of the Holy Cross. This was in 1845, an event that did something to redeem that otherwise inauspicious year. The moving spirit was Dr Pusey, aided by William Ewart Gladstone, and a group of highly aristocratic laymen.

The somewhat grudging permission of Blomfield, Bishop of London, and Howley, Archbishop of Canterbury, having been obtained, the community was founded as a body of the Sisters of Mercy on the model of the French *Soeurs de Charité*, founded by St Vincent de Paul. It was offered as a memorial to the Poet Laureate, Robert Southey, who had himself advocated the foundation of some such order in the Church of England, but had died two years before it could be accomplished. Its parish was Christ Church, Albany Street, whose vicar William Dodsworth was helpful and sympathetic until, after the Gorham Judgment, he went over to Rome.

In 1848 the sisters were visited by a Miss Lydia Sellon. She had been invited by Dr Phillpotts, Bishop of Exeter, to undertake work in the slums of Devonport, and, desiring to found a community to assist in the task, had come at the instance of Dr Pusey, to see how things were done in the Sisterhood of the Holy Cross. The result was the foundation of the Society of the Holy Trinity at Devonport in 1849. When the Crimean War was under way and Florence Nightingale instituted her nursing organization, sisters from the two communities provided her with some of her most devoted assistants. Collaboration in this field led ultimately to a closer association between the two organizations. In

1856 they were amalgamated and are now known as the Society of the Most Holy Trinity. Its mother house is at Ascot Priory, Berks. The nature and objects of the society have been modified until it has now become a semi-enclosed order. Its purpose is 'the adoration of the Holy Trinity, together with continuous intercession for the conversion of the sinful and the consolation of the dying, to which has been added latterly the unity of Christendom. No work is undertaken outside the convent precincts, but, within their mitigated enclosure, the nuns have a hospital for convalescents and a grammar school for day scholars living in the neighbourhood as well as senior and junior boarders.' A distinctive feature of the community life is that in choir the nuns recite the Sarum Breviary in its entirety.[2]

It was, perhaps, hardly to be expected that the first tentative efforts at the revival of the religious life would be rewarded by a vast accession of numbers. Greater success in this respect was achieved by the next foundation, that of the Community of St Mary the Virgin, generally known as the Wantage Sisters. This community was founded by the Vicar of Wantage, the Rev W. J. Butler, in 1848, with the original intention of doing educational work. Actually it began with moral welfare, adding important educational ventures later, together with mission work at home and abroad, and crowning all with a special interest in the study of plainsong. Today it has no fewer than twenty-six branch houses in England, three in India, and five in Africa.

Another incumbent who was instrumental in the foundation of a great religious order was the Rev T. T. Carter, Rector of Clewer, who was responsible for the Community of St John the Baptist, popularly known as the Clewer Sisters (Windsor, Berks). They were founded in 1852 'to serve God in works of charity'. 'The Community works among women and children who need moral and spiritual help; cares for the sick, aged, and needy; educates the young; and undertakes home and foreign mission work and such other works of charity as it may be called upon and be able to perform.'[3] It now has nine branch houses, all in England.

In 1855, Dr Neale, the noted liturgiologist and Warden of Sackville College (an endowed set of almshouses for the aged poor), founded the Society of St Margaret, East Grinstead. The Sisters began their work by nursing the poor in their own cottages. It soon extended to the neighbouring St Margaret's Orphanage and presently included schools and other educational work. Now there are fifteen branch houses in the United Kingdom, five in Ceylon, and five in South Africa. Also exist three affiliated houses, one of which is the St Margaret's Convent,

Boston, USA. One of the best known and most appreciated works is the home for the dying on Clapham Common.

A somewhat later foundation, the Community of the Sisters of the Church, which flourished in numbers, is often known as the Kilburn Sisters, because it opened an Orphanage of Mercy in that part of North London in close connection with the imposing church of St Augustine's. Actually, however, they were originally founded (1870) in Chester by a Miss Emily Ayckbowm, who had already shown her capacity in the inauguration of the Church Extension Association six years earlier. The community now has its headquarters at Ham Common, Surrey. That it still maintains the intention of its founder is shown by the charge laid upon the Sisters that 'they are called to a life of unceasing toil for the extension of Christ's Church, the salvation of souls and the relief of misery'.[4] This threefold aim is, of course, subject to the prime purpose of every conventual body, 'to perfect holiness in the fear of the Lord'. The community has thirteen branch houses in England together with five elementary schools in London, and it has nine branch houses overseas, three in Canada and six in Australia.

It would be impossible to sketch even in outline the history of the many women's communities. The above must be taken as examples. It will be noticed that they are mainly active communities, their work being done largely outside the chapel, which is the centre of their life and devotion. There are, however, a number of contemplative communities, whose life is confined within the walls of their convent and whose work lies almost entirely within their chapel. Perhaps the best known of these is the Community of the Sisters of the Love of God, whose mother house is the Convent of the Incarnation, Fairacres, Oxford. It began in a small artisan's cottage in 1906, but continued to outgrow such accommodation until by stages the sisters attained their present satisfactory home and beautiful chapel designed in baroque style by Paul Waterhouse. Their founder was Fr Hollings, SSJE, and they have always been supported by the Cowley Fathers whose own mother house is hard by. There are branch houses at Boxmoor, Hertfordshire, and at Burwash, Sussex. 'The spiritual aim of the Community is the contemplative life of prayer, intercession, and reparation. The rule is not founded on that of the Carmelites or any of the older Orders. [It was drawn up by the former warden, Fr Cary, SSJE, who was a well-known authority on the contemplative orders.] The whole of the Breviary Offices are said in English; the Night Hours being said at 2 a.m. There is continuous intercession throughout the day and during part of the night. A strict rule of silence is observed.'[5]

Anson suggests that the renewed desire for the contemplative life was due to the contemporary interest in mysticism aroused by the writing of Dean Inge, Baron von Hügel, Bishop Chandler, and Evelyn Under-hill. Certainly there was much interest in mysticism at the time, but it is noticeable that of the books mentioned only Inge's was published before this sisterhood was founded. It is significant of the drawing together of the 'schools of thought' in Anglicanism that the community was invited by the evangelical Bishop in Jerusalem, Graham-Brown, to establish a branch house in the Holy Land.

The extent of the change seems the more remarkable when it is remembered that another contemplative order, that of the Community of the Servants of Christ had felt constrained in 1918 to move out of the diocese of Chelmsford because its bishop could not allow them to reserve the Blessed Sacrament in their chapel. This enclosed community is now happily established in the House of Prayer, Burnham, Bucks.

It may well be asked what, in the meantime, was happening to the religious life for men. We have already mentioned some of the un-successful efforts to found communities for them. The first to attain stability was the Society of St John the Evangelist (the Cowley Fathers). It was in 1865 that Richard Meux Benson and two companions entered together into a novitiate to try out their vocation to the religious life. During Christmastide of the following year they took their life vows on the feast of their patron St John. The Society was not modelled on any of the great medieval orders but was a new society fashioned after Richard Benson's own knowledge and insight. It was intended to be primarily a society of priests, but laymen were from the first welcomed into it and have provided a valuable element in its common life. Originally expected to be a body of missionary priests for India, the fact that it was founded in Oxford led to its development as an example of the 'mixed' life, a combination of the contemplative and active ideals. As early as 1870 it had expanded sufficiently to allow the opening of a daughter house in Boston, USA, which soon ripened into an independent province. The Society is now an organization of three Congregations of equal status, English, American, Canadian. A Central Council of the whole Society, consisting of the three Superiors and their Assessors, meets every five years. The American congregation has a daughter province in Japan. The English congregation has two provinces besides the home province, one in India, the other in South Africa. Thus the original missionary intention of the Founder has been amply fulfilled.

The second order for men to have achieved world-wide fame is the Community of the Resurrection. It was founded in 1892, by Charles

Gore, who was its first Superior, and later became Bishop of Oxford. Gore and his five priest companions deliberately based their rule on the endeavour to resuscitate the life of the first Christians, who, as we are told in Acts ii, 42–44, 'continued steadfastly in the apostles' teaching and fellowship . . . and had all things common'. Laymen with a trade or a profession are admitted, together with those ordained, into full membership of the Community. After a number of moves the society settled into headquarters in the House of the Resurrection, Mirfield, Yorks, from which circumstance the monks are generally known as the Mirfield Fathers. There they have set up, in close connection with Leeds University, an important college for the training of ordinands. The community has other hostels or training colleges—St Teilo (Cardiff), St Peter's Rosettenville and St Augustine's Penhalonga (S. Africa), as well as Codrington (Barbados). 'There has been a steady growth and expansion of the Community in recent years. The novitiate is now larger than it has ever been. . . . In spite of the enormous extension of exterior work, the founder's ideals are still maintained, of keeping in their right order—Prayer, Study, and Work.'[6]

A third famous community of men is the Society of the Sacred Mission (the Kelham Fathers), founded by Herbert Kelly in 1894. Kelly was the most colourful character among the founding fathers of Anglican monasticism. Since he lived to the age of ninety, he was able to stamp a clear impress of his personality on the work he inaugurated. It began simply as a project for training missionaries for Korea; it so functioned until, four years later, in 1894, the six men who were its backbone realized that what they were doing could be better done by a body of people under vows. Together they entered upon their novitiate and took their present name. From the first they insisted on three points as their guiding principles: freedom of opportunity, thoroughness of education, and reality of sacrifice. Their main work has always been education, with the special intention of enabling boys of the lower middle classes to fulfil their vocation to holy orders. They take the boys at an earlier age than other Anglican training colleges, and so are able to integrate the whole of their life and their religion with a thoroughness that is not usually found elsewhere. Kelly himself was known to say on occasion when his team was losing a football match that 'the boys could not be in a state of grace'. Today there is a magnificent college at Kelham with accommodation for over a hundred students. The Society does much the same kind of work in Australia and South Africa. Individual members also do extensive parochial work both in England and overseas.

A community of special interest, not because of its numbers (it has only about forty members), but because of its intrinsic character and its example of triumph after repeated failure, is the Benedictine House at Nashdom (Burnham, Bucks). Abortive efforts to found a Benedictine establishment in the Anglican Communion had been made at Caldey and Llanthony but the monks had seceded to Rome. A new effort under the inspiration of Lord Halifax was made at Pershore. Again, however, the Superior crossed the border to Rome; the few postulants and novices were left under the care of an oblate, the Rev Denys Prideaux. Fr Denys, however, was a man of considerable genius, a more or less self-taught scholar and linguist, who nursed the community until it grew too big for its home and had to move. It found a new and stately house in Nashdom (which apparently is Russian for 'our home') originally built for Prince and Princess Dolgorovski. There was developed Benedictinism at its purest. The three elements of the common life so strongly insisted upon by St Benedict—prayer, study, and manual work—still maintain their original order of priority. The first is exemplified in the care given to the daily chanting of the Chapter Mass. Dom Gregory Dix, with his brilliant if wayward scholarship, has been a conspicuous example of the second. In addition to normal manual work, the activities of the monks include a certain amount of external clerical labour such as sermons and retreats. It has even included a notable incumbency of All Saints', Margaret Street, by Dom Bernard Clements.

A very different type of the religious life is that practised by the Friars. Everyone knows the effect produced by their early witness to the inspiration of holy poverty, and by their preaching and teaching, in thirteenth century England. It was almost inevitable that in the general resurgence of coenobitic ideas some place should ultimately be found in the Anglicanism of the twentieth century for the expression of this type of service. True, there was no great quantity of lepers shrinking furtively along the country roads and needing loving attention. But during the bad slump between the two world wars there was a terrible amount of unemployment, and many of the sufferers were homeless and tramping the roads. Among them a truly Franciscan type of ministry might be valuable, if it reproduced the original ideals of prayer, works of mercy and apostolic preaching. In 1921 a few men started such a ministry at a farm near Batcombe in the lovely Dorset country. Ten years later the Bishop of Salisbury received the vows of the first three brothers. A number of 'Homes for Wayfarers' had by this time been opened; but as the manhood of the country became absorbed in the new war effort they were handed over for other purposes. The government, however, were anxious for the friars to help with recalcitrant boys from the remand homes. The brothers also took on a school for maladjusted boys at Hooke, Dorset, about ten miles from the parent Friary at Cerne Abbas. Just as the original friars found their work extending to the universities in the middle ages, so their Anglican successors have found a home and a church at St Benet's, Cambridge. Also they have ventured overseas and are now responsible for a training college for Papuan natives in New Guinea. But always their main work is among the poor; and their ministry to the seamen and coloured people of Cable Street, London, E1, is beyond praise.

This account of the restoration of community life in the Anglican Communion has perforce dealt mostly with England, and where it has mentioned other countries it has been to show how the revival spread to them from Great Britain. It would be a mistake, however, to think that other parts of the Anglican communion enjoyed no similar indigenous revival of their own. Australia, for instance, has its own particular version of it in the Bush Brotherhoods that do invaluable work in areas too remote for ordinary parochial organization. It has also a couple of more conventional communities for women wishing to live the full conventual life, the Society of the Sacred Advent (Queensland) and the Community of the Holy Name (Victoria), in addition to several branches of English communities transplanted overseas. New Zealand similarly has two women's communities. India has two for men and one for women, while South Africa has seven for women, three of them especially for natives. But it is in North America that such foundations have been most plentiful. There has been, it is true, the usual crop of abortive attempts. There are now eight communities for men which came to birth there and have attained a stable maturity. The most venerable of them is the Order of the Holy Cross, West Park, New York, founded in 1881. For women there are fourteen separate communities in addition to four that were founded from England.

One feels apologetic for giving so cursory and perfunctory an account of modern monasticism in the Anglican Church. The excuse must be that it assumes so many different forms that no writer, unless he were producing a complete brochure on the subject, could expect to cover all the ground. One may hope, however, that sufficient has been said to give some idea of the extent and importance of the movement. From its very nature monasticism refuses to court publicity and in consequence it is relegated to an obscure place in contemporary histories.

It would, however, be difficult to exaggerate its importance in the external work of Anglicanism of today and even more its effect upon the Church's internal life.

CHAPTER ELEVEN

THE PARSON IN HIS PULPIT

Methods of recording sermons and teachings—The Friars—Preaching at Paul's Cross—Bishop Hugh Latimer—Sermons as a means of argument between Anglicans, Roman Catholics and Puritans—Teaching and exhortation—Liturgical, proclamational and instructional sermons—changing styles of sermons

IT MIGHT naturally be thought that an easy way to discover the genius of Anglicanism would be to examine its homiletical literature. Surely if the character of a church is to be made known, it will be most clearly seen in the exposition of its faith and practice that proceeds in vast quantity from its pulpits.

There is much to be said in favour of this view, and, as we shall see presently, Anglicans have one historical asset that puts them in an uniquely favourable position for making such an effort. However, there are some qualifications to be made in this optimistic estimate of the method. One of the most important arises out of the very style of sermon delivery. It might have been supposed that, since a sermon is by nature a direct appeal in God's name to his people, it would have been delivered *extempore* and would therefore be almost impossible to put on record. We know, however, even from Old Testament examples that that disability is often overcome. It is hardly likely that those whom we call the great Writing Prophets originally proclaimed their message by other means than direct oral address to their audience. Yet somewhere the message got itself taken down and committed to manuscript for the benefit of its own and future generations.

In the New Testament a preacher like St Paul ensured permanence for his teaching by enshrining large portions of it in his correspondence. The tendency of modern criticism is to suggest that a good deal of homiletic material found its way into other epistles, such for instance as I Peter. When we get into the patristic period we find that many of the fathers, while preaching *extempore*, employed a number of shorthand writers to put their utterances into more permanent form. Anglican preachers have from time to time employed all these methods. We have therefore far more material on which to base an estimate than we might have expected.

During the medieval period preaching became a much less normal activity of the clergy, the emphasis of their duty shifting to the sacraments and the confessional. Preaching, however, might break out into violent activity for a special purpose, such as the proclamation of the first crusade by Peter the Hermit. But it really came into its own in the work of the friars, who usurped the function to such an extent that it was hardly even expected of the parish priests. The preaching of the friars was of the homeliest description; it used all the arts of popular appeal, including story-telling, emotional excitation and even visual aids. But being thus simple and direct it was necessarily ephemeral, and we have comparatively few records of it.

In the later middle ages the enthusiasm for the spoken word died down. There were indeed spasmodic efforts on the part of authority to convince the faithful of their duty to hear sermons. In view of what is often said about the failure of the pre-Reformation clergy to preach, it is interesting to find the Bishop of Rochester at the end of the fourteenth century complaining that the laity will go a day's journey to see a wrestling match but will not walk a mile to hear a sermon.[1] It was hardly therefore a case of 'the hungry sheep look up and are not fed'. It was rather that preaching was the friar's *métier*. When his style had lost its appeal, the parochial clergy failed to find anything to replace it until the new learning and the new knowledge of the text of scripture rekindled fires that had been long dead.

The style of the friars was no doubt the same all the world over— except in the universities, where they also had a great vogue and adapted themselves to their learned audiences. Its importance in the history of Anglican preaching is that it formed a model for the first great English preacher after the separation. Hugh Latimer would have been reckoned a great orator in any company, but as an ecclesiastic his eloquence was turned into genuine preaching by his devotion to the gospel, his understanding of affairs, and his interest in people. His courage, his wit, and his journalist's eye for a situation were all made to subserve his real aim, which was to bring his hearers fully and con-sciously within God's plan of salvation.

This is perhaps the best place to mention the great and unique asset possessed by Anglicanism for a general estimate of its preaching. That is nothing less than the institution of St Paul's Cross, which was the great propaganda centre for the whole country. Formally under the control of the Bishop of London, in time of special stress it became of unique interest to the government, and was often used for official pro-nouncements or for partisan purposes. We are fortunate in having a scholarly volume from the pen of Professor Millar Maclure which gives particular attention to the history of the Cross from 1534 to 1642 and even produces a register of sermons for that period—a most welcome contribution from the university of Toronto to the history of Anglicanism.[2]

A cross on this site probably ante-dated the church itself, and marked the place where even in Anglo-Saxon times official proclamations were made and formal assemblies sometimes held. The earliest documentary evidence belongs to 1241, when Henry III met the citizens of London there to discuss with them the question of the French war. The earliest known sermon preached there was on the occasion of the excommunication of Lewis of Bavaria in 1330. A few years later we find the Archbishop of Armagh there, preaching a whole series of sermons against the friars. This was indeed to turn the friars' weapon against themselves. From that time the sermon at St Paul's Cross became a regular feature of English church life. It was there that in Mary's reign (1554) Bishop Gardiner announced that England had been received back into the Papal fold, and there that details were announced of the defeat of the French at St Quentin (10th August 1557).

Naturally the sermon was not always a great occasion calling for a celebrated preacher. Often it was delivered by some young don from the university, who was given an opportunity to prove his worth and attract favourable notice. Such beneficiaries of the Cross were Richard Hooker and Jeremy Taylor. The benefit received was not always immediately obvious or substantial. A young and struggling scholar might not find it easy to pay his travelling expenses or the cost of several days' lodging. The Bishop of London had to solicit the aid of the City to find a suitable resting-place and an adequate fee for the visitor. The City's help, if a trifle grudging, was at least continuous. Even today, although the sermon has been moved from the cross to the nave, the Lord Mayor never fails to send his bottle of sherry for the refreshment of the preacher.

But to return to Hugh Latimer, Bishop of Worcester, who became one of the best known preachers at the Cross.* In 1536 he was there twice. On 12th March he lashed about him in fine style, condemning the hierarchy and the nobility as 'strong thieves' and finding no harm in the eating of meat in Lent and on Fridays so long as 'it be done without hurting of weak consciences'. On 17th June he defended himself against the charge that he had withdrawn what he had previously said about the folly of confession and the worshipping of saints. On 12th May 1538 he had to preach at the condemnation of a friar, John Forest, who had obstinately denied the royal supremacy. Latimer's exhortation to the

*There is an edition of his sermons in the 'Everyman' series.

audience to pray for him resulted in no change of mind and the poor fellow was burnt at the stake ten days later. After this Latimer did not appear at the Cross for ten years, during eight of which he was, according to Stow, altogether silent.

In January 1548 he seems to have preached on eight occasions at the Cross, at one time urging obedience on the part of all, high and low, to the clergy, who 'sit in Moses' chair'; at another drawing his famous analogy between the two ploughs, one for the sustentation of the body, the other for the sustentation of the soul; the one being hindered by enclosures, the other by 'lording and loitering' among the clergy. One of the main characteristics of Latimer's style was his thoroughly medieval use of anecdote. Take for instance his story of the lady who had had a sleepless night and was now going off to the sermon at St Thomas Acres as she 'never failed of a good nap there'. Another was his fondness for personal reminiscence, as when he told how his father taught him to shoot, 'how to draw, how to lay my body in my bow, and not to draw with strength of arms as other nations do, but with strength of the body'. Still another characteristic was his devotion to the good of the 'little man'. He never tired of preaching against the oppression of the poor by the rich. He thought that it was chiefly the yeoman who maintained not only the realm of England but the Kingdom of God. He was never afraid of trying to improve material conditions, and in his last recorded sermon at the Cross on 11th December 1552, he actually complained of the insanitary conditions of St Paul's churchyard. Even the English pulpit, which prides itself on its practicality, has seldom if ever seen such a combination of plain common sense and gospel fervour as was displayed by Hugh Latimer.[3]

His influence on the national style of preaching might have been even greater, had it not been for the terrible controversies in which the preachers of the period were necessarily engaged. If one looks through the early pages of Maclure's register one wonders whether there could have been any spiritual gain at all in such discourses. From 15th January 1534, when the customary prayer for the Pope was first omitted, controversy, even where not openly expressed, always hovers in the background. At Easter that year Cranmer forbade preaching on 'the King's matters', though the speakers could fulminate against the Pope at will. Later that year, from 3rd November to 18th December, each Sunday while Parliament was sitting the Cross was mounted by a fresh bishop, denying that the Pope was head of the Church.

The following year the ill-fated monks of Charterhouse were bidden to attend the sermons at Paul's Cross so that they might learn the error of their opinions. Four of their number, who were doing penance for their refusal to acknowledge the royal supremacy, suffered the mortification on 27th February 1536 of hearing the mild Tunstall, Bishop of Durham, declare the Pope's authority 'usurped'. On 23rd September young Matthew Parker, then Dean of Stoke College, was appointed to preach by Thomas Cromwell, who had heard of his 'learning and uncorrupt judgment', and who no doubt wished to enlist the help of the rising intelligentsia in the King's cause.

On the other hand the doctrinal balance was redressed when two Lutherans had to recant of their heresy. A bricklayer, who had dared to preach from a tub in his garden, was compelled to carry a faggot, a fate shared by a renegade priest who had denied the merit of Christ's passion and the value of exorcizing bread or water. No wonder Hilsey, Bishop of Rochester, on being called upon to preach the sermon at the Cross, said he had never been so afraid in his life. But he had less cause for fear than had the Kentish priest who, on 8th February 1545, did penance for counterfeiting the blood of Christ by cutting his finger and letting it bleed over the host. Nor was he in such bad case as Nicholas Shaxton, formerly Bishop of Salisbury, who on 1st August 1546, wept bitterly while recanting his heresy in denying the corporal presence of Christ in the sacrament of the altar.

The following year saw Edward VI on the throne. The arrival of Lent gave an opportunity for denying that the season had any divine authority. The pace at which the old religious landmarks were being removed was too fast even for some of the advanced guard. November finds Nicholas Ridley complaining of lack of reverence in the approach to the altar. William Barlow, however, the Bishop of St David's, on the last Sunday in that month produced two images, which the St Paul's clergy had carefully hidden in the cathedral, and publicly destroyed them. Writers have not infrequently drawn a parallel between the mendicant friar and the puritan preacher. This readiness to use a 'visual aid' may be reckoned as one of the more intriguing points of the comparison.

The congregation had still opportunity to hear each side of the controversy. Both Gardiner of Winchester and Bonner of London came to clear themselves of the charges made against them by other preachers. They showed themselves pliant on the subject of the royal supremacy but adamant on the corporal presence of Christ in the sacrament. The Duke of Somerset brought in Matthew Parker, now Vice-Chancellor of Cambridge, while Cranmer brought in Hooper, afterwards Bishop of Gloucester, to state the other side. But one of the most powerful preachers was Thomas Lever, Master of St John's Cambridge, who followed

Latimer in inveighing against social injustice. He warned the public against wilful rebellion, and urged that particular attention should be paid to the deplorable condition of the universities.

The 9th July 1553 found Nicholas Ridley, Bishop of London, himself preaching at the Cross and using the occasion to support the claim to the throne of Lady Jane Grey, and declaring both Mary and Elizabeth illegitimate—an ill-fated sermon which was to cost him dear. Even after Mary had come to the throne, John Rogers, afterwards to be martyred, spoke boldly in favour of the religion taught under Edward VI. Protestant preachers were not the only ones who required courage. On 13th August the Queen's chaplain, preaching in praise of Bonner, was attacked by the crowd and rescued with difficulty. The next Sunday the preacher was provided with 200 of the Queen's guard. But on 10th June 1554 Bonner's own chaplain was shot at while preaching and the bullet nearly hit the Lord Mayor. Gardiner and Tunstall of the old guard are still found preaching. On 2nd December the former published, in the presence of the King (Philip II) and Cardinal Pole, the Pope's commission to receive England back into the fold.

With the accession of Elizabeth confusion was at first worse confounded. Preachers flatly contradicted each other, until for nearly six months sermons had to be forbidden. Even after they had been resumed and Grindal on 14th May announced that the Edward VI Prayer Book was to be used again, the canons of St Paul's absented themselves on the ground that they were still using the Latin services. In rapid succession the newly appointed bishops were invited to preach and to show themselves on the principal platform of the Church. Presently Anglicanism began to reveal itself as a particularized form of the Christian creed. On 26th November 1559 John Jewel, Bishop of Salisbury, threw down his first 'challenge to the papists to prove their doctrines by authority'. The old opinions lingered in unexpected quarters. Early in 1561 James Calffeld, Canon of Christ Church, moved the congregation to tears by describing the wiles with which the papists ensnared the young men at Oxford—a complaint repeated by other preachers in 1566–97. Evidently an emotional style of preaching was not yet regarded as bad form.

In the middle of the year catholics and protestants were blamng on each other the catastrophe that had occurred in the burning of the steeple of old St Paul's. Obviously it was a sign of God's displeasure, but against whom? On 26th January 1564 the Romanists were equally condemned for the recent visitation of the plague. When the controversy over vestments became violent in the following year some preachers, by whom appointed is not known, took the opposition side, and Archbishop Parker was moved to suggest to Cecil that preachers at the Cross should in future be licensed. Cecil did thereupon submit a list of preachers suitable for Lent, which was duly settled by Parker. Jewel, who was one of the most frequent and favourite preachers at the Cross, defended the vestments on the not very enthusiastic ground that they were of only secondary importance and not worthy to be made a matter of conscience. Later there were preachers who openly stated that the English Reformation had not yet gone far enough and pleaded for the imposition of the Puritan discipline. These of course had to be answered. Jewel's work was carried on by John Whitgift, then Master of Trinity, later to become Archbishop of Canterbury. By the end of 1581 Richard Hooker, a young Oxford don, joined the list of apologists—and Anglicanism came into its own.

This did not mean the end of controversy. A glance through the subjects mentioned in the remaining pages of Dr Maclure's register is enough to show how urgently the Anglicans had to defend their position against both Papist and Puritan, and how the representatives of the official point of view had to struggle against the fifth column of puritans in their own midst. Indeed there were among the preachers themselves dissidents of many kinds. One fulminates against the King, another against the House of Commons, another against the wickedness of the city and the pride of its merchants. Some are found bold enough to speak against the Spanish match, in spite of express orders to the contrary. Preachers evidently did not let their normal fears prevent them from speaking out on public matters. They were mostly on the safe side in denouncing the Essex rising; but even so it is interesting to find Bancroft leaving nothing to chance, but giving the preacher on that subject a brief which had previously been submitted for Cecil's approval.

Bancroft himself preached a sermon which stoutly maintained the doctrine of the divine institution of episcopacy. A modern note is struck when a preacher bemoans the tendency of the younger members of the clergy to find fault with the bishops. John Donne is among those who defend ecclesiastical vestments and ornaments as conducive to piety. In view of the importance of the royal supremacy in Anglican history it is natural to find the preachers speaking in highest terms of the sovereign, whether Elizabeth, James, or Charles, but the fulsome terms of their flattery are often nauseating to modern ears. The surprising thing is that, in spite of the tight hold of the establishment on the pulpit, so many of the preachers should have found it possible to take an individual line.

Happily many of them were men of real piety who obviously felt that the essential point of a sermon was to teach a spiritual lesson. As the period wore on a less controversial tone was observable. A plea against bitterness is all the more welcome for being rare. Thomas White, founder of Sion College, in two sermons drew attention to London's sins and called for a cessation of discord in the Church. John King, Bishop of London, used the occasion of James's recovery from illness to preach a notable sermon on death; and a year after, on the only occasion when James attended at Paul's Cross in person, the Bishop ventured to make a fervent appeal for the restoration of his very dilapidated cathedral.

Plainness in style was now being demanded, and a complaint was even made against a preacher who ventured to quote the Fathers in defence of his argument. The subjects chosen were more often such as would lend themselves to the simpler method of composition. The love of God, the mystery of the Blessed Trinity, the sin against the Holy Ghost take the place of more political or controversial themes. A truly Anglican note is struck by a quite new plea for toleration, an eloquent praise of freedom, and a defence of establishment.

The sermons still display what must seem to us an intolerable complexity of division and sub-division. But that was made almost inevitable by their length. Laud thought that they should last not less than an hour and a half nor more than two hours. But it was by no means unknown for a preacher at the end of the second hour to turn his hour-glass again. On 1st November 1552, Nicholas Ridley after the morning service, in which for the first time he had introduced Edward VI's second prayer book, preached an afternoon sermon which went on till five o'clock and so wearied the Lord Mayor that he refused to go into the church afterwards for the usual leave-taking. The gradual shortening of the sermon in subsequent centuries has probably done more than anything else to alter its style. George Herbert thought that an hour was an adequate length, but Bishop Burnet of Salisbury thought that half an hour was likely to produce a better composition from the preacher and closer attention on the part of the congregation. Today it is only lecture-sermons such as the Bamptons at Oxford and the Hulseans at Cambridge that dare go beyond the half-hour and, if the BBC is to be trusted, fifteen minutes are as much as can be sympathetically endured by the average listener.

But this is to anticipate. What we now have to do is to trace the development of the Anglican sermon in the meantime. Maclure, to quote him once again, sums up the changing purpose of the exhortation at Paul's Cross as follows:

'For most of these preachers who made no pretence to literary ability, the sermon was an instrumental, not absolute, form: in the time of the Reformation an instrument of demagogic propaganda; in the time of Elizabeth, of controversy; in the Jacobean period, mainly of social criticism; in the last days, of controversy once more, in defence of the Laudian establishment against a second Reformation.'

The Laudian system was effectively settled at the time of the Restoration when monarchy came into its own again in the person of Charles II. Strange though it may appear, he seems himself to have been something of a sermon-taster and to have approved the simpler style that was now coming into vogue. That style was largely due to the severely classical genius of the Cambridge Platonists. In the person of Benjamin Whichcote indeed it had become aphoristic, but clarity and purity of diction were the seeds from which his epigrams came to fruition. Charles, with his French training, had a cultivated taste for this sort of thing. He also no doubt appreciated the shorter length of discourse that went with it. There was very little else to make him lean towards the Latitudinarians who developed this style.

A precursor is to be found in Jeremy Taylor (1667), Bishop of Down and author of *Holy Living* and *Holy Dying*, who denounced the idea that the pulpit was a place for mere oratory. In his view 'the business of the sermon is to preach a holy life, obedience, peace and love for our neighbours. Backbiting and intemperance are to be dealt with severely. The most frequent themes are to be: death, judgment, heaven, and hell, the life and death of Jesus Christ, God's mercy to repenting sinners and his severity against the impenitent.'[4] It will be seen that, as was to be expected from the author of *Ductor Dubitantium*, the first Anglican book on casuistry, questions of moral conduct now begin to occupy a special place in the preacher's thoughts.

Early representatives of the new style were Ussher of Armagh (+1656), Wilkins of Chester (+1672), Lloyd of St Asaph (+1717) and Robert South (+1716). But the great representative of it was Tillotson (+1694) who began life as a Presbyterian and ended it as Archbishop of Canterbury. He had a puritan up-bringing but was fortunate enough to be brought in contact with the Cambridge Platonists at the university. As a preacher he eschewed even the poetic imagery of Taylor, who could speak of marriage as 'the nursery of heaven', and of false accusation as 'the blood of dragons'. He kept everything as flat and unemotional as he could, relying for his effect upon the sheer commonsense of his teaching and the ease with which it could be understood. In literary style he was at the opposite pole to the modern poet. In religious and moral teaching he was utterly indifferent to the romantic, the adventurous, the glamorous. He had no use for stories or illustrations. His sermons sounded fresh because he abandoned the 'clichés', the pedantry, and the interminable sub-divisions of the old style. He had his own clear structure which was an adequate scaffolding for a well thought out and balanced theme.

The result was that he was not only widely read by the laity but served as a model for generations of his fellow clergy. Parson Woodforde of the famous diary, whose life carried over into the nineteenth century, was still, like many of his contemporaries, following in Tillotson's footsteps. Indeed he not only took the great preacher as a model, but would on occasion quote him *in extenso*, making up a whole sermon for his rustic flock out of excerpts from one of Tillotson's longer discourses. This slavish plagiarization meant the ultimate end of the style. If the high-flying, coloratura style of the Caroline divines had crashed under the manipulation of less skilful practitioners, the earth-bound, unambitious, monochrome style of Tillotson became unutterably dull in the hands of mediocre clergy who lacked his skill, knowledge and experience. It petered out in the long, written discourses of the early Victorian period. It came to be scarcely expected that anyone would closely follow the sermon. 'What?' exclaimed an intelligent teacher, recalling his early manhood, in reply to someone who had expostulated with him on this score, 'if the old parson got into the pulpit and began to read, I thought it was just part of the liturgy.' It was only when some topical reference was made or some national event had stirred imagination that the congregation would sit up and take notice. An exception to prove the rule could of course be found in London, where a popular preacher would be as much of an entertainment to country visitors as a successful play is today.

A new breath of life was infused into preaching by the two great revivals, Evangelical and Catholic. Preachers had something fresh to say; congregations had had their interest stimulated. There were in both cases many enemies, but new controversy sharpened the edge of attention. In particular it put a premium on *extempore* preaching, particularly among the evangelicals. To bring individuals to the shock of a sudden conversion was not easy when reading a manuscript; it needed the challenge of the speaker's eye, the pointing finger, the voice directed to the personal conscience. For the catholics, with their greater emphasis on history, doctrine, and sacramental custom, the need was not so urgent. Exposition rather than challenge was their métier. But even among them it was often found useful, as their appeal penetrated the parishes, to abandon the manuscript in favour of direct address. It is true there was no fixed rule or custom. The fervent exhortations of Wesley and Whitefield on the one side gave place to the carefully prepared addresses of Charles Simeon, all ready for publication. On the other the great example of Newman's literary masterpieces (a style which he himself abandoned after his conversion to Rome) was at first continued by Liddon, Church, Newbolt, Scott Holland, but eventually replaced by the short, homely addresses of Dolling and Stanton. In the meantime liberal churchmanship was not without its prophets. Charles Kingsley's skill as a novelist helped to ensure the liveliness of his sermons. Robertson of Brighton showed a rare insight both psychological and social. Overseas, Phillips Brooks of Boston, USA, produced a manual for preachers which has never been surpassed. The fruit of it was seen in the eloquent, if lengthy, discourses of Bishop Brent of the Philippines, who made so profound an impression on his audiences in England and particularly on the ecumenical movement.

If one compares all this historical material with the typical Anglican preaching of today one is struck by the tremendous contrast. Compared with much that we have considered the modern sermon scarcely seems to belong to the same genre. This contrast is often placed to the grave discredit of the present generation of Anglican clergy. It is said that while they have busied themselves about the sacraments they have left the art of preaching to their non-conformist brethren. Some colour was lent to this charge by no less a person than Randall Davidson, Archbishop of Canterbury. Speaking at the Eastbourne Church Congress in 1925 he said, 'complaints of the inadequacy of our sermons are rife, and the fact of the inadequacy is beyond dispute'. Of course no preaching can ever be adequate, but it was a dangerous sentiment for a prelate to express. One remembers the general feeling at the time that the rebuke would have come home with greater force if the good Archbishop's own preaching had been more obviously adequate. However, it must be admitted that there was a period when the recovery of enthusiasm about the sacraments was so fresh and vigorous that Anglican clergy were inclined to forget that they were also ordained to be ministers of the word.

On the whole it can safely be said that the period when sermons were despised is now past. Although the Anglican clergy are never likely to be able to give so much time to sermon preparation as their non-conformist colleagues, it can be said that they do take seriously the double duty of ministering both word and sacraments. Moreover, considerable attention is nowadays given to training in the arts both of teaching and preaching in the seminaries or theological colleges. The clergy today are much better equipped than they were even at the beginning of the present century in the technique of their profession. It must be said too that as a result preaching is much more simple and direct than it used to be. It confines itself almost exclusively to spiritual issues. In consequence it provides fewer stories for the press, but it probably speaks more directly to men's souls.

The process has been helped by the gradual supersession of the written sermon. It is true that some of the last generation, like N. P. Williams of Christ Church and Bishop Kirk of Oxford,[5] consciously modelled themselves on classical patterns and produced sermons in the great style. According to the publishers volumes of sermons are being sold in much greater numbers than before the war. It would therefore be a great pity if such models were entirely lost, but they are generally left nowadays to the younger dons or preachers of academic tastes. In the various parts of the Anglican communion beyond the seas it is hardly likely that any preacher would ever dream of reading from a manuscript; even if he had prepared one, he would leave it in his study or hand it to the press on proceeding to the church. In England it is to be hoped that the written sermon will continue to have a useful life, but for most purposes the so-called extempore sermon is generally preferred.

Three of the greatest examples of the style in modern times were Boyd Carpenter, Bishop of Ripon, Charles Gore, Bishop of Oxford, and Studdert Kennedy, Rector of St Edmund, Lombard Street. All of them were extempore preachers but all were regular writers and all avoided the fatal fluency which is the temptation of most public speakers. Studdert Kennedy, who was the most eloquent and possessed the greatest capacity to sway a big audience, even when he was about to address a body of troops would have every word carefully typed, although he intended to leave the typescript at home. Gore was the most intellectual of the three and his argument was always most carefully articulated in every detail. Boyd Carpenter could take one through an Old Testament story with such clarity and point that the memory of the presentation still lingers in the mind half a century later. But after all, if we want to know what is characteristic of Anglican preaching we must turn our gaze from the giants and see how the ordinary parochial clergy tackle their task.

Anyone who tries to make a just estimate of Anglican preaching today must first reckon with the fact that there is so much of it. Leaving week-days out of consideration, one finds services spread over the whole

Sunday, and no service except an early Communion is considered complete without a sermon. If the old adage is true that 'he who preaches twice prates once', what can be said of the man who has regularly to preach twice and sometimes three or even four times a Sunday? If there is here some reason for a decline in quality, there may also be some explanation of the decline in length.

Again leaving out the 'occasional' sermon (that is the sermon preached on some special occasion and not in the course of ordinary routine) there are roughly three classes into which Anglican sermons fall.

The first is a highly characteristic resuscitation of the medieval 'prone' or liturgical sermon. The prone was originally the grill or screen at the chancel steps from which notices were given out at the appropriate point in the Mass; it gave its name to that moment in the liturgy. When a short exhortation came to be added at this point it too took on the name that was already given to that section of the service. Today, when throughout the Anglican communion there is a growing tendency to regard the Sung Eucharist as the family service for the week, it has become customary to attach to it a short sermon generally explanatory of the special lections or intention of the day. The prone thus occupies an important place as part of the service; it fits in with the thought of the day, and unites itself with the act of worship so as to achieve the unity of one whole in a way that is hardly possible, however desirable, in other services.

Since time is an important factor in such services, the prone cannot be long. Owing to the mixed character of the congregation it must be simple and direct. The preacher must know exactly what he wants to say, and he must say it at once. A new type of sermon, practical and popular, is thus being developed, and it may be regarded as characteristically, although not exclusively, Anglican.

The other two classes of sermon follow the division which Professor Dodd has taught us to see in the New Testament between *kerugma* and *didache*, proclamation and teaching. By derivation 'preaching' should be confined to the former, but teaching is an essential part of preaching. Anglicans have never felt inclined to separate sharply the one from the other. Depending so much, as they do, upon the appeal to reason, they have never been able to exclude teaching from their sermons. There are indeed many, both of the clergy and of the laity, who would like them to indulge in far more teaching than they do.

The *kerugma*, or preaching strictly so called, is the proclamation of the gospel. It is the announcement, necessary in every generation, of the good news of God's plan of salvation, and a challenge to every individual soul. There is no sign that in modern times such a proclamation is likely to lose its importance. To many continental theologians it is the essential word of God. Bultmann, with his strongly existentialist philosophy and his despair of ever arriving at the truth of historical details in the gospel, thinks that in this challenge lies the only revelation. Anglicans are not likely to go so far as that. They are not tied to existentialism and they have a great liking for history. But they do recognize the necessity of each individual accepting for himself the claim of Christ. The emphasis of the Methodists upon sudden conversion may have been toned down by the more formal Anglican spirit but the Anglican's fondness for retreats and parochial missions shows that he realizes the essential need for the application of the gospel to the individual soul. And when the parson is really preaching he has that very much in mind.

This homiletic task the Anglican shares with all Christian preachers. He becomes rather more characteristically *sui generis* when he uses the sermon as an opportunity for teaching. This he is well able to do because of the popularity of the choir office. Matins and evensong are in themselves services that require a certain amount of intelligence adequately to follow, and it is appropriate that the sermon in such a service should make an intellectual appeal.

It cannot be said that the clergy have yet realized to the full their modern opportunity. Old habits die hard and there are many who think of the sermon mainly as a means of exhortation. Many also are afraid of appearing too much like school-masters in the pulpit. Yet such apprehension is generally misplaced. It is certain that the present-day congregation becomes restive under open exhortation. On the other hand they are of a more enquiring turn of mind than their parents and they have a real thirst for information.

Other organs of communication have been quick to recognize this trait and have even done something to cultivate it. The BBC performed a service of real value to the present generation when it began the practice of inviting experts to read fifteen minute papers as introductions to their subject. It is a pity that more of the clergy do not treat their congregations in the same way and introduce them to the theological subjects they themselves have learnt at college. Old Testament, New Testament, Church History, Doctrine, Apologetics, Ethics—all could form the themes of whole series of sermon-lectures, which the clergy are well qualified to give. If one is afraid of becoming too academic, one can remember that under different forms these subjects are all ways of thinking about the spiritual realities of religion. They are all sections of theology and should lead us direct to God. Faith itself is likely to be more vivid and more strongly held if it has explored the intellectual territory in which its object is to be found. The 'teaching sermon' is not meant to consist of undigested gobbets of dogma, but of real efforts to make Christian people aware of the conditions in which their creed was born and grew to its present maturity. We have travelled a long way in reaching the present style of sermon, but there is every probability that it will prove at least as effective as its predecessors.[6]

CHAPTER TWELVE

THE PARSON IN HIS PARISH

The parson's position and duties today—Historical development of the parson's position—The parson overseas—Influence of business efficiency on parochial administration—Influence of the parson's family

INEVITABLY AN organization must be judged very largely by its officers. Although Anglicans do not identify the Church with the clergy, yet the common expression 'go into the church', implying not baptism but ordination, is sufficient to show that the clergy are regarded as a class apart and as representing the Church in a more specific manner than the laity.

It is a curious idiosyncrasy also that by the clergy is generally meant the class sometimes known as 'the inferior clergy'. It is common form to speak of 'bishops and clergy' as if the two bodies were not essentially one. This usage is not altogether to the disadvantage of the lower status. Just as it is usual to say of an army that it would do much better if it were better led and that if it were not for the admirable competence of the NCOs there really would be no army at all, so, in regard to ecclesiastical matters, it is common to contrast the ineptitude of the bishops as a body* with the extremely fine work done by the front-line clergy. The latter part of the estimate at least is fully endorsed by our contemporary ecclesiastical historians, who are specially loud in their praises of the nineteenth and twentieth century parish priest. The laity in the parishes would probably qualify the severer element in the judgment so far as to express some respect for the bishops, whom they often regard as their natural protectors against the vagaries of their incumbent.

The attitude of the laity as a whole to the clergy is not easy to define. Certainly there is none of the violent anti-clerical feeling that one sometimes encounters on the continent. Nor, on the other hand, is there anything like the adoring reverence that the Irish Catholics display towards their spiritual leaders. If the Anglicans do not feel so strongly the numinous atmosphere surrounding the dispenser of the sacred mysteries, they at least expect from him as a 'man of God' a life of irreproachable morals and willing helpfulness.

In Victorian times there was a certain barrier between the clergy and

*Though not separately; the individual bishop is generally popular, not least in his own diocese.

the bulk of their parishioners because the former had been finally recognized as belonging to the gentry. Today, when social barriers have been to some extent broken down and the clergy are drawn from almost every class of society, it is to be expected that there will follow a closer understanding and sympathy between the two halves of the Church. This is the more likely since the laity are learning to help the clergy more wholeheartedly in the spiritual side of their work.

Also the educational barrier has almost disappeared. Instead of being the only scholar in the parish, the parson is often less equipped academically than many of his parishioners. There will, of course, always be a section of the clergy who will occupy a foremost place in learning and literature, so that the scholarly reputation of the ordained ranks will not be entirely lost. But it still remains to be seen how vitally the new diffusion of learning will affect the relations between the parish priest and his people. Certainly it ought to be a great advantage to both sides if they can learn to speak the same language.

It is to be hoped that fuller understanding will reveal to the general public a feature of clerical life that they have never yet grasped—its extraordinary variety. The average person thinks of the clergyman in his church on a Sunday, preaching, or leading the worship of his people, and quite probably imagines that his duties begin and end there. Even those limited duties in point of fact demand a certain versatility. It is not always easy to find a man who can sing and read and also preach acceptably.

If the sympathetic member of the public were able to follow the parson outside his church, he would find how many other tasks he has to carry out, each demanding its own, and often quite unrelated, skill. He visits the sick and the whole, teaches in the schools, prepares individuals for the sacraments, gives spiritual direction wherever required, chairs committee meetings, and tries to run a purely voluntary society as efficiently as a great business; he acts as an amateur journalist in publishing a monthly magazine; he lectures on all sorts of subjects to adults; and in addition to all this he supplies spiritual drive and leadership for the whole parish in its attack on the general apathy and indifference of the multitude. The variety of tasks is so great that the average parochial clergyman has no excuse to find life dull or monotonous. He never has the opportunity to pursue one piece of work for long together; he must always be turning to the next thing in hand. That is the reason why the parson can work so many more hours at a stretch than most people, and can continue to do it as a matter of daily routine for the whole of his life.

Now this kind of thing could be said *mutatis mutandis* of practically all ministers of religion. But it is true in a quite special sense of the Anglican clergy, and that for a specific reason. In view of its particular history, the Anglican Church has been impelled to cultivate a number of different ideals of the priestly life. As these have been successively presented to her, she has not dropped the old while trying to grasp the new; she has kept them all in hand together, until today the vocation of the priesthood in the Anglican communion is the richest and most diversified in content of any profession under the sun. The 'massing priest' of the Middle Ages is shown in a most attractive light as Chaucer's 'poor parson of a town'. But he probably left to his chantry brother the educational tasks that he would have had to shoulder if he had lived after the Reformation and had been capable of them. If he had lived in George Herbert's time he would have had to visit his parishioners on all occasions, and not only when they were sick. If he had lived on till the evangelical revival he would have begun to feel the strain of incessant preaching. If he had lasted till the Tractarian epoch he would have had to train himself and his people for 'fully choral' services several times a Sunday, to say nothing of conducting numerous guilds during the week. A little later and he would have been launched into the full spate of schools, committees, organizations characteristic of Bishop Wilberforce and his 'good churchmen'. While if he had lasted until today he might well have been expected to take his part in the symposium of the air on radio or television either alone or with his whole choir and congregation.

All this will probably become clearer if we consider in a little more detail the position of the Anglican parson at various periods of his history.

As far as he was concerned, the Elizabethan Settlement did not at first settle very much. The changing policies of the previous reigns had meant considerable upheaval. It was some time before people knew where they were and whether they had reached any haven of stability. As the dust of battle settled down and he had opportunity to look about him, he found that while he had at his back an Act of Uniformity and an authorized Prayer Book, he was assailed by determined opposition on either hand and faced by a wall of apathy in front. It has been estimated that, while 7% of the people were definitely antagonistic, 75% were indifferent to the changes in religion so long as their own customs were not interfered with.[1] But it was not altogether possible to leave them alone. The trappings of worship were greatly changed. The churches had lost much of their colour and decoration. The altar was drawn out from the east end and placed table-wise during a celebration. The priest did not wear his old vestments; few of them wore a cope; and some could net even be induced to put on a surplice. No doubt, he knew that some churchwardens had hidden away the choicest of the old vestments and vessels in hope of a return to sanity, but more had just made off with what was no longer used or needed. The parson, if he was faithful to the new regime, must stir up the 18 % of the people who were staunchly and devotedly 'Anglican' to adapt themselves to the new Prayer Book and use it as best they could to express the old feelings of worship and to imbibe fresh strength for their daily life.

But on either hand there were determined enemies. On the right were the recusants, who remained steadfast to what they believed to be the old religion. They had not renounced their allegiance to the Pope, and even if they attended for form's sake the services in the parish church, they valued more highly the ministrations they could still receive at the hands of some Roman priest, tutor-in-hiding to a local gentleman's family, or travelling in disguise from one secret refuge to another. Such adherents of the old ways did not amount to more than 5 % of the total population. They did, however, represent a danger to the safety of the country so long as Mary, Queen of Scots, lived to provide them with a rallying point, and while rumours grew thick about the organization of a Spanish armada. But when those two dangers were removed the Romanists were no longer important to the statesman or politician.

Much more trying were the partisans on the extreme left, the Puritans. They did not number more than 2 % of the population but they made a far greater outcry than their numbers warranted. Indeed, for a time it looked as if they might conquer Parliament and overturn the Church of England from within. Unfortunately, their relative numbers were greatest among the parson's clerical colleagues. Even after the weeding out consequent upon the publication of the *Book of Discipline*, with its open attempt to supersede the Book of Common Prayer and to replace episcopacy by the presbyterian polity, which led to the eviction within six years (1558–64) of about 200 beneficed clergy, there still remained about 350 Puritan incumbents out of a total of roughly 8,000.[2]

How persistent was the Puritan attack we can judge from its temporary triumph eighty years later under Cromwell and the Commonwealth. We make it harder for ourselves to understand the reason for its partial success through our unhistorical refusal to see any good in it. No doubt the verdict of history is accurate in detecting a real division between the Puritan and the Anglican spirit. The latter was humanist and in the main conciliatory. The former was intransigent and fanatical.

Perhaps the worst that we have said against the Puritans is that they came near to suggesting that everything nice was bad. That at least was the judgment of Kenneth Hare:

> 'The Puritan through life's sweet garden goes,
> To pluck the thorn and throw away the rose,
> And hopes to please by this peculiar whim
> The God who fashioned it and gave it him.'

Nevertheless it is easy to exaggerate this trait. No nation that counts Milton among its greatest poets can accuse the Puritans, without qualification, of having no love for art or beauty. And they did most certainly introduce a much needed note of seriousness into public and private life and work for the improvement of clerical efficiency.

During most of the Elizabethan reign the status of the clergy was lamentably low. For one thing there were not nearly enough to go round. In order to supplement their efforts resort was made to the modern-sounding expedient of 'lay readers'. Even so, a minimum supply of clergy could be maintained only by ordaining too great a proportion of tradesmen, servants, artisans and men of no education at all. Modern research into diocesan records has enabled reliable figures to be compiled showing how serious was the situation. Elizabeth and her archbishops set to work to remedy it as far as possible, insisting wherever they could on university training and a degree. But that was really a long-term policy. Before the candidates could be adequately educated a beginning had to be made to get the grammar schools in order and then to rescue the universities (which were the real training grounds for the ministry) from their poverty and disorder.

In this situation the Puritan 'prophesyings' could be regarded as a valuable attempt to raise at once by voluntary emulation the whole tone of clerical life. They were generally weekly gatherings at which the clergy listened to one another expounding scripture and offered their criticism, very much as they do on a somewhat broader basis in the usual clerical meeting today. Such gatherings could, of course, become breeding grounds of fanaticism and even of sedition. From time to time they were for that reason forbidden. Regulations went even further and, at a time when the sermon was beginning to occupy the principal place in worship, forbade preaching altogether except by those licensed for the purpose. At the same time the government provided authorized homilies to be read when there was no licensed preacher. If the incumbent was himself licensed, he would preach once a month; if he were not, he would be expected to provide a licensed preacher once a quarter. Needless to say, the regulations were often neglected.

Harassed by such a situation in his parish, the parson was not always happy in his own home. Edwardian regulations had allowed him to marry: Marian had driven his wife away: Elizabethan allowed her back again, but with a frown. The Virgin Queen's dislike of clerical marriage is still illustrated in a curious anomaly. If a cleric receives a knighthood his wife does not, like that of the layman in similar circumstances, take the corresponding feminine title.* Elizabeth's attitude did not make it easy for her clergy to find suitable wives, and there was a good deal of ill-natured talk about them. A particularly trying circumstance was that by the injunctions of 1559 clergymen had to obtain not only the sanction of their marriage but also approval of the bride from the bishop and the justices of the peace. It was not until 1604 that the clergyman's normal right in this matter was fully and officially recognized.

One addition made to the parson's duties at this time has proved ever since of great value: he was now provided with a register in which he had to record 'every wedding, christening and burial'. This was the first time that records of the kind were adequately kept. In order that there should be no doubt about it, the churchwardens were bidden to provide him with a chest, lock and key, by use of which the registers would be properly preserved. Some of them indeed have lasted until this day, although others have perished through fire, flood or gross neglect. The few that remain are still the happy hunting ground of American visitors searching for a pedigree.

A thing the parson did not have to bother about was the provision of a congregation. That task was taken out of his hands by the government, which expected every parishioner to present himself at divine service and fined him if he did not obey. The difficulty was still to provide an adequate ministry. By the beginning of James's reign matters were straightening themselves out. Half the beneficed clergy had by this time been licensed to preach, pluralism was on the decrease, and a greater proportion of the incumbents had university degrees.

Normally the Anglican incumbent was now less harassed by Puritan opposition. Archbishop Bancroft had dealt leniently but on the whole

---

*This protocol enabled a gentleman of the Household in congratulating a bishop who had just received a knighthood to add the remark 'I'm afraid, however, that you will never be able to make your wife a lady.'

successfully with the menace. The most common point of division rested curiously enough in the wearing of the surplice, which to the Puritan was a 'rag of Popery'. After repeated admonitions and prolonged argument those who refused to comply with this and other regulations for the decent conduct of services were extruded from their benefices. How many incumbents thus suffered is not certain. The Puritans put the number at about three hundred, but the official figures as given by Bancroft point to the conclusion that it was really no greater than fifty.

The Puritans, however, did not admit themselves defeated. They founded afternoon lectureships which, not being statutory services, did not fall under the regulations. The Puritan minister who functioned as lecturer had no need to wear a surplice or use the Prayer Book. This peculiar device did as much as anything to keep puritanism alive and to give it some sort of rallying point against the times to come.

The advent of the Stuarts revealed an important political difference between Anglican and Puritan. Our parson, having learnt to accept the royal supremacy in the Church, had gone on to admit the doctrine of the divine right of the sovereign in secular affairs. That had been boldly stated by no less a person than James I himself in his book *True Law of Free Monarchies*. While the bishops gave him their support, the Puritans were stern in opposition, basing their political hopes on some sort of constitutional government. A matter of greater concern to the parson's congregation would be their contrasted attitude to the observance of Sunday. The Puritan identified the Sunday with the Sabbath and transferred to the first day of the week all the taboos that Jewish law had concentrated on the seventh. The normal Anglican expected, after fulfilling his duty of church attendance, to be allowed to follow his own devices, either completing his harvest or engaging in any sport or festive occasion that offered. The royal *Declaration of Sports* first issued in May 1618 endorsed the latter point of view.

In the following reign the parson felt the urgent hand of Archbishop Laud, who, fully supported by Charles I, was determined to press on with his policy of Thorough and to bring back the Church to what he believed to be its earlier standard of decency. The parson, if he had any leaning at all towards the doctrines of Calvin, found himself forbidden to preach them by a royal proclamation of 1628. Any time between 1633 and 1636 he might find himself engaged with Laud's metropolitical Visitation, which was being particularly used as an opportunity to see that the altar was back again by the east wall and securely fenced in, with the Ten Commandments as its main background.

One circumstance is not likely to have caused our representative parson as much heart-burning as its recurrence certainly would today, and that is the possible institution to some neighbouring parish of an incumbent whose only ordination had been at the hands of clerics of ill-defined status in some continental church. That instances of the kind did occur is beyond dispute, just as it is certain that a century later SPCK in default of Anglican clergymen used the services of Lutheran missionaries overseas. What is in dispute is the precise significance of the anomaly. The question is of particular importance at the present juncture in view of the place occupied by the credentials of the ministry in all ecumenical discussions. It would be outside our purpose to pursue the point here. The interested reader can see the evidence for himself in Dr Norman Sykes's *Old Priest and New Presbyter*[3] and a re-examination of the same evidence arriving at opposite conclusions in A. L. Peck's *Anglicanism and Episcopacy*.[4] What we can perhaps say is that while Anglican authority certainly regarded episcopal ordination as necessary in the case of its own members brought up in its own midst, it was not prepared to condemn the order of others brought up in other lands where episcopal ordination was not available, or invariably to insist on their re-ordination if they were appointed to serve under Anglican authority. The absence of full-dress debate on the subject at least shows that it was not then so burning a question as it is today. In such circumstances to use the available evidence of that period as determinative of Anglican theology on the ministry for all time would be at least unwise.

The kind of life lived by the parson at this period has been admirably summed by Tindal Hart.[5]

'What of the parson himself? The Elizabethan and early Stuart parish priest was expected to live up to an ideal. Except under necessity he was prohibited from entering a public house; he might not engage in trade or "servile labour"; he was forbidden to touch cards or dice; and, clothed in suitable attire, was expected to expend his leisure in studying the Scriptures and improving his learning. Canon Law, as we have already seen, ordered him to preach (if licensed) or read the homilies, catechize, conduct the Prayer Book services in surplice and hood, and visit the sick. But he also played his part in the secular life of the village. No labourer could leave the parish without his signed certificate; he recorded the whippings of the sturdy rogues, and sent them back to their place of origin; he was responsible for his parishioners eating fish on the statutory fast days; and also for keeping the churchwardens up to the mark in presenting offenders. A convicted recusant had to make his public confession and submission before the incumbent at divine service; and the latter saw to it that the penance imposed by the ecclesiastical court was duly carried out.'

With the execution of Laud and Charles I the Anglican parson suffered an eclipse. Cromwell, who enjoys an undeserved reputation for tolerance, could not tolerate Papists or Anglicans. The Book of Common Prayer was banished and nearly 2,500 incumbents were evicted. The parson's lot was indeed hard. A Commission of Triers was instituted, consisting of thirty-eight persons, whose duty was to examine all candidates for benefices, and they were followed by others who examined those already in possession. By these means most of the clergy were dispossessed, and the Triers even managed to exclude Dr Pococke, the greatest Orientalist in Europe.[6]

This temporary triumph, however, did not go to the Presbyterians. Cromwell was an Independent, and so were most of his soldiers. They had no use for the Calvinist discipline, and, consequently, even in the hour of victory Puritanism was far from being an undivided movement. In any case, few things could have been better calculated than such persecution to stir up the people as a whole to a greater love of the Prayer Book. When Cromwell died in 1658 many congregations at once fetched their parsons back to pray from the Book of Common Prayer, copies of which had been carefully concealed during his Protectorate.

With the King the parson came into his own again. Political even more than ecclesiastical reasons prompted a violent reaction. After the abortive Savoy Conference of 1661 the policy of comprehension was abandoned; church and state went hand in hand; and for the next century and a half squire and parson were to be the leading figures of parochial life. An Act of Uniformity of 1662 compelled all ministers to use the Book of Common Prayer on pain of losing their benefices. On St Bartholomew's Day that year a number of Puritan incumbents variously estimated at twelve hundred to two thousand, who refused to comply, were evicted. They left their parishes to help form the dissenting congregations that were to exercise so important an influence on future history. The parson now suffered from the mistaken zeal of his friends. The politicians tried to put down nonconformity by act of parliament. The Clarendon Code contained three regulations, the first of which brought a number of occasional communicants to his altar in order to justify themselves as office-holders by a formal partaking of the Sacrament; the second prevented any assembly for worship outside his church if it embraced more than five persons beyond the normal number of the household concerned; and the third forbade any of his rival preachers to come within five miles of any town where they had formerly worked, unless indeed they had in the meantime taken the oath against arms. Such measures culminated in the Test Act of 1673, which ordered all holders of civil and military office to take the oath of supremacy, to declare against transubstantiation, and to receive Holy Communion according to the Anglican rite.

These legal regulations were not well calculated to make the parson popular with certain sections of his parishioners. *Non tali auxilio.* Nevertheless, the majority took them as a matter of course, and the example of what happened in the American colonies shows that whatever party had been in power the same intolerance would have been displayed. Perhaps the worst effect of the system was that it tied the clergy so close to the monarchy that they became, in effect, the official propagators of the doctrine of divine right. It is all the more to the credit of the bishops that, when James II went too far, seven of them were prepared to resist him and to risk in doing so not only their liberty but their life. Certainly they had no intention of setting in train any series of steps that would lead to a change in the monarchy. Events, however, were too strong for them, and from being public heroes some of them became the leaders of a tiny minority. When William and Mary were placed on the throne they felt unable to change their allegiance, and so started the unfortunate Non-juror schism.[7]

With the change in the dynasty the idea of divine right was surrendered by the country as a whole and drastic changes in ideology occurred almost simultaneously. A Toleration Act of 1689 removed the main disabilities of dissenters. The new science was getting under way; the age of Deism and the Enlightenment was approaching. Dutch William had no sympathy with Anglican theology or worship, and felt under no particular obligation to its bishops and clergy, who as a whole had given him so cool a reception. Everything combined to break the alliance between the clergy and the throne. The bishops, it is true, being nominated by the crown soon began to form a strong element in that Whig party on which the new monarchy chiefly relied. But that alliance involved a widening breach between the bishops and the parochial clergy. Apart from a brief interval in the reign of Queen Anne, when the high churchmen enjoyed an Indian summer of popularity, the eighteenth century saw a gradual deterioration in the standards of clerical life. The quarrels of bishops and clergy led to the practical suppression of the convocations in 1717 so that, for the rest of the century and beyond it until 1852, the Church was left without any common voice of its own. As there were no diocesan or any other conferences, the parson was left generally on his own, to be dealt with occasionally by the archdeacon on behalf of an absentee bishop.

In the circumstances it is somewhat remarkable that clerical standards did not fall still lower. Even in their deterioration the clergy did no more than reflect the general tone of public life. Abuses of every kind, which today would be regarded as little less than criminal, were tolerated, and even expected, as normal. A service and sermon on Sunday with a certain amount of catechizing of children and apprentices, and sick-visiting during the week, in addition to the occasional offices, were all that were likely to be expected of the conscientious incumbent.

This did not mean that he had no other contact with his parishioners. He would be expected to share in their social life at different levels. He might farm his own glebe and so be as close to the land as any of them. He would be expected to entertain them at a tithe dinner, to arrange a parochial festivity at the harvest-home or church ales for the raising of money. George Herbert had thought that all parishioners should be invited to the Rectory in turn. If he were himself a scion of the nobility occupying a family living, the parson would be a frequent guest at the great house. In any case, he might well ride to hounds and be hand in glove with the squire. Apart from such casual contacts, he might easily have a more serious association with certain members of his flock as a magistrate or justice of the peace. The incumbents as a class were much sought after to perform this public office. It was a bad thing in so far as it gave some of them a reputation for severity and destroyed the relation of affection that should subsist between a pastor and his people. But it increased the opportunity for good in so far as it gave the parson a position not merely of influence but of authority. It is within living memory that a country rector driving his dog-cart could pull up beside a rough-looking labourer and say to him 'You were drunk on Saturday'; 'Yes, sir'; 'Then see that it doesn't happen again'; and could drive on with the comfortable assurance that for a time, at any rate, his behest would be obeyed.

By the latter part of the eighteenth century, as we have seen, the obligation to say the daily office was widely disregarded. The fact that his church was not expected to be in use every day made it easier for the parson to get away. This was one of the contributory causes, together with the need to ensure an adequate income, for the terrible increase in the twin practices of non-residence and pluralism. In a statistical return made shortly after the end of the century it was revealed that not more than 42% of the incumbents in England and Wales were actually resident upon their cures.[8] The failure to reside often meant the deterioration of the parsonage house, and this was later used as a further excuse for non-residence. Not all non-residents, therefore, were pluralists, although the fact that the latter included a number of bishops and of senior clergy, who might have been considered already well-placed, caused mounting scandal. It was this kind of thing that led at long last to a second reform of the Church in the earlier half of the nineteenth century, which in the opinion of many is comparable in importance to the better known reformation of the sixteenth century.[9]

In the meantime we have to allow for the other side of the picture by reminding ourselves of the founding of SPCK and SPG and the various societies for the mending of manners. In 1729 the Methodist Society was founded at Oxford and the evangelical revival soon brought an immense change in ideals to the clergy affected by it. At the same time we have to remember the work done in defence of the faith by the learned clergy of the period such as Waterland, Sherlock, Berkeley, Butler, Law. But if he were not of an academic turn of mind, our parson might still find much to interest him and engage both his duty and his affection. *Nihil humani alienum*. The diaries of James Woodforde (who was at least Fellow of New College) and William Cole (who was an antiquarian and friend of Horace Walpole) as well as the careers of Robert Walker and George Crabbe show that, given a real sense of vocation, there is no limit to the opportunities of service to God and man wherever one's parish is found. As we know from George Herbert's advice to his wife, medical attention had long been numbered among the parson's duties. Most of the more zealous incumbents seem so to have accepted it. George Crabbe was somewhat unusual in having been trained to medicine before his ordination, but he does not seem to have been more successful in practice than an amateur like James Woodforde with his herbalist remedies.[10]

The effect of the evangelical movement was to quicken individualist zeal rather than to improve the position of the Church in the country. Indeed, the result was rather the opposite, for it gave a new life to non-conformity and was fertile in producing a fresh crop of dissident sects. The privileged position of the Anglican clergy was largely destroyed and the remaining disabilities of non-Anglicans removed, by the repeal of the Test Act in 1828. The growing antipathy between 'Church' and 'Chapel' was strengthened by the Tractarian Movement, which laid tremendous emphasis on the Church as the only legitimate corporate representative of Christianity. The original tract had called upon the clergy to recognize themselves as the lineal descendants of the apostles.

By the middle of the nineteenth century the parson's attitude to his work was revolutionized. There was much more of it. His church was open every day and he resumed the practice, which had died down in the latter half of the previous century, of reciting the daily office in public. He remembered that he was a dispenser of the sacraments as well as of the word; the quarterly or monthly celebration of the Eucharist became first a weekly, then also a saints' days, and finally in many cases a daily, celebration. To his preaching, which had by this time become frequent and regular, was now added the need for many instructions to guilds, bible classes and confirmation classes. We must also recognize the growing practice of the laity to resort to the parish priest for the individual direction of their spiritual life.

The clergyman who was anxious to fulfil the obligations of his office and yet was not prepared to accept all the doctrinal presuppositions of the Tractarians might still find the pace of life immeasurably quickened by the bustling activity of Samuel Wilberforce (1805–73). He is generally regarded as the originator of an entirely new ideal of episcopal duty. But the parish priest was equally affected. Wilberforce, even before he became Bishop of Oxford, introduced a new ideal of professional competence. He was no longer content to leave the training of ordinands to the normal arts curriculum of Oxford and Cambridge. He saw that adequate performance of clerical duties demanded a varied technique, and he set himself to provide the opportunity to acquire the necessary skills. Even before he was able to instigate the foundation of seminaries or theological colleges, he had begun to train men himself. Today the whole elaborate machinery of selection boards, pre-college training, and the network of theological colleges, as well as training-colleges for teachers, is the fruit of his far-sightedness and abounding energy.

No detail of parochial life escaped the eye of this doughty diocesan. A MS still exists at the Bodleian in which Wilberforce kept note of every important circumstance connected with each parish during the twenty-five years of his reign in the diocese of Oxford. It was during this period that many of the characteristic Anglican organizations, whose purpose we have considered elsewhere, came into being. Under the new régime of activity inspired by Wilberforce they began to affect the parishes. No self-respecting incumbent of a parish of reasonable size could regard himself as properly equipped unless he had a number of those organizations at work. The care of them, added to the activities already mentioned, changed the tone of clerical life from one of dignified ease to one of continuous and business-like service.

If the daily round and common task were thus changed, it must be said also that there came, through the missionary activity that blazed up in the mid-nineteenth century, a tremendous widening of horizons. The Anglican Church was no longer an insular institution centred in the British Isles but a world-wide communion offering the most varied opportunities to any who entered its service. Nor was it merely a question of going overseas to act as preceptor to Christians, native or other, who were in tutelage to the parent-body at home. Already great national churches like those of America and Australia were developing missions of their own.[11] The very term 'missions' soon began to give place to the name 'younger churches' until they at length became 'the sister churches' of the Anglican Communion. The effect of this expansion on the clergy was noteworthy. They were under no obligation, as were the Moravians, to spend some part of their active ministry in foreign missionary work, nor had they as much pressure brought upon them to do so as the Methodist ministers.

Inevitably, however, as the call sounded more clearly, many of them found their way overseas. It was the evangelical clergy, under the organization of CMS, who led the way in this gallant enterprise—all the more gallant since it was generally looked upon not as a temporary expedient but a life-long self-dedication. Today, with the increased facility of movement, there is a far greater interchange between home and overseas. Indeed, as the mutual knowledge of the main centres of Anglicanism is being increased by exchange of pulpits and the holding of pan-Anglican congresses, to say nothing of the growing importance of Lambeth Conferences since their first inauguration in 1867, it is becoming increasingly difficult to say which is 'home' and which is 'overseas'.

Today the chief difference thrust upon the notice of the English priest doing temporary duty in other parts of the Anglican Communion is the lack of all the privilege and prestige that are supposed to bolster a state church. No doubt these are often replaced by tangible advantages of another order. He may find the concessions allowed to the clergy of all denominations on the railways and on the rates, in such countries as USA and Australia, are far better than any financial privileges allowed him in his own country. At the same time his work is necessarily affected by the difference in status. He is no longer under any statutory obligation to render his ministrations to parishioners not actually of his flock. In fact, the very idea of the parish as an ecclesiastical unit tends to become somewhat nebulous, and to be replaced by that of the congregation, at least in the larger towns. Consequently, the parish priest is not expected to spend a considerable part of the day in house-to-house visiting. If he keeps in touch with the homes of the actual members of his congregation, that is about as much as is normally expected of him in that way.

In the wider sphere of the diocese and province, to say nothing of the national church, the difference made by the absence of an 'established' church may be quite marked on public occasions. There is no one church to take the lead, and governments that are indifferent or hostile may refrain from including a religious element in their programme on the pretence of not desiring to raise the denominational issue. In America the clergy are rigorously excluded from the state schools. On the contrary in some parts at least of Australia they are accorded a much prized 'right of entry' and are generally welcomed when they come at specific hours to teach their own faith.

The English visitor may well conclude that in other countries church administration, whether on a parochial or higher level, is more efficient than in his own. This is natural where the Church has had to make its own way instead of relying on the generosity of past generations. In USA every town parish of any size expects its incumbent to run an office with a paid secretary and a proper filing system. Indeed, since so much has to be done through the post, there would soon be disaster if the office part of the administration were not well run. The parish priest normally keeps office hours like any business man. That is the more necessary as he often lives at a considerable distance from his church. In Commonwealth countries this side of the organization is not usually so far advanced, except perhaps in Canada. But the practice is now almost universal (and has even made its way to England) for the parish to make an allowance to the incumbent for the expenses incurred in administration. Thus has been lifted a burden that has lain heavily on the shoulders of the English rector for several generations. But it must be admitted that with it something of the old family relationship has disappeared.

This development in efficiency is very largely due to the increased part taken by the laity in the government of the Church almost every-where. They have brought in their own ideas of business methods and consecrated them to religious service. The result can be seen most markedly in the better quality and upkeep of church buildings and plant. It is mostly in England that the policy of 'mend and make do' still applies for the Church. There, it is not so much a war-time legacy as a heritage from generations of past history.

The business-man's entry into church affairs has not been entirely easy. He has met with one great stumbling-block in the shape of the parson's freehold. Relics of this ancient privilege still remain even in parts of the Anglican communion where the Act of Uniformity no longer applies. The capacity to remove an unsatisfactory official is one of the mainstays of business efficiency. But in respect to the tenure of his office the parson is found to enjoy an almost unique immunity. However, he who pays the piper calls the tune. The business-men were not slow in finding out that if they could not remove an unwanted rector by direct action, they could starve him out by withholding their subscriptions to his stipend. That procedure is impossible in England where the only part of the incumbent's income derived direct from his parishioners is the annual Easter offering. In his security of tenure the English parson can, therefore, still regard himself as having an advantage over his colleagues in other lands. Whether that is for the good of the Church as a whole is an open question.

That the clergy are not entirely given up to the effort to maintain their freehold is shown not only by the numbers of them who enter monastic life, but also by that gallant band who volunteer for missionary service. 'Foreign missions' we used to call their sphere of service in days before we began to recognize that no land can be foreign to the cause of Christ. Now that so many of the churches owing their foundation to modern missionary effort have arrived at the status of independent provinces, the sphere of missions, strictly so called, has become much smaller. Of the areas totally untouched by civilization hardly any remain today outside New Guinea. That in itself is an eloquent testimony to the work of the missionaries. Little has been said of them here, because the task of recording their achievements would have been far too great for the present volume. In fact, everything that we have recorded is the result of the work of missionaries at some period or other.

One cannot conclude this consideration of the parson in his parish without drawing attention to the benefit conferred upon the nation by the clerical families. Much fun has been made of the size of these families, particularly in Victorian times. But their size often led to the vicarage becoming a valued educational establishment for the sons of the gentry. Together with the children of the incumbent, the young people taught there grew up to fill many of the most important posts in the civil and military services. It would not be too much to say that the commendable standard of character and service displayed by this ruling class throughout the whole British Empire in its heyday was dictated by the Anglican rectory. Of the bishops during the last century not far from half have been sons of the clergy. Of those sons as a whole Francis Brown says:

'England owes them a great debt, which she has in part repaid by the respect generally accorded to the clerical order. Clerical marriage has served to prevent the social segregation of the priesthood as it has forged links with a clergyman's neighbours. It has also given the Church a good deal of influence since few men in high places, other than *novi homines*, have no clerical connections, intimate or remote.'[12]

In any estimate of the importance of the Anglican clergyman in the social life of the day due place must be given to the influence exercised through his wife, his sons and daughters.

CHAPTER THIRTEEN

CONCLUSION

A dialectic theology—Practical, tolerant, incarnational—Organization adaptable—Church and State—Authority and freedom—Communal spirit—New questions—Vitality—Imperial outlook —Lay interest—The common task—Its demand—The inner reaches—The ultimate aim

WE MUST now try to draw together the somewhat discursive thoughts we have so far generated on Anglicanism and the Anglican Communion. It is already obvious that to present a clear and bold outline is no easy task. It is no easier than an attempt to explain the English character. The exercise may be no more successful than the effort of a team of *ingénus* to explain on television what they mean by the doctrine of the Trinity. Still the very complexity of the subject gives it a fascination of its own. And in any case we are pledged to the attempt.

Dialectic Theology

We might as well begin with the most knotty problem of all. It is sometimes said, even by its friends, that the trouble with Anglicanism is that it has no theology. That surely must be wrong. Did Hooker and Jewell, Pearson and Bicknell live in vain? If it is meant that we have no comprehensive and articulated system like the *Institutes* of Calvin or even the *Decrees* of the Council of Trent, it is true enough. But it is already something of a theology to deny the necessity for binding such burdens, grievous to be borne, on men's shoulders. If it is meant that we have no special and peculiar doctrines of our own, that too may be taken as part of our glory. We claim to believe what is in the Creeds and in the Bible, that is to say, what is common to all Christendom. We have our Catechism and our Articles, although we regard them as on a lower level of authority than the creed. The Lambeth Conference of 1888 declared that missionary churches 'should not necessarily be bound to accept in their entirety the Thirty Nine Articles of Religion'.[1] It is probably just this refusal to be wise above what is written or to regard every doctrinal issue as closed that makes the critics regard Anglicans as lacking a theology.

A sounder view has been put forward by Professor H. E. W. Turner in an effort to explain Anglicanism to Scandinavians. He describes it as a dialectic faith, a faith that deliberately accepts the tension between different points of view. This is something very different from a compromise. It gives each side the opportunity to maintain the full truth as it sees it, and to work towards a full understanding between both sides, in which a satisfactory synthesis may be reached. It pre-supposes that the prospect of eternal salvation rests less on precision of intellectual belief than on an attitude of the whole personality. It encourages openness of theological discussion in order that none of the richness of eternal truth may be lost.

Certainly the tendency of the Anglican church as a whole has always been to keep the obligatory essentials of the faith to the fewest and simplest, thus giving opportunity for the greatest possible comprehensiveness. Such a policy is natural for any national church, but it was congenital in Anglicanism and was brought about, as we have seen, through the exigencies of English history. It has since been serviceable in leaving us open to every wind that blows without subjecting us to unhealthy influence from any particular quarter. Theological interest is as wide in Anglicanism as in any branch of Christianity. If it is less massive than the German, and less clear-cut than the French, it is more practical than either. It has produced its own movements to left and right, but it is not subject to the extreme change of fashion so often noticeable elsewhere. At any rate it has resulted in what an admirer has called 'the most spacious home in Christendom'.

Practical

It is observable that when the strong medicine of continental theology is introduced to Anglican circles it generally suffers considerable dilution before it is accepted for the cure of souls. Anglican theology is too closely allied to the altar and the pulpit to permit of its themes being handled as if they were primarily intended for the lecturer's desk. This has given to Anglican theology a magisterial and judicial quality which may not be as exciting as the qualities demanded of the pioneer and explorer but is probably even more valuable for helping souls in the way of pastoral care. Neither Calvin nor Luther, Barth nor Bultmann can claim any proprietary right in Anglican theology, though the influence of all would be admitted in varying degree.

Anyone who wishes to know what Anglican theology is like and does not wish to burden himself with too many details could do worse than read the volume entitled *Doctrine in the Church of England* published under the editorship of William Temple by SPCK in 1938, to which some reference has already been made, but which has been so neglected in recent years that no apology is needed for referring to it again in the hope of promoting some revival of interest. The sixteen years devoted to its composition had been well spent, and the spirit in which it was written was as nearly objective as could be. Naturally it did not please everyone, and some searching criticisms were offered in a slim volume by Fr Hebert, SSM, in the following year.[2] Theological studies have not stood still since that date but taken together the two books still give the best and most balanced account of Anglican theology today.

Tolerant

What will inevitably strike the reader of the former volume is its liberalism, or what some of its kindlier critics would call its tolerance. It is sometimes suggested that this tolerance is a modern feature developing out of indifference or amateurishness. But one finds so able a historian as Dr Norman Sykes pointing out the lack of rigidity even in an exceptionally stiff Anglican like Archbishop Laud. 'If Laud stood for a fixed liturgy and uniformity of rites and ceremonies, he championed also a free pulpit; whilst his opponents stood for a free liturgy and a rigid theological system.'[3] It was no doubt this freedom of thought rather than any views on the freedom of the will that led to the application of the epithet 'Arminian' to the English Church during the seventeenth and eighteenth centuries. In the same spirit one of the more recent apologists for Anglicanism, Archbishop Garbett, emphasizes the compatibility between the two essential qualities of authority and freedom, recalls with horror that Calvin towards the end of his life had only one thing to retract, namely an earlier plea for toleration,[4] and quotes with approval George Tyrrell's statement that the proper application of this double attitude is the perennial problem and that 'the church which solves it will sweep the world into its net'.*

Incarnational

It is a common criticism of Anglicanism, especially by such sticklers for dogmatic precision as the Eastern Orthodox and the Lutherans, that it is 'too lax and ambiguous in doctrine'. An extremely friendly Norwegian critic has described it as 'the most elastic Church in Christendom'.[5] G. F. S. Gray[6] agrees that there is no special Anglican system of theology in the sense that, for example, there is a Calvinist system; nor is any one doctrine given such overwhelming importance as Lutherans give to the doctrine of justification by faith alone. But neither scholar would take this elasticity to imply that Anglicanism has no theology. 'Anglicanism maintains the doctrines of the ancient and undivided Church, and rejects medieval developments . . . Anglican

---

*Tyrrell, a Roman Catholic, actually thought that the C. of E. came nearest this ideal.

doctrine is in fact a synthesis; it upholds on the one hand respect for the authority of tradition and revelation, on the other hand freedom for the individual to follow his conscience and to search for truth.' That is how Gray sees the position, while Molland says that if the Orthodox is the 'Church of Easter', and the Lutheran the 'Church of Good Friday', the Anglican is the 'Church of Christmas'.[7]

Most observers would probably agree that this association of Anglicans to an especial degree with a theology of the Incarnation, shows a good deal of penetration. Certainly it is the special 'slant' of many modern theologians such as Maurice, Westcott, Gore, Thornton, Scott Holland and William Temple. The emphasis on the Incarnation, the taking of the manhood into God, has led to the recognition of a diffusive aspect of the grace and power of God, and this in turn has prevented Anglican claims from becoming exclusive. Anglicanism manages to be authoritative without claiming infallibility, liberal without lapsing into mere vagueness.

Organization Adaptable
Much the same might be said of its constitutional organization. To the Anglican it is as important to have the right order as to have the right doctrine. (*Hinc illae lachrimae.*) But strict adherence to the three-fold order of bishop, priest and deacon is accompanied by a remarkably free expansiveness in general administration. It is well known that Hooker's polity proves so adaptable that many critics question whether the last three books of his monumental work can really have been written by him. While in the earlier books his characterization of the royal supremacy fits in with the practice of Tudor autocracy, in the later the monarch is made subject to the law and can only exercise dominion over the Church in accordance with the Church's own law. However that may be, in the long run it was just this adaptability that enabled a very insular and nationalist body to become the parent of a world-wide communion. In fact, contrary to what is often affirmed, the parent appears today more concerned to shake off the relics of insularity than some at least of the offspring. An Australian professor very properly complains 'the very name which has been enshrined in our constitution —"The Church of England in Australia"—has an expatriate flavour. It suggests an institution which is maintained in Australia in somewhat the same spirit as Captain Cook's cottage, moved stone by stone from its Yorkshire village, is maintained in Melbourne's Fitzroy Gardens.'[8] But then it must always be remembered that to the Australian, England, with its long history, its 'cloud-capped towers, gorgeous palaces', is just

as much the home of romance as are the wide open spaces of the Australian bush to the Englishman.

Church and State

It is an interesting question how far English secular and ecclesiastical development have acted upon each other. In the discussion of origins it is not difficult to show that there was an English Church before there was an united English Kingdom and that the representatives of the Church meeting in their national councils led the way to national unity.* In the later days of expansion the missionaries sometimes followed the flag and sometimes the flag followed the missionaries. In the South Seas it is sometimes said that when the missionaries first came they had the Bible while the natives had the land, whereas now the natives have the Bible and the missionaries the land. Much worse things might be said with perhaps greater show of justice about the whole of the colonial system. The fact is that the Church, like the secular concerns, through its very enterprise acquired a stake in many countries. Our present point is that the civil and the ecclesiastical organizations, developing side by side, inevitably affected each other.

The Church with its long tradition and its carefully ordered life both fostered among colonists a nostalgic feeling for the life they had left, and provided a structure within which the newly aroused energies of natives could be trained. At the same time the state, developing along new lines of democratic freedom, taught the Church valuable lessons in the art of self-management. Even where slavery was a part of social life this kind of inter-action was not greatly impeded. It was to the credit of Anglicanism that it learnt as quickly as it did the difference between what was essential and what was purely adventitious in its own system of government. Indeed the leaders of the Church sometimes showed themselves more far-sighted than secular opinion either at home or abroad, as for instance in their desire to appoint bishops for the American colonies. If it took a long time to plant episcopacy without prelacy overseas, it was not altogether the fault of unenterprising bishops at home.

Authority and Freedom

In the long run this development of Anglicanism in countries where it lost the status of an established church not only brought into greater prominence the elements which were essential to its ecclesiastical

---

*The first time the English Church 'deliberated and acted as a unity' was at the Council of Hertford, AD 672.

character, but also revivified ideas about the real nature of the Church which had lain almost dormant. It became clear to the man in the street and even to the professional lawyer that to be the Church was not the same thing as to be an establishment. The question inevitably arose, 'What is the Church?' Before the Reformation the question would not have been necessary, but since that time the idea of the Church as a separate entity had suffered gradual dilution until in the early nineteenth century it represented little more than the State on its spiritual side. The Oxford Movement called vivid attention to the true character of the Church as a spiritual organism. Like other organisms it developed its own external organization. Looking into its past it could recognize how in its own history it had combined elements both from the Classical and from the Semitic worlds; it had drawn from the Roman law its conception of a collective personality and from St Paul the doctrine of the Body of Christ. The corporate life thus envisaged had continued down the ages, finding its own expression in the changing environment of secular law under which it functioned. Now the newly developing Anglican communion must find an outward organization which would give full play to its double conception of authority and freedom. Under the former head it stuck to the old traditional order of ministry, creed and sacrament. Under the latter it dovetailed with the traditional order its own unique type of government by debate, carrying the old conciliar spirit into the framework of worldwide communion, national church, province, diocese, rural deanery and parish.

This combination of authority and freedom secures the relative independence of each member church while maintaining the unity of the whole. There is no infallibility and no authoritarianism. Nor is there any mere counting of heads. The effort is always to arrive at a common mind under the guidance of the Spirit. Even the resolutions passed by the Lambeth Conference are not binding except in so far as they are accepted by any diocese, and no diocese would be likely to accept them unless it felt that they would be supported in the parishes. The unity is thus that of the common mind that is inspired by love. No doubt this development has been made all the easier because of the way in which parliamentary democracy has grown up in Britain and the United States and has communicated itself to the countries for which they had some responsibility. But if the Church has benefited by the example of the State it has enjoyed the greater initial advantage and has on the whole proved the greater benefactor. It is not to be expected that, so long as human imperfection remains, the city of this world can in all respects imitate the City of God. Nevertheless international organizations like the British Commonwealth and the United Nations could probably learn a great deal by giving close attention to the way in which so varied and diverse a body as the Anglican Communion holds together. It is not suggested that mere machinery is enough. There must go with it a certain disposition which alone can ensure the smooth running of the organization. Anglicanism offers no panacea for national or international ills, it has no specific or peculiar doctrine of its own. But it can at least encourage a certain temper of mind and heart. Even although it cannot always command such a disposition for itself, it believes in the virtue of reasonableness based on charity of judgment.

Communal Spirit

This is what Anglicans would strive to make typical of their own communal spirit. They like to be thought 'broadminded' although they would generally resent the label 'Broad Church'. They associate the latter term with a certain vagueness or haziness of belief which they do not consider to be truly characteristic of themselves. They would contend that they are comprehensive rather than broad, maintaining within their own body a dialectic between high and low, between catholic and evangelical, which they regard as conducive to a deepening knowledge of the truth.

At least this continual discussion enables them to distinguish between what is central and what is on the mere fringe of faith. The theologians have reduced the necessary elements to the famous quadrilateral of creed and ministry, bible and sacraments. The man in the street may not be prepared to commit himself to much more than God, the life hereafter, and the ethics of Jesus. Even after he has taken his place in the pew and begun to learn more he will be slow to make further commitments and will argue somewhat inarticulately most of the way. Also among the clergy there is generally some difference of opinion between the higher and the lower ranks. A fair proportion of the bishops in any generation have been trained as university dons, and it is always easy for the practical parish priest to accuse them of selling the pass when they are found to favour some new type of theological methodology. A certain element of distrust of the hierarchy has been endemic among the rank and file of incumbents ever since the open hostility of the eighteenth century, which resulted in the silencing of convocation, and the attempts of the bishops to suppress the enthusiasm engendered first by the Methodists and then by the Oxford Movement. However this antagonism normally amounts to no more than the disgruntlement usually felt by the members of any society in the presence of those in authority.

New Questions

It is perhaps fortunate that other differences cut right across the barrier between bishops and 'clergy'. The long distinction between catholic and evangelical is as obvious to-day on the episcopal bench as elsewhere. But the difference is no longer so important as it was. The spirit of 'live and let live' has largely corroded the old determined opposition. There is of course a fringe of irreconcilables on the edge of either extreme, but the bulk of both parties recognize that they have to live together and make the best possible arrangements for doing so. Nowadays anyone who wishes to draw attention to this particular difference of ecclesiastical colour is met with the faint distaste that usually greets the outmoded and old fashioned. In any case other differences are continually cropping up to distract attention and provide new points of debate. Should there be women priests? Ought the method of electing bishops in England to be changed? Would it be wise to overhaul the whole parochial system? Should we give a thorough revision to the liturgy? Ought the proposed new canons for the regulation of the Church of England to be pressed in every detail whatever parliament may say? Should the organization of the whole Anglican Communion be carried to the point of centralization or should it be left in its loosely federal condition? Should the organization of provinces be intensively elaborated or should the dioceses be left as far as possible to look after themselves? Ought the Church in USA to take to itself archbishops or not? Should the day of missionary societies be reckoned to have ended or should they be encouraged to continue and given a new lease of life? Should Anglicanism strain all its powers to further the cause of ecumenism or should it spend its energies on strengthening its own position? Should it be willing to lose its distinct identity piece-meal or should it consider its own perfected character the best contribution it could make to the reunited Church of the future? What is the truly Christian attitude to pacifism, unilateralism, and the colour-bar?

These are questions of varying importance drawn from different spheres of interest. But they are modern questions and they cut across the old lines of demarcation. They give something fresh to talk about and the old points of debate begin to look less significant. Added to this there have been real gains that have put the old issues out of date. In the sphere of liturgiology for instance so much more is known about primitive and classical patterns that in some suggested revisions 'high' and 'low' seem to have changed places. It is not the evangelicals today who are inviting their people to evening communion and making their altars look as much like supper-tables as possible. It is, however, a movement from both sides that has stressed the importance of a 'family communion' at an hour when all the family can attend.

Vitality

Gains of a more material kind have been plentiful. The multiplication of organizations may be regarded as a mixed blessing, but it is at least symptomatic of great vitality in the Church. The growth of the religious communities is an even more remarkable and more permanent sign of life. The development of administrative machinery and the consequent loosening of state control has assisted the whole communion to establish its own independent identity, which has been strengthened by the readiness of the various parts of it to assemble together with growing frequency for mutual consultation and advice.

The fuller recognition of the Church as a spiritual entity has had its effect on the training and efficiency of the clergy. It is recognized that the priesthood is a profession as well as a vocation and that it demands an expert technique. To be an 'educated gentleman' is no longer sufficient to make a priest. For good or ill the general level of education has fallen while the special training has risen to make possible the emergence of a new body of ministrants who at least know their job as pastors of a spiritual flock, even if they are poor classical scholars and theologians.

The two great movements of the nineteenth and twentieth centuries, the spread overseas and the groping after unity, have had a great effect not only upon the growth of the Anglican Communion but also on its effectiveness in the world. They have also had a profound influence on its spiritual maturity. They have given it a sense of urgency in the effort to fulfil God's will. The world must be won, the Church must be recognized as one, in *our* time. Here lies the great hope not only for the ecclesiastical organization but for the secular world of states and nations. No other proffered remedy for current ills can inspire such enthusiasm. This is true even in such isolated patches as are stirred by a bastard nationalism disguised as communism or by communism disguised as nationalism. It is because the Gospel is the hope of the world that, in spite of all the material drawbacks, so many men are still induced to seek its ministry.

More remarkable in recent years, at least as far as Anglicanism is concerned, has been the awakening of lay interest. The man in the pew is no longer content to sit and listen. He recognizes that the Church is something more than the congregation of which he is a member. It is a world-wide organization imbued with one life. And as that life throbs in his veins it demands some specific expression in active work and service. The growing readiness of lay men and women to take their part in furthering the spiritual work of the Church is perhaps the most marked feature of Anglican development in our time.

Imperial Outlook

It may be the consciousness of triumph over so many obstacles both of space and thought that has given to the Anglican clergy the particular brand of happiness noticed by Archbishop Garbett,[9] and to the whole Anglican Communion that imperial outlook which may be interpreted either as superiority or as statesmanship according to one's point of view. Or it may be held to reveal lingering traces of Balliol and of British colonialism. Certainly a certain aloofness has been often detected on the part of the established hierarchy by their colleagues of other denominations. It is also a frequent topic of humorous comment in the USA. But in that country it is precisely the same quality that is alleged by their countrymen against the Episcopalians. It still depends upon the point of view. One is reminded of the reply of a visiting prelate to an Australian reporter's question: 'What do you think of the Oxford accent?' 'I don't notice it, I've just come from there.' An American gossip-writer on the occasion of Queen Elizabeth's visit to his country was much attracted by Her Majesty and wrote a charming comment: 'Elizabeth is quite a nice girl for one who talks English with such a foreign accent.' Perhaps we could go back for the emergence of our typical imperialism as well as of the correct accent to the period of the first Elizabeth and the establishment of the first empire. Neither in State nor Church have we entirely lost the spirit of Raleigh.

That spirit may be reflected in the manners of the *grand seigneur* even when all excuse is lost. But it is seen to better effect in the breadth of thought of a Hooker who combined reason and revelation in such a way that all knowledge could be drawn into his studies and all seen to be a gift from God. The humanism thus engendered is with us still. Anglicans have always found it difficult to separate sharply between the sacred and the profane. When God created the world 'he saw that it was good'. If now the world 'lieth in the evil one', it is there for rescue; and it is our business to rescue it by transforming it into the Kingdom of God, the realm in which God's rule is recognized and obeyed. It is indeed a typical Anglican temptation to take too activist a view of this possibility, and to think that, if we adjust the material situation aright, the Kingdom will be here. We find it hard to learn the lesson that in the last resort the Kingdom can come only from God out of heaven and that all *we* can do is to prepare the way for its coming. Nevertheless the fact that the Anglican is in the long run an optimist, firmly convinced of a happy future which he can himself do something to secure, gives him a wide outlook, prevents him from sinking into a mere cloistered piety, and removes him as far as possible from the mental attitude of a sect.

Lay Interest

It may be that this imperial (not to say imperious) character is just the other side of the Anglican's passion for liberty. No doubt he is suffering for that just now, when the general tendency of a disordered world is to cry out for someone to put it to rights and many young people are asking for authority to preserve them from the jeopardy in which they are placed by the modern chaos. The typical Anglican is still unwilling to forfeit any portion of his liberty. Roger Lloyd says that there is no liberty anywhere so absolute as that of the Anglican parish priest.[10] Like priest, like people. In many respects the Anglican communion is a real layman's Church. He is so much at home with it that he is not in the least afraid of breaking its rules. Norman Sykes affirms[11] that 'it was a byword amongst reformed churches for its lack of a proper discipline of the laity'. No doubt the Anglican way is extremely easygoing where the laity are concerned. As a result the laity have fallen badly behind in their knowledge of the Christian faith and of the flood of new light that modern research has thrown upon its history. Archdeacon Mayfield[12] puts the point clearly: 'The saying popular in the 1920s that the laity, in their knowledge of the Christian faith and its developments, lag fifty years behind the clergy, is still true, though the period needs increasing.'

However, there is another side to the picture. No one whose business it is to lecture on such subjects can fail to be aware that there is growing up an ecclesiastical intelligentsia, lay men and women who make themselves thoroughly conversant with the conclusions of scholarship in biblical studies, apologetics, church history, and doctrine. If this kind of interest spreads, as it shows every sign of doing, the Anglican method of treating its members as adults will be amply rewarded.

It is among an intelligent and instructed laity that the liberty of the clergy will be most appreciated. They will want to know what the Church stands for, but they will want to be told, not simply on authority, but by someone who is allowed sufficient freedom of thought to be acknowledged as sincere and whole-hearted in his statement. Such a laity will always expect their clergy to retain some of the amateur status of the gentleman, and they will not be unduly elated by news of increased professional skill. However, with the endemic perversity of the human race they will resent any failure in professional competence and they will always want to 'have it both ways'. In the long run the laity get the kind of clergy they deserve. (After all, they themselves produce them!) This tendency may help to explain the somewhat indefinite status of the Anglican clergyman, not quite surrounded by the numinous halo of the Roman Catholic priest and yet not quite to be treated as 'no different from anybody else', like his opposite number in non-conformity. How he is treated will depend largely upon himself. At the worst he is ignored, as in some industrial areas; at the best he is treated as a friend, in whatever circles he moves. Always he is expected to display a higher standard of morality than his neighbours. The fact that he is generally a married man means that his family must share his example, and the vicarage is expected to be a pattern for other homes in the parish.

Comparison with his neighbours on grounds of business efficiency is not so easy as it was. The parson who farmed his own glebe has almost died out, and has hardly been replaced by the new type that works beside his parishioners at the lathe or on the assembly line. There are many more who are schoolmasters or who have already completed some other professional career before entering Holy Orders. But none of these things, nor even the shedding of the clerical collar, obliterates the distinction in the popular mind between priest and layman. From whatever social stratum he is drawn, the 'clergyman' is treated with the respect due to his cloth (how typically Anglican the phrase sounds!) until by his own act he forfeits it. Where he tries to deserve it he is met with much more than a distant respect. In public life today there are no ties of affection and loyalty so strong as those which unite the parish priest to his people. In many cases those ties still endure half a century after the priest has left the district. So easily does the pastoral relationship pass over into that of intimate personal friendship.

The Common Task

It is against the background of such a relationship between clergy and people that it is necessary to view their common task. As together they constitute the Church, so it is together that they must accept responsibility for the work the Church is intended to do, whether that work is called evangelism, or the salvation of souls, or preparing the way for the Kingdom of God. The special difficulties today are three: the drift of the masses away from religion, the wastage in Church membership, and the shortage of man-power. These difficulties are not felt with equal force in all parts of the Anglican Communion. In the United States for instance the current seems to be setting decidedly the other way. No doubt many of the missionary dioceses could say the same thing (except that they need more men and money to take full advantage of the opportunity offered). Unfortunately perhaps the English experience is more generally typical.

Here the drift of the masses away from religion is glaringly obvious. There is no need to exaggerate it. The common saying that 'not one person in ten ever darkens the door of a church' is quite obviously untrue, as could be seen at once by anyone who took the trouble to reckon up the number of people who attend the places of worship throughout the country on any normal Easter Day. Nevertheless the attendance at church on ordinary Sundays is a good deal less than it used to be. That is evidenced by the fact that many churches once fitted with galleries to accommodate great congregations are now glad to see them taken down or else converted into offices and club rooms. It is important, however, to realize that the members of the congregation thus lost did not belong to the 'masses'. The Church never had many of them, nor did the Free Churches, whose custom of selling or renting the whole of their seating accommodation kept out all but the 'respectable' classes. The charity seats, so much condemned in the old parish churches, did at least give the very poor a chance of attending church if they wished. In fact the free seats were normally occupied, but there were too few of them. So we never had the masses and we have never succeeded in capturing them.

An equally serious problem from the pastoral point of view is the Church's failure to bring her own members to the full practice of their religion. Out of nearly 27 million baptized there are rather less than 10 million confirmed, while the annual number of communicants at Easter does not amount to two and a half million. It is not to be supposed that this falling off represents a rejection of religion or even of the Anglican faith. Far from it. It is indeed a common contention on the part of those who stay away that they are just as good Christians as those who attend regularly. No doubt the great and rapid rise in social amenities and easy entertainment, together with the upheaval caused by two world wars in one generation, has had much to do with the emergence of this strange phenomenon of a professing but non-practising population. Some of it must also be due to the shrinkage of numbers in the clerical profession. There are now in round figures only fifteen thousand clergymen serving in the two provinces of Canterbury and York. That means that during the last few years, while the population increased by about five million the number of ordained men at work has decreased by about five thousand. It is true that to the total clerical number we have to add over seven thousand full-time lay workers, but it is still evident that by the old standards the ministerial provision must be regarded as gravely inadequate. The situation is closely paralleled on the Continent, and also among other denominations in Britain. A source of consolation is the fact that the position is beginning to improve. It is unlikely that it will be completely restored, but at least the fall in the number of candidates for the ministry seems for the moment to have been arrested.

It must unfortunately be recognized that, in spite of all possible excuses, the Church fails to make her services attractive to a large proportion even of her own members. Or, if that is the wrong way to put it, she does not succeed in arousing in them the consciousness of a need for regular worship. Among those who do attend frequently the middle classes provide the large majority. It is the trading and professional classes that still form the backbone of the Church. There may be some connection here between Anglicanism and respectability. If so it is none the worse for that. It is at least worth noticing that neither a more corybantic nor a more esoteric type of worship has succeeded any better in capturing the adherence of the rest of the population at either end of the social scale. This observation holds good not only in Britain but in such other parts of the Commonwealth as Australia and New Zealand. In the United States on the other hand the ratio between membership and attendance is probably higher than anywhere else except in the purely missionary districts.

The Demands of Anglicanism

Of course it may be that Anglicanism demands something that not a great many even of its own members can give consistently. At least that is what the Bishop of Chester seems to think.[13]

'To be an Anglican requires many qualities which even some men of highest religious genius have lacked. It requires the courage to apply the individual conscience to the challenge of the Faith; it needs the patience to wait till the answer to some problem not yet obvious is revealed, and the honesty on occasions to say, "I don't know". It needs the love to be tolerant with those whom we think misguided or foolish in the expression of their opinions. It needs the self-discipline to accept the demands of our faith, not because we are told we must do so, but because we believe such things to be true. Here is the true genius of Anglicanism; and it is very precious.'

Perhaps the atmosphere is a little too rarefied, the tone pitched a little too high, for truly popular appeal. On the evidence of friend and critic alike the three most obvious features of Anglicanism are tolerance, restraint, and learning. None of them is characteristic of mankind in the mass. Taken all together they may well prove a strange and un-attractive climate for the man in the street.

Meredith Dewey[14] carries the analysis a step further and adds to the main characteristic of Anglicanism the twin traits of realism and pragmatism.

'If I were briefly to describe the ethos of our Anglican tradition thus illus-trated, I would say its distinctive quality is realism. It is anchored to fact and ascertainable fact. Its debate perpetually returns to the ordinary experience of ordinary men. It is not philosophically speculative, nor does it pay great regard to abnormal mystical phenomena. Its approach to Scripture is not rarified, isolating texts or passages here and there to erect a theory, plausible and imposing, but without bearing much relation to life. It continually returns to the consequences of believing, to man's moral experience, his spiritual experience and to his common sense. In this sense it is pragmatic. It is pragmatic not in the sense that it defines truth by experience, by what works, but it is pragmatic because it is based on pragma —on fact, on the nature of God and his purpose for man.'

One might have thought that this realism might have lent increased importance to the great central body of moderate opinion. Such, however, is not the judgment of at least one qualified observer. Arch-deacon Mayfield[15] thinks that central churchmanship has declined in recent years and that the two wings of catholics and evangelicals have in consequence drawn closer together. The catalytic element has been provided by the new stress on episcopacy.

'The closer relation of the Church of England with other episcopal and non-episcopal churches has emphasized the place which the Anglican episcopate occupies as a focus of unity for Catholic and Evangelical alike. As a result of this *rapprochement*, the central or moderate tradition has declined in impor-tance. Whereas formerly this central tradition could provide a link between the greater and far more positive traditions, today the link is found directly in deeper mutual understanding and sympathy. Such tensions as may be engendered by the existence within one communion of Catholic and Evangelical traditions were seldom more relaxed than they are today.'

It should be pointed out that the bishops are not alone in their endeavour to ignore or surmount the barriers between parties in the Church. A great deal has been done in recent years by the principals of theological colleges, who have steadfastly refused to regard their institutions as seminaries for the close in-breeding of any one type of churchmanship. Even while remaining loyal to the general standpoint of their foundation they have taken care that the students shall become familiar with other aspects of churchmanship than their own. Just as in 1827 it was a combination of interests from all sides of the Church that made possible the immense sales of Keble's *Christian Year*, so today the average student is once again becoming anxious to know every side of a question and even to hear leaders who are not of his own favoured school. No one now thinks it possible to restore unity either in the Anglican Communion or in Christendom as a whole by the imposition of a stern uniformity. It can be done only by the ungrudging recognition of legitimate interests and by giving full play to their expression. If Anglicanism can do this adequately within its own borders, it will give a welcome assurance to Christians throughout the world that unity can be sufficiently won and established, not on a basis of centralization and magisterial authority, but by a harmony of autonomous parts held together by a common faith and mutual service. That at least seems to be the practical conclusion to which experience is leading the bishops. It is to be hoped that they have not got too far ahead of their followers.

The Inner Reaches

If one is inclined to think that all this is rather superficial and concerned only with the externals of religion, it is well to be reminded that the *via media*, which is so characteristic of Anglicanism, is to be found also in the inner reaches of its spiritual and pastoral life. Anglican spirituality is neither so emotional nor so speculative as that to be found elsewhere. It aims at a level-headedness which has often been reproached as lack of enthusiasm, but is also mercifully far removed from the semi-hysteria or quasi-obsession which sometimes makes one feel uneasy in the presence of religious fervour. The fact that there is so frequent an interchange between pastoral and academic posts helps to preserve the balance between emotion and reason among both clergy and laity. The speculative and affective strains characteristic of all true religion are maintained in harmony, and superstition, whether in thought or practice, is kept at arm's length.*

This desire to balance opposites is the true *via media*. It is often mistaken for weakness or woolliness. There may be left in it some residuum of the Britisher's love of the amateur but it is more likely to arise from an ability to see both sides of a question. It may often arouse suspicion because it makes impossible a plain answer to a plain question. Some

*This is the gist of the teaching on spiritual direction by Martin Thornton.

churches prefer to give their downright answer at once, and then, when it has been assimilated, to bring out the necessary qualifications. The Anglican thinks aloud in public about all the qualifications first, and then proceeds to give an answer that tries to satisfy all the conditions. It must be admitted that the latter procedure is more likely to satisfy the academic temper than to meet practical and pastoral needs. 'It is always easier to obey a rule than to apply a principle.' Yet our Lord himself seems as a teacher to have chosen the more difficult way. He more often asked questions than answered them, and sometimes he would reply to one question merely by asking another. People must be taught as far as possible to think for themselves. We must be adults, not robots. And in religion truth is even more important than practical expediency.

Another aspect of this *via media* is to be found in Anglican worship, where the professional expert is never allowed to run away with the theme and get too far ahead of the general public. The four main principles on which the arrangement of the liturgy has proceeded ever since the Reformation are quite clear: the congregation must be allowed to worship in its own mother tongue; the priest and people must share together, with a proper vocal part for the latter; all must be in accord with the plain teaching of the Bible; and due contact must be maintained with the ancient forms of worship from the Church's historic past. These are the basic principles that animated Cranmer and the compilers of the early editions of the Book of Common Prayer. They were so successfully applied that interest in the science of liturgiology almost died out. It was spasmodically revived by the Non-jurors and by the leaders of the Oxford Movement. But it is only in our own day that it has really come to life again. Now it is part of a general interest that has spread far beyond the bounds of any one communion. What is known as the Liturgical Movement can be found working in all the main branches of Christendom from Rome to Edinburgh. Nowhere has it had greater effect than in the churches of the Anglican communion, as witness the excellent work done in the revision of the liturgy in places so far apart as Canada and India. If imitation is the sincerest form of flattery Anglicans can note with satisfaction the approximations made to their standards in churches both of the Pre-Reformation and Post-Reformation traditions. This change has manifested itself in the way of increased intelligibility on the one hand and of increased order and variety on the other.

Whether it can ever be possible to frame a Prayer Book which at one and the same time is intelligible throughout to the totally inexpert and also provides an all-round satisfaction for the needs of the practised and regular churchgoer may be doubted. At the same time, even as things are, the Church is the only institution in any parish which provides for all the members of the population of both sexes and of every age and calling. 'All other community-making activities are for this section or that, the boys, the mothers, the workers, the employers. None but the Church is for all.'[16] The one activity in which the whole congregation joins together is its worship. It is this that settles their attitude to God and to each other, this indeed that settles their whole attitude to life. The man who *worships* his Creator has an entirely different view of existence from any other. No wonder that the action of worship appears important and that Anglicans should take pains to establish it on the highest level. Where it is well done in sincerity and truth, whether in some homely village church or in the reverberating spaces of some vast cathedral, it has about it a numinous quality which brings the participant within the very gates of heaven and returns him to earth with something of its glory still radiating from him. 'The Anglican tradition of public worship is not only one of the chief bonds which unite Anglicans all over the world, but one of its greatest contributions to Christendom as a whole.'[17]

The Ultimate Aim

To the Great Church of the future Anglicanism is ready to commit much more than this, even itself. It has no desire to perpetuate itself in isolation, still less to subdue others to itself. It looks forward to a re-united Church in which itself and all it has stood for will form but a part. It expects a world-wide Church which will be truly Catholic and Evangelical but not necessarily Anglican. That was the spirit of the Lambeth Appeal in 1920 and that is the spirit in which the negotiations over South India were undertaken. Certainly Anglicans will want to take steps to prevent their communion from being dismembered and distributed piece-meal among existing Christian bodies. There is no existing body that, as it now is, stands for all the things in like proportion for which the Anglican Communion stands. They are a great heritage and they should certainly form a part of the united church of the future. It ought not to pass the wit of man, under the guidance of the Holy Spirit, to find a way in which they can be preserved within the framework of the universal Church.

NOTES

INTRODUCTION

1. *Oxford Dictionary of the Christian Church* s.v. Anglicanism.

CHAPTER I: HISTORICAL TURNING POINTS

1. Fr Cary-Elwes, *The Sheepfold and the Shepherd*, p. 205.
2. Collingwood and Myres, *Roman Britain* (Oxford, 1936), p. 270 f.
3. Gee and Hardy, *Documents Illustrative of English Church History* (London 1921), p.1.
4. Collingwood and Myres, *op. cit.*, p. 271.
5. Bede, *Ecclesiastical History*, III, IV.1.
6. Professor Bréhier, *L'Art Chrétien*, p. 172.
7. Bede, *op. cit.*, XXVII.
8. Oakeshott, *The Sequence of English Medieval Art* (Faber and Faber, 1950), p. 11. Note especially the map showing exchange of cultural influences.
9. I. P. Shaw, *Nationality and the Western Church*, pp. 18–19.
10. Gee and Hardy, *op. cit.*, p. 56.
11. Professor Darlington, *The English Church and the Continent* (Faith Press), pp. 11, 12.
12. C. M. Ady, *The English Church* (Faber and Faber, 1940), pp. 58 ff.
13. Maitland, *Constitutional History of England*, pp. 11, 509.
14. J. W. C. Wand, *The Second Reform* (Faith Press, 1953).
15. Hensley Henson, *The Church of England* (CUP, 1939), p. 7.
16. I. P. Shaw, *op. cit.*, p.33.
17. A. F. Pollard, *Henry VIII* (Longmans), p. 61.
18. Gee and Hardy, 25 Henry VIII c. 21 Peter Pence Act 1534, *op. cit.*, p. 225.
19. C. M. Ady, *op. cit.*, p 178 f.
20. Sir J. E. Neale, *Elizabeth I and her Parliaments* (Jonathan Cape, 1953) passim.
21. Norman Sykes, *From Sheldon to Secker* (CUP, 1959), pp. 205 ff.
22. Hans Cnattingius, *Bishops and Societies* (SPCK, 1952), pp. 72 ff.

CHAPTER II: ITS SISTER CHURCHES

1. Dawley, *The Episcopal Church and its Work* (Seabury Press, 1955), p. 40.
2. Sperry, *Religion in America* (CUP, 1945), p. 79.
3. Latourette, *History of the Expansion of Christianity* (Eyre and Spottiswoode, 1943), Vol. V pp. 326 ff.
4. Cockshut, *Anglican Attitudes* (Collins, 1959), ch. V.
5. Stephen Neill in Wand, *Anglican Communion* (OUP, 1948), p. 90.

CHAPTER III: FAITH

1. Sir Thomas Browne, *Religio Medici* (Everyman's Edition), p. 3.
2. More and Cross, *Anglicanism* (SPCK, 1935), pp. 15, 16.
3. William Chillingworth, *The Religion of Protestants. A Safe Way to Salvation* (1638).
4. Quoted in J. S. Whale, *Christian Doctrine* (CUP), p. 16.
5. More and Cross, *op. cit.*, p. 95.
6. Col. 3[11].
7. Zech. 4.
8. More and Cross, *op. cit.*, pp. 689–90.
9. More and Cross, *op. cit.*, p. 695.
10. C. M. Ady, *The English Church*, p. 157.

CHAPTER IV: A WAY OF LIFE

1. Dr Richard Niebuhr, *Christ and Culture* (Faber, London, 1952).
2. Joseph Addison, Hymn 297 in *English Hymnal*.
3. Swinburne, *Hymn of Man*.
4–11. Quotations rom More and Cross, *Anglicanism* (SPCK, 1935).
12. E. E. Reynolds, *Three Cardinals* (Burns and Oates 1958), p. 36.
13. cf. *The Report on the Commemoration of Saints and Heroes* (SPCK, 1957).

CHAPTER V: THE HISTORIC PARTIES

1. Gal. 5^1.
2. T. A. Lacey, *The Anglo-Catholic Faith* (Methuen, 1926), p. 23.
3. Addleshaw, *The High Church Tradition* (Faber, 1941), pp. 9, 10.
4. Owen Chadwick, *The Mind of the Oxford Movement* (London, Black 1960).
5. E. A. George, *Seventeenth Century Man of Latitude* (London, 1908), p. 109.
6. Quoted in Balleine, *History of the Evangelical Party*, from *Fraser's Magazine* (Jan. 1878), p. 22.

CHAPTER VI: MODERN LIBERALISM

1. Ensor, *England* (Oxford 1936) p. 527.
2. London, 1915.
3. Moorman, *History of the Church in England*, p. 391.
4. Philippians 2.

CHAPTER VII: HEY-DAY OF ANGLO-CATHOLICISM

1. Unfortunately these chapters were written before the appearance of Archbishop Ramsey's Hale Lectures '*From Gore to Temple*' (Longmans 1960). This book is strongly recommended as a fuller account of the development of Anglican Theology between *Lux Mundi* and the Second World War (1889–1939).

CHAPTER IX: INSTITUTIONS AND SOCIETIES

1. H. P. Thompson, *Thomas Bray* (SPCK, 1954), p. 16.
2. T. S. Johnson, *The Story of a Mission* (SPCK, 1953), p. 23.
3. Hans Cnattingius, *Bishops and Societies* (SPCK, 1952), p. 227.
4. Warre Cornish, *History of the English Church in the Nineteenth Century*, Part I, p. 38; and Lowther Clarke, *History of SPCK*, p. 104.
5. Violet B. Lancaster, *Short History of the Mothers' Union*, and G. Payne-Cook, *Recollections of a Vice-President of the Mothers' Union*.

CHAPTER X: RELIGIOUS COMMUNITIES

1. P. F. Anson, *The Call of the Cloister* (SPCK, 1955), p. 5 ff.
2–5. *Guide to the Religious Communities of the Anglican Communion*, (Mowbray, 1951).
6. P. F. Anson, *op. cit.*, p. 131.

NOTES

CHAPTER XI: THE PARSON IN HIS PULPIT

1. Charles Smyth, *The Art of Preaching* (SPCK, 1940), pp. 14 ff.
2. M. Maclure, *The Paul's Cross Sermons* (OUP, 1958), No. 6 in the Studies and Texts Series of the University of Toronto Department of English.
3. Maclure, *op. cit.*, p. 201.
4. H. Trevor Hughes, *The Piety of Jeremy Taylor* (Macmillan, 1960), p. 116.
5. E. W. Kemp, *N. P. Williams* (Hodder and Stoughton, 1954), and *Beauty and Bands* (Hodder and Stoughton, 1955).
6. Examples of current styles in preaching can be studied in F. D. Gifford's *The Anglican Pulpit Today* (London–Mowbray, 1953).

CHAPTER XII: THE PARSON IN HIS PARISH

1. Dr A. Tindal Hart, *The Country Clergy in Elizabethan and Stuart Times* (Phoenix, London 1958), p. 18.
2. Dr A. Tindal Hart, *op. cit.*, pp. 18–19.
3. Cambridge University Press, 1956.
4. Faith Press, London, 1958.
5. Dr Tindal Hart, *op. cit.*, p.78.
6. J. W. C. Wand, *History of the Modern Church* (Methuen), p. 129.
7. J. W. C. Wand, *The High Church Schism* (Faith Press, 1951), and Overton, *The Non-jurors* (London, 1845).
8. C. K. F. Brown, *History of the English Clergy* (Faith Press, 1953), p. 15, 36 ff.
9. J. W. C. Wand, *The Second Reform* (Faith Press, 1953).
10. Dr A. Tindal Hart, *The Country Priest in English History* (Phoenix, London 1959), p. 76.
11. G. F. S. Gray, *The Anglican Communion* (SPCK, 1958).
12. C. K. F. Brown, *op. cit.*, p. 222.

CHAPTER XIII: CONCLUSION

1. Resolution 19.
2. Memorandum on the Report of the Archbishops' Commission on Christian Doctrine (SPCK).
3. *The English Religious Tradition* (SCM, 1953), p. 38.
4. C. Garbett, *Claims of the Church of England* (Hodder and Stoughton, 1947), pp. 27, 45.
5. Einer Molland, *Christendom* (Mowbray) 1959), chap. 6.
6. G. F. S. Gray, *The Anglican Communion* (SPCK, 1958), p. 111.
7. Molland, *op. cit.*, 148.
8. L. Webb, *Conciliar Element in Anglican Tradition* (Canberra, 1957), p. 2.
9. C. Garbett, *op. cit.*, p. 268.
10. Roger Lloyd, *Church of England in the Twentieth Century* (Longmans, 1956), I, p. 225.
11. Norman Sykes, *English Religious Tradition*, p. 2.
12. Mayfield, *The Church of England* (Oxford, 1958), p. 175.
13. Ellison, *The Anglican Communion* (Seabury Press, Connecticut 1960), p. 84.
14. Dewey, Ratcliffe and Sykes, *Anglican Tradition* (SPCK, 1959), p. 4.
15. Mayfield, *op. cit.*, p. 191.
16. Roger Lloyd, *op. cit.*, I, p. 161.
17. G. F. S. Gray, *op. cit.*, p. 133.

BIBLIOGRAPHY

The subject is so vast that no attempt can be made at an exhaustive list. The following is to be viewed merely as a series of suggestions for further reading. Preference is given to the more modern works, and those only in English. Except where otherwise stated they are published in London.

For the purely historical side of the subject the eight-volume *History of the English Church* edited by Stephens and Hunt (1901–10) is indispensable. Of the single-volume histories the latest is J. R. H. Moorman's *History of the Church in England* (1953). *Documents Illustrative of English Church History*, Gee and Hardy 1921, and *Anglicanism*, More and Cross are invaluable for reference to original sources. The works of leading Anglican divines can be found *in extenso* in the many volumes of the *Library of Anglo-Catholic Theology* and their Protestant counterpart the publications of the Parker Society, all of which appeared around the middle of the nineteenth century.

CHAPTER I: HISTORICAL TURNING POINTS

ORIGINS
The background in *Early Church History* can be studied in the large books by Duchesne, 4 vols. (1909), Kidd, 3 vols. (1922), Carrington, 2 vols. (1957), or in the single volume work by J. W. C. Wand, 7th ed. (1962). The early contacts with continental Christianity are discussed in the first two volumes of the *Oxford History of England: Roman Britain and the English Settlements* by Collingwood and Myres (1936), and *Anglo-Saxon England* by F. M. Stenton (1943). The pre-Norman church is dealt with at length by A. Plummer in *The Churches in Britain before AD 1000* (1911), while its relations with the rest of Europe can be studied in *England and the Continent in the 8th Century* by W. Levison (1946) and *The English Church and the Continent* by R. M. Darlington (1959).

On the REFORMATION period the following are specially worthy of study: *Henry VIII*, A. F. Pollard (new edition 1951); *Cranmer and the Reformation under Edward VI*, C. Smyth (1926); *Nicholas Ridley*, J. G. Ridley (1957); *The Reign of Elizabeth*, J. B. Black (1936); *Elizabeth and her Parliaments*, J. E. Neale (1953); *Elizabeth's First Archbishop*, F. J. Shirley (n.d.); *Whitgift and the English Church*, V. J. K. Brook (n.d.); *John Whitgift and the Reformation*, P. M. Dawley (1955); An old favourite is *The Reformation of the 16th Century* by Charles Beard (1883).

On the EXPANSION period the last five volumes of K. S. Latourette's seven-volume *History of the Expansion of Christianity* (1945) is the fullest record. As far as the Church of England is concerned the beginnings of it can be seen in *Church and State in England to Death of Queen Anne* by H. M. Gwatkin (1917). The results can be seen in *Christian History in the Making* (1946) by J. McLeod Campbell. Valuable information on the discussions to which it has given rise can be found in *Bishops and Societies* by H. Chattingius (1952) and *The Lambeth Conferences (1867–1948)*, a selection with an introduction published by SPCK in 1948. *An Atlas of Christian History* by Dell and Fullard (1960) will also be found useful. For questions of government one should consult H. L. Clarke, *Constitutional Church Government in the Dominions* (1924), and R. A. Giles, *The Constitutional History of the Australian Church* (1929).

CHAPTER II: ITS SISTER CHURCHES

These are covered seriatim in *The Anglican Communion* edited by J. W. C. Wand (1948). For the Protestant Episcopal Church in the United States information from a non-Anglican can be found in W. C. Sperry *Religion in America* (1945). The most compendious account is in *The Episcopal Church and its Work* by P. M. Dawley (Greenwich, Connecticut 1955), and *Men and Movements in the American Episcopal Church* by E. C. Chorley (New York 1946) should also be consulted together with *A History of the American Episcopal Church* by W. W. Manross (New York 1935). For Canada see *Our Church in Canada* edited by C. W. Vernon (Toronto 1933).

For India see Eyre Chatterton *History of the Church of England in India* (1924) and C. J. Grimes *Towards an Indian Church* (1946). For South Africa A. H. H. Baynes *South Africa* (1908) and Osmond Victor *The Salient of South Africa* (1931). Some account of the Church in Australia will be found in *Australia* (Handbooks of Church Expansion) by A. E. David (1908), *Australia's Greatest Need* by J. W. S. Tomlin (1914); of the Bush Brotherhoods in C. H. S. Matthews *A Parson in the Australian Bush* (1926); and of the formation of new dioceses in J. W. C. Wand *White of Carpentaria* (1946), and in E. S. Rowland *A Century of the English Church in New South Wales* (n.d.). For New Zealand recourse may be had to H. T. Purchas *History of the English Church in New Zealand* (1914) and L. Creighton *G. A. Selwyn* (1923). For China one should consult V. K. Shebbeare *China* (1933), G. Barker *Changing Scene in China* (1946) and M. Bruce *Opportunity in China* (1947). But unfortunately no book exists to describe the present state of the Chinese Church. For Japan one should see H. St. G. Tucker's *History of the Episcopal Church in Japan* (1938) and C. K. Sansbury *Japan* (1947). For Africa there is no book that covers the ever-changing situation but one may see A. H. Baynes *South Africa* (1908); one poignant problem is dealt with in *Colour Conflict* by G. W. Broomfield (1943). Borneo is dealt with in L. B. Currey's *Borneo* (1933) and the West Indies in *The Diocese of Jamaica* by J. B. Ellis (1913).

The sister churches in the British Isles have their own individual histories. The following books may be found useful: Anthony Mitchell *Scotland's Church* (Dundee 1933), J. Ritchie *Reflections on Scottish Church History* (1927), W. A. Phillips *History of the Church of Ireland* (3 vols.) (Dublin 1933), Johnson-Robinson-Jackson *History of the Church of Ireland* (Dublin 1953), D. A. Jones *A History of the Church in Wales* (Carmarthen 1926), J. W. James *A Church History of Wales* (Ilfracombe 1945).

Most of the churches mentioned in this chapter publish their own annual year book, which brings one up to date. The earlier history, at least of those of modern foundation, is embodied in the annals of the great missionary societies—*History of the Church Missionary Society* by E. Stock (4 vols., 1899–1916) and of SPG *Into All Lands* by H. P. Thompson (1951). The architectural aspect of their growth can be seen in *Anglican Cathedrals outside the British Isles* by B. F. L. Clarke (1958).

A full-dress history of missions is the seven volumes of K. S. Latourette's *History of the Expansion of Christianity* (1945) and a short introduction is Mrs Creighton's *Missions* (Home University Library, n.d.).

CHAPTER III: FAITH

The classical statement is to be found in the *Works of Richard Hooker* (2 vols.) (1890). It can be filled out from the quotations from the eighteenth century to be found in *Anglicanism* by More and Cross (1935). *Bicknell on the Thirty-Nine Articles* has become a classic and has been ably edited by H. J. Carpenter (1955). A careful statement of limits within which variation is allowable is to be found in the official report of the Archbishops' Commission *Doctrine in the Church of England* (1938). An epoch-making book was *Lux Mundi* edited by C. Gore, of which a twelfth edition appeared in 1891. The movement of thought is traced in *Development of English Theology in later 19th Century* (1952) and *English Thought 1860–1900* (1956) both by L. E. Elliott-Binns, *Religious Thought in England from 1850* by C. C. J. Webb (1933), and *From Gore to Temple* by A. M. Ramsey (1960. Quite admirable but appeared too late to be used in this book).

Current individual views may be found in Cyril Garbett *Claims of Church of England* (1947) and *Church and State in England* (1950), and J. W. C. Wand *What the Church of England Stands For* (1951). See also *The Doctrine of the Church in Anglican Theology 1547–1603* H. F. Woodhouse (1954).

CHAPTER IV: WAY OF LIFE

A good introduction can be found in *The Kingdom of Christ* F. D. Maurice (1838); *Crockford Prefaces,* a selection issued in 1947; *English Church Life from the Restoration to the Tractarian*

Movement, Wickham Legg (1914); and *Introduction to Canon Law in the Church of England*, E. W. Kemp (1956). On Anglican humanism one should read *The Platonic Tradition in English Religious Thought* by W. R. Inge (1926). *Amor Dei* by J. Burnaby (1938), *Authority and Freedom* by A. E. J. Rawlinson (1933), and *Nature, Man and God* by William Temple (1934). On moralism one should read *Dr Whichcote's Aphorisms* edited by W. R. Inge (1930), *The Philosophy of the Good Life* by C. Gore, *Christian Morality* by H. H. Henson (1936), *Faith of a Moralist*, A. E. Taylor (2 vols., 1932), *The Vision of God*, K. E. Kirk (1931).

On Anglican piety one must be familiar with such classics as Law's *Serious Call*, *The Whole Duty of Man*, Andrewes's *Preces Privatae*. An excellent discussion of such works is to be found in C. J. Stranks *Anglican Devotion* (1961). Other examinations of Anglican piety are *Studies of English Mystics* by W. R. Inge (1905), *Chronicles of Little Gidding* by A. L. Maycock (1954) and (very interestingly by a Methodist) *The Piety of Jeremy Taylor* by H. T. Hughes (1960). For worship and its adjuncts one should read *Worship* by E. Underhill (1936), *The Worship of the Church* by M. H. Shepherd (Greenwich, Connecticut, 1952), *The Worship of the Church* by A. R. Bellars (c. 1933), *History of Christian Worship* by O. Hardman (1937), *Liturgy and Society* by A. G. Herbert (1935), *Liturgy and Worship* edited by W. K. Lowther Clarke (1932), *Music and Worship* by Davies and Grace (1935), *Church Music in History and Practice* by W. Douglas (1937).

CHAPTER V: THE HISTORIC PARTIES

The history of the High Church party can be traced in *The Nonjurors* by J. H. Overton (1902), *History of the Nonjurors* T. Lathbury (1845), *The High Church Schism* J. W. C. Wand (1951), *High Church Tradition* G. W. O. Addleshaw (1941), *High Church Party* G. Every (1956), *The Oxford Movement (1833–45)* R. W. Church (1891), *Short History of the Oxford Movement* S. L. Ollard (1915), *The Oxford Movement and After* (1932), *The Mind of the Oxford Movement* (an anthology with excellent introductory essay) O. Chadwick (1961), and a quite admirable Lutheran account in Yngve Brilioth's *The Anglican Revival* (1925).

The origins of the Broad Church Party can be traced in E. A. George's *Seventeenth Century Men of Latitude* (1908) in F. J. Powicke's *Cambridge Platonists* (1926), J. de Pauley's *The Candle of the Lord* (1937), A. S. Farrar's *Critical History of Free Thought* (1862), P. Gardner's *Modernism in the English Church*. For social repercussions one should see *The Church and the World* by Hudson and Reckitt (3 vols., 1940), and *Charles Kingsley and his Ideas* by G. Kendall (1946).

The rise of the evangelical or Low Church School can be followed in *A Short History of the Evangelical Movement* by G. W. E. Russell (1915), *History of the Evangelical Party* by G. R. Balleine (5th ed., 1933), *Early Cornish Evangelicals* by G. C. B. Davies (1951), *Activities of the Puritan Faction* by I. M. Calder (1957), *Simeon and Church Order* by C. Smyth (1940), *Charles Simeon* by Hunnell and Pollard (1959) and *The British Anti-Slavery Movement* by R. Coupland (1933).

CHAPTER VI: MODERN LIBERALISM

For this subject the more noteworthy symposia should be studied: *Essays and Reviews* (1860), *Lux Mundi* (1859), *Foundations* (1912), *Essays Catholic and Critical* (1926). *Modernism in the English Church* by P. Gardner (1926) should be again consulted as well as *English Thought* (1860–1900) by L. E. Elliott-Binns (1956). A particular aspect is dealt with by Duncan Forbes in *The Liberal Anglican Idea of History* (Cambridge 1952). O. C .Thomas gives a typical example of the way Anglican liberalism works out in *William Temple's Philosophy of Religion* (1961). A. O. J. Cockshutt discusses some of the more important controversies with admirable detachment in *Victorian Attitudes* (1959). Liberal views as they affect the doctrine of the ministry can be studied in *The Historic Episcopate* edited by K. M. Carey (1954) with the reply by A. L. Peck, *This Church of Christ* (1955), and *Old Priest New Presbyter* Norman Sykes (1955) with the reply, again by A. L. Peck, *Anglicanism and Episcopacy* (1958).

CHAPTER VII: ANGLO-CATHOLICISM

Several of these books have been mentioned before but should be consulted again: T. A. Lacey *The Anglo-Catholic Faith* (1926), W. L. Knox *The Catholic Movement in the Church of England* (1923), H. L. Stewart *A Century of Anglo-Catholicism* (1929), S. L. Ollard *The Anglo-Catholic Revival* (1925), C. P. S. Clarke *The Oxford Movement and After* (1937).

The effect on education can be seen in K. E. Kirk *Story of the Woodard Schools* (1937): and on industrial life in W. G. Peck *The Social Implications of the Oxford Movement* (1933). For its influence on thought one should read *Dean Church—The Anglican Response to Newman* by B. A. Smith (1958), *Gore, a Study in Liberal Catholic Thought* by James Carpenter (1960), and two biographies by E. W. Kemp—*N. P. Williams* (1948) and *Life and Letters of K. E. Kirk, Bishop of Oxford* (1959). Its effect on the lives of humbler parish priests is portrayed in *The Life of Father Dolling* by C. E. Osborne (1903), *A. H. Mackonochie* by E. A. Towle (1890), and *Father Wainwright* by L. Menzies (1947). Newman's *Apologia* (1864) remains a literary and theological classic.

CHAPTER VIII: ECUMENISM

The two most important books are *Christian Unity* by G. J. Slosser (1929) and *History of the Ecumenical Movement* by Rouse and Neill (1954). A smaller volume is *The Ecumenical Movement* by N. Goodall (1961). A very considerable symposium is that edited by K. Mackenzie *The Union of Christendom* (1938). Individual books on the Anglican attitude are S. L. Ollard *Reunion* (1919), A. C. Headlam *The Doctrine of the Church and Christian Reunion* (1920), H. L. Goudge *The Church of England and Reunion* (1938) and G. K. A. Bell *Christian Unity, the Anglican Position* (1948). There is a considerable mass of smaller literature; a bibliography was published by H. R. T. Brandreth *Unity and Reunion* (2nd ed., 1948). Three series of *Documents on Christian Unity* were published by G. K. A. Bell (1924, 1930 and 1948). An excellent account of Orthodoxy can be found in Nicolas Zernov's *Eastern Christendom* (1961).

CHAPTER IX: INSTITUTIONS AND SOCIETIES

Besides the literature published by the several societies much information will be found in the annual Year Books of the various churches especially the *Official Year Book of the Church of England* (SPCK) and, for USA *The Episcopal Church Annual* (Morehouse-Barlow Co., New York). For the historical and general background one might consult *The Church of England in the Twentieth Century* by Roger Lloyd (2 vols., 1946), *The Church of England, its Members and its Business* by Guy Mayfield (1958), *The Second Reform* by J. W. C. Wand (1953). As was to be expected the Venerable Society has received the lion's share of literary attention: *History of SPCK* W. K. Lowther Clarke (1959), *Henry Newman* L. W. Cowie (1956), *Thomas Bray* H. P. Thomson (1954), *Joshua Watson* A. B. Webster (1954). The Church Army is to be studied in *Wilson Carlile and the Church Army* by E. Rowan (4th ed., 1933) and *Wilson Carlile* by S. Dark (1944); a noted clerical charity in *The Sons of the Clergy* by E. H. Pearce (1904); the Mission to Seamen in *The Flying Angel* by L. A. G. Strong (1956); Moral welfare in *The Story of a Beginning* by J. E. Higson (1955); the more official institutions in *The Foundations and Early Years of Queen Anne's Bounty* by A. Savidge (1955) and the story of the Church Commissioners in *The First Five Years* by P. B. Wilbraham (1953).

CHAPTER X: RELIGIOUS COMMUNITIES

The story is for the most part embedded in the histories and biographies. The following have a special bearing on the subject: *Guide to the Religious Communities of the Anglican Communion* by The Advisory Council on Religious Communities (1951), *The Call of the Cloister* by P. F. Anson (1955), *Religious Orders in the Anglican Communion* by R. H. Weller (Milwaukee 1909), *Edmund Keble Talbot* by G. P. H. Pawson (1954), *The C. R. Diamond Jubilee Book* (1952), *Letters of Richard Meux Benson* edited by Congreve and Longridge (1916), *Further Letters*

(1920). *Priscilla Lydia Sellon* by T. J. Williams (1950); adumbrations of the 'religious' life may be seen in the Australian Bush Brotherhoods and in the organization described in *The Lee Abbey Story* by J. C. Winslow (1956). See also the *Directory of the Religious Life* published by the Advisory Council on Religious Communities (1943).

CHAPTER XI: THE PARSON IN HIS PULPIT

The best known Anglican book on preaching is that by the American Phillips Brooks *Lectures on Preaching* (Yale 1877). A history of the subject from 747 to 1939 is *The Art of Preaching* by Charles Smyth (1940). A fascinating description of a particular pulpit is to be found in Millar MacLure's *The St Paul's Cross Sermons* (Toronto 1958) of which great use has been made in the text. Specimens of modern Anglican preaching can be found in *The Anglican Pulpit Today* by D. Gifford (1953), *Religious Experience* by William Temple (edited by A. E. Baker 1958), *The Archbishop Speaks* (Geoffrey Fisher, edited by E. Carpenter 1958) and in the two biographies by E. W. Kemp already mentioned, *N. P. Williams* (1954) and *Kenneth Escott Kirk* (1959). See also *Beauty and Bands* by K. E. Kirk (1955), *Durham Essays and Addresses* by M. Ramsey (1956), *The Preacher's Theme Today* by W. Temple (1936), *The Search for Perfection* by W. R. Matthews (1957), *Strangers and Pilgrims* by the same author (1945), and *The Ministry of the Word* by F. D. Coggan (1945).

CHAPTER XII: THE PARSON IN HIS PARISH

For the history one should read the *History of the English Clergy* by C. K. F. Brown (1953), *The English Clergy* by H. Thompson (1947), *The Country Clergy in Elizabethan and Stuart Times* by A. Tindal Hart (1958), *The Old Time Parson* by P. H. Ditchfield (1908), *The English Country Parson* by William Addison (n.d.). The diaries are a great help in building up a comprehensive picture: *Diary of a Country Parson* (James Woodforde 1758–1802), selections by J. Beresford (1935), *Journal of a Somerset Rector* (J. Skinner 1772–1839) by Coombs and Box (1930). Also useful are *Victorian Period Piece* by J. S. Leatherbarrow (1954), *Church and Parish* by Charles Smyth (1955). Contemporary clerical activities are described in Peter Green *The Town Parson* (1919) and Joost de Blank *The Parish in Action* (1954).

Clerical ideals are set forth in George Herbert *A Priest to the Temple* (1652), W. C. F. Newbolt *Priestly Ideals* (1898), E. Graham *The Pastoral Lectures of Bishop King* (1932), H. Latham *Pastor Pastorum* (1890), R. C. Moberley *Ministerial Priesthood* (1897), C. R. Forder *The Priest at Work* (1947), A. L. Preston *The Parish Priest in his Parish* (1933), L. S. Hunter *A Parson's Job* (1931), H. H. Henson *Ad Clerum* (1937).

CHAPTER XIII: CONCLUSION

Two reference books of first-class importance are the *Dictionary of English Church History* by Ollard, Crosse and Bond (3rd ed., 1948) and the *Oxford Dictionary of the Christian Church* F. L. Cross (1957). Of the older histories of the Church of England Stephens and Hunt (9 vols., 1910) and H. O. Wakeman (5th ed., 1898) are still indispensable, and that of E. W. Watson in the Home University Library (1961) 3rd ed., has an important individual slant. Of the more modern S. C. Carpenter's three volumes *Church and People* has now been issued by SPCK in a paperback and Stephen Neill's *Anglicanism* is in the Pelican series. The most up-to-date students' handbook is J. R. H. Moorman's *History of the Church of England* (1953), but R. H. Malden *English Church and Nation* has some out-of-the-way information and J. W. C. Wand *History of the Modern Church* (10th ed., 1961) sets Anglicanism against the background of general church history. Books dealing with the character of Anglicanism (in addition to those by Dr Garbett already mentioned) are *The Anglican Communion in Christendom* by A. E. J. Rawlinson (1960), *The English Church* by C. M. Adey (n.d.), *The Church of England* H. Hensley Henson (Cambridge 1939), *The Genius of the Church of England* Charles Smyth (1947), *The Anglican Tradition* by A. T. P. Williams (1947). Two books exhibiting the Anglican tendency to self-depreciation are *Essays in Anglican Self-Criticism* edited by D. M. Paton

(1958) and *One Army Strong?* by Peter Kirk (1958). The case for authority is stated in *Authority in the Church* by T. A. Lacey (1928) and *Authority in the Church of England* by Gordon Crosse (1906). But the essential character of Anglicanism could be more easily discerned in that unique piece of ecclesiastical journalism *A Bundle of Memories* by H. Scott Holland (1915) or in the lives of the seven Anglican worthies depicted by Margaret Cropper in *Sparks among the Stubble* (1955) or of the 'nine great Anglicans' in H. A. L. Rice's *The Bridge Builders* 1961. If Anglicanism does not canonize its heroes it seldom fails to pay them the honour of a biography. Inevitably such 'lives' form a fruitful source for the better understanding of the Anglican type of mind. Some of the more recent are: *Randall Davidson* G. K. A. Bell (1935), *Charles Gore* G. L. Prestige (1935), *John Sharp* A. Tindal Hart (1949), *Richard Hooker* F. J. Shirley (1949), *Winnington Ingram* S. C. Carpenter (1949), *Cosmo Lang* J. G. Lockhart (1949), *William Temple* F. A. Iremonger (1948), *Charles Kingsley* G. Kendall (1947), *Jeremy Taylor* C. J. Stranks (1952), *William Lloyd* A. Tindal Hart (1952), *Wolsey* A. F. Pollard (1953), *Henry Philpotts* G. C. B. Davies (1954), *The Protestant Bishop* (Compton of London) E. Carpenter (1956), *Thomas Haweis* A. S. Wood (1957), *White Kennett* G. V. Bennett (1957), *Thomas Ken* A. L. Price (1958), *Evelyn Underhill* M. Cropper (1958), *Lancelot Andrewes* P. A. Welsby (1958), *William Thomson* H. Kirk Smith (1958), *Cyril Foster Garbett* C. Smyth (1959), *Arthur Cayley Headlam* R. Jasper (1960), *Dean Inge* Adam Fox (1960).

INDEX

Act of Uniformity, 1662, 218, 224

Additional Curates Society, 100–101

Africa, 135; creation of bishoprics in, 26; Anglicanism in, 44; theological colour of its churches, 116–17; missions to, 169

Africa, South, 26, 190, 193; the Anglican Church in, 39–41; her Church Railway Mission, 40–41; effect of the Colenso case on her Church, 107–108, 116

Aidan, St (d. 651), 10

Alban, St (fl. c. 305), 4

Albert Hall, Anglo-Catholic meetings in, 143–4

America, creation of bishops for, 24–5; her missions to Japan, 44n†; Bray and, 166-7, 168; see also United States

Andrewes, Lancelot (1555–1626), 22

Alexander II, Pope (d. 1073), 12

Anglican Communities, 183–5, 187–93

Anglican, the, definition of, xiii; what is his attitude to life? 70–71; the qualities he admires, 75–8, 233; his attitude to conscience, 78; and goodness, 79–81; peculiar quality of his piety, 81–5; his form of worship, 89–91; his attitude to religion, 120–21; and the new Liberals in, 128–9; and Mysticism, 131–2; his passion for liberty, 237

Anglican Communion, the, variations of churchmanship in, ix–x; reflects its British origins, x, xiii; definition of, xiii; development of, 3–4; the Lambeth Conference and, 26–7, 63; no central government in, 27, 47; the clergy in, 28, 210–23; contribution of the American Church to, 32–4; its unifying influence and Australia, 38; founded on the continuity of doctrine and ministry, 52; rationalization of its churches, 63; variety of services in, 85–6, 89, 96; its need for variety and simplicity, 90–91; independence of its overseas branches, 108; different colour of its dioceses, 116–17; its responsibility in respect of reunion, 118; effect of the Catholic Revival on, 144–8; Christian humanism within, 152; unity of Bible and Church in, 155–6; and the Ecumenical movement, 157, 160, 161; and monasticism, 183–94, 235; its colonial system, 231, 235; its new organization, 232, 235; modern questions in, 234; its Imperial outlook, 236; closer union within, 241–2

X Anglicanism, definition of, xiii–xiv; its development from the early Church, 3–4; importance of the Reformation to, 15–16; effect of Mary's papalism on, 19; its emergence under Elizabeth I, 20–22, 200–201; Hooker and, 21–2, 51, 60, 65, 72, 97; its

national expansion, 22–4; its overseas expansion, 24–6, 67, 231; early history of, in N. America, 29–36; its influence in India, 42; boasts no exclusive doctrine, 46, 68–9, 233; virtues and defects of its comprehensiveness, 47–51, 117–18; Calvinism and, 48–9; division into evangelical and catholic in, 49–51, 95, 234; importance of its comprehensiveness to Christendom, 50–51; the continuity of its doctrine and ministry, 51–5; and episcopacy, 53–4, 217; the official attitude to non-episcopacy, 54; its use of the Bible, 56–8; and the interpretation of the Bible, 59–62; its authority in matters of faith, 60; its emphasis on nationalism in religion, 62–3, 65, 68; position of the clergy in, 67; does it accept or reject the world, 70ff.; the Cambridge Platonists and, 74; and humanism, 74–5; and moralism, 75–81; peculiar character of its piety, 81–5; its vernacular and traditional form of worship, 85; union of old and new in, 86–7; its division into Low and High Church, 95ff., 109; its fate under the Commonwealth, 99; and Broadchurchmen, 103; emergence of liberalism in, 104, 229; answers Latitudinarianism, 106; effect of *Essays and Studies* on, 107; widening of its vision, 120; its summer period, 121; and the challenge of new ideas, 122; Liberalism and, 127; effect of Mysticism on, 131–2; its propensity for Religious Societies, 165ff., 174–5; development of monasticism in, 186–94; development of sermons in, 202ff.; and episcopal ordination, 217; its theology, 227–30; adaptability of its organization, 230; a professing but non-practising religion, 239; what it demands, 240–41; character of its spirituality, 242–3

Anglican Evangelical Group Movement, 127–8

Anglo-Catholic, xiii; as a term of abuse, 102, 147

Anglo-Catholicism, its original meaning, 102, 143; moves towards Rome, 102–103; and the new Liberalism, 128, 139; its hey-day, 143–4; effects of its revival, 144–8, 154

Anglo-Saxons, the, and Christianity in Britain, 5–7; increase papal power, 13

Anson, P. F., *The Call of the Cloister*, 183, 184, 185, 186, 190

Apartheid, the Church in S. Africa and, 41

Apostolic Succession, the Anglican attitude to, 54

Ariminum (Rimini), Council of, 5

255

258